A LIFE BEGUN ON THIRD BASE

JOHN S. MARTIN JR.

Catalina Press

Catalina Press, LLC
Tucson, Arizona
www.catalinabookpress.com
books@catalinabookpress.com

Follow us and our authors on:
Twitter: @CatalinaPress
Facebook: @CatalinaBookPress
Instagram: #CatalinaBookPress

© 2020 John S. Martin Jr. All Rights Reserved

ISBN 978-1-953721-02-0

Printed in the United States of America

Revised edition

Contents

Preface   v
Introduction   vii

1. Our Roots   1
2. My Parents   7
3. Early Life   17
4. Peggy Conroy and Our Family   25
5. Mentors   49
6. My Introduction to the Law   53
7. Assistant United States Attorney   61
8. Country Lawyer   83
9. Supreme Court Advocate   87
10. Private Practice   103
11. United States Attorney   135
12. Return to Private Practice   165
13. District Judge   181
14. Retirement   233
15. What I have Learned in Eighty-Five Years   267

Preface

For my birthday in May 2019 my daughter Meg gave me a subscription to Storyworth, an online service that sends you reminders once a week to write something about your life. The basic idea is that over the course of the year you will write a memoir about your life that can be passed on to future generations.

I thought about how much I wish I knew more about the lives of my parents and grandparents and I decided that it would be worthwhile to write a book for future generations of Martins. As I undertook that effort, I recognized that, through no fault of my own, I had a range of interesting experiences that might be of interest to a wider group of readers.

As a boy of 12 I took a road trip with the Brooklyn Dodgers during Jackie Robinson's first year with the team. As an adult, I would meet and become a friend of Thurgood Marshall. As a young lawyer, I prosecuted cases as a Assistant United States Attorney in the Southern District of New York and I would later serve as the United States Attorney in that District and as a United States District Judge. My career also included service in the Solicitor General's office where I argued eight cases before the Supreme Court of the United States and

Preface

had major responsibility for a series of cases in the District Courts that led to the enactment of the Foreign Intelligence Surveillance Act. During my years in private practice I had a number of high-profile cases and cases involving interesting issues.

Thus, after writing the memoir for my family, I have edited it to remove details that would only be of interest to future Martins. What follows is the result of that effort. My hope is that it will provide those considering a career in the law, as well as the general public, with a better idea of what lawyers do and the day to day work of prosecutors and judges. I hope you will find it of interest.

Introduction

Barry Switzer, a famous football coach, is credited with the saying "some people are born on third base and go through life thinking that they hit a triple." I recognize I was fortunate to be born on third base and, if I accomplished anything in this life, it is because I had wonderful parents, an exceptional wife and family, great professional role models and the help of many people with whom I worked over the course of my career.

I also recognize there is a great deal of serendipity in what happens to you in life. As a lawyer, I achieved the distinction of serving as United States Attorney for the Southern District of New York and as a United States District Judge in that district. None of that would have happened had my father's brother Bill, a lawyer, not been a friend of Leonard P. Moore, a judge of the United States Court of Appeals for the Second Circuit, who hired me as his law clerk, where I met Thurgood Marshall, then a judge of that court, who would later hire me to be one of his assistants when he was the Solicitor General of the United States, which impressed Senator Moynihan who was responsible for me becoming both United States Attorney and a District Judge, and I probably would never have met Senator Moynihan had I not taken a summer job while in law school at a firm where I met

Introduction

Chester Straub, who was later a member of Sen. Moynihan's Judicial Selection Committee and who, I believe, played a significant role in Senator Moynihan's decision to recommend me for those offices.

In recognizing how lucky I was to meet the people who had such a great impact on my professional career, I do not mean to suggest that they lowered their standards to advance my career or totally denigrate the importance of my own efforts to whatever success I achieved. I doubt Judge Moore would have hired me had I not been a member of the Columbia Law Review, or that Solicitor General Thurgood Marshall would have hired me had he not been impressed by my appearances before him when he was a Circuit Judge. However, there are number of lawyers with talent equal or better than mine who have not had the good fortune of meeting the right people at the right time in their career. I cite this simply as a reminder that success and failure in one's career may often be the result of things over which we have no control.

The most important thing that happened to me as a result of my serendipitous introduction to Thurgood Marshall in the fall of 1962 is that, five years later, he brought me to Washington to serve in the Solicitor General's office. It was while I was working there that a friend said to me: "I know a girl in Washington you should look up." I did. Her name was Margaret Mary Conroy, better known as Peggy. We would marry less than six months after our first date, and she was the best thing that ever happened to me. Together, and mostly to her credit, we raised four wonderful children who gave us nine incredible grandchildren. This memoir is for them.

ONE

Our Roots

Although we were born in Brooklyn, we thought of ourselves as Irish. Both of my mother's parents were born in Ireland and we spent more time with them than with my father's parents.

I never knew Pat Larkin, my mother's grandfather, who was the first of my mother's family to come to the United States. He left his wife and children in Ireland and, as soon as he could afford it, he brought them to the United States. My grandmother, Susan Larkin was the last of her family to come to the United States. She made that ocean voyage with her young sister, Mollie — both of them probably no more than 12 or 13. When they arrived in this country, their father—whom they hadn't seen in several years—was there to greet them. However, in the intervening years he had grown a mustache and his appearance had changed so significantly that they did not recognize him. Because the two young girls denied that the man seeking to take them from immigration custody was their father, he had to return to Brooklyn to get their mother.

My grandfather, Michael O'Donohue, was born in County Cork and came to this country as a teenager, as did most of his brothers and sisters. They left behind their parents and one or two siblings, whom they would never see again. As both a parent and a child, I find it hard to comprehend the dire financial circumstances that would persuade me to separate permanently from my parents or my children. Yet countless immigrants did just that.

How or when Mike and Susie met I do not know. They married and had seven children, Joe, Marie—my mother— Elizabeth, Lucille, Helen John, Frank, and Edmund. Elizabeth died during childhood and Frank was killed in a plane crash during training in the Second World War.

Like many Irishman of his time, Michael O'Donohue joined the New York City Fire Department. He rose through the ranks to become a fire chief. He was apparently somewhat of a legend in the fire department and when the Normandy, a major ocean liner, caught fire, the first Fire Chief to respond at the scene sent in a third alarm because as he said, "I knew that would bring me Mike O'Donohue."

Chief O'Donohue's last assignment in the New York City of Fire Department was as Chief of Public Assembly. He was in that position in 1945 when the Second World War ended. Had he been corrupt, Public Assembly could have made him a rich man because Public Assembly regulated the number of people who could assemble in theaters, restaurants and sports facilities and the safety equipment those facilities required.

It is ironic that the Chief lost his job with the election of William O'Dwyer, whom he enthusiastically supported when O'Dwyer ran for Mayor. Indeed, the day my uncle Eddie returned home from fighting the war in Europe, the Chief made him leave his welcome home party to go and register to vote because O'Dwyer, "one of our own" was running for mayor. Shortly after O'Dwyer took office, the Chief was removed from Public Assembly by O'Dwyer's new fire Commissioner, who was subsequently convicted and sent to jail.

My mother's mother, Nana Sue came to live with us after we moved to Nyack. Susie lived alone after the Chief's death but she suffered from diabetes and had a series of operations removing toes and ultimately one of her legs. She lost her leg as a result of an exploratory operation to determine the amount of damage the diabetes had done. Since the amputation had not been planned, we were all worried about how Susie would react to losing her leg. One of the strange things about an amputation is that the nerves running from the leg continue to operate and you can feel your toes even though the leg is gone. It took Susie about three days to realize that her leg was gone and her reaction was to say, "what a dope am I that I did not realize for three days that I didn't have a leg." She took it with great grace.

My dad arranged for one of the great moments in Susie's life. 1960 was the last full year of Dwight Eisenhower's presidency and also the 45th anniversary of his graduation from West Point. The class of 1915 held its reunion dinner at the Bear Mountain Inn with Eisenhower in attendance. As the Manager of the Inn, Dad greeted the President at the entrance to the Inn and escorted him to the reception, which was in a room behind the dining room. Knowing the route the President would take, Dad positioned Susie in her wheelchair just outside the entrance to the room where the reunion was being held. As they were approaching the spot where Susie was, Dad said to Eisenhower, "Mr. President would you say hello to a gold star mother (a mother who lost a child in the second world war)." Eisenhower leaned over and grabbed Susie's hand. Below is the picture of that event which appeared on the front page of the New York Daily News. My brother Mike and my dad can be seen in the background.

JOHN S. MARTIN JR.

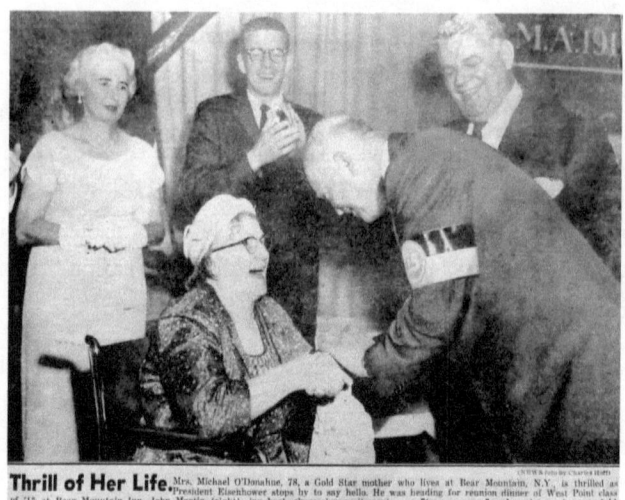

Thrill of Her Life. Mrs. Michael O'Donahue, 78, a Gold Star mother who lives at Bear Mountain, N.Y., is thrilled as President Eisenhower stops by to say hello. He was heading for reunion dinner of West Point class of '15 at Bear Mountain Inn. John Martin (right), inn host, shares her excitement. —*Story on page 2; other pictures in centerfold*

Nana Sue meets Dwight Eisenhower

We knew much less of the background of my father's parents. She was Blanche Sherwood and he was William Martin. We ultimately met her brother, Will Sherwood, who had operated the Fifth Avenue Coach Company in New York and a similar operation in Chicago.

My father was the second of six children. His older brother Bill became a successful lawyer and was a great help to me in my career. His brother Edgar was a Jesuit who was a prisoner of war in the Philippines where he was serving as a missionary. Dad had two sisters, Blanche and Susan, a brilliant woman with a PhD who suffered from psychiatric problems for most of her adult life. His youngest brother Paul was also in the restaurant business and operated a diner in Greenwood Lake New York.

My grandfather Martin was for some period of time a salesman and, when he retired, he decided to open a diner. He thought that since he had eaten in hundreds of diners, he knew what the customers wanted: hearty food at a low price. While the hearty food brought in customers, the low price brought bankruptcy.

My grandfather's bankruptcy turned out to be a blessing for my father, who had left high school to work in his father's diner. When my grandfather went bankrupt, dad took over the business and ultimately paid off all his debts. The diner located on 56th St. between 10th and 11th Avenues served as a launching pad for my dad's successful career in the restaurant and hotel business.

My mother, Marie O'Donohue was introduced to my father by his sister Blanche who was mom's high school classmate. She was 18 when they married and he was 24.

TWO

My Parents

My mother was an important influence in my life and she bore a vast amount of the responsibility for raising us because my father worked seven days a week for 14 or 16 hours a day. However, I find it hard to recall specific incidents that would demonstrate what an incredible woman she was. Hers were simply the day-to-day chores of raising a family of six and doing her best to see that her children wanted for nothing and became responsible human beings. She was very close to her family and they often came to stay at Bear Mountain. After I married Peggy, I noted that one of the things that she and mom had in common was they were both women who friends and relatives would come to for advice when they faced a problem. Mom was beloved by many people. She died at age 51 while having a minor ear operation. We were convinced that an anesthesiologist killed her, but dad did not want her body desecrated by an autopsy.

I wish I knew my father better. It is not that I did not see him regularly and spend time with him—from the time I was 14 I spent my summers and some of my weekends working for him. When I graduated from college, I worked with him for a year before deciding to go to law school. I knew him as well as most sons know their fathers; as a loving dad, a good provider for the family who paid fully for my college and law school as he did the education of all the children. But I did not know him as his friends must have known him. I find it hard to articulate the qualities that enabled a boy from Brooklyn, who dropped out of high school to take over a bankrupt diner, to build a career in the restaurant and hotel business where he became a minor celebrity and a close friend of some of the leading sports figures of the time. He was affable and made friends easily, but he was also a tough boss who knew how he wanted things done. Yet, like many tough bosses about whom I have read, such as Vin Lombardi and Steve Jobs, most of the people who worked closely with him loved him.

Marie and John Martin

Dad's first big break came shortly after he and mom were married. A major portion of the US fleet anchored in New York Harbor and the public was invited to board. To service the crowds that would gather in the park along the Hudson River, the New York City Parks Department licensed a number of food concessions. Dad, who was operating the dinner, formed a partnership with a man named Melton Lagakis, who operated the Terminal Cafeteria next door to the Chief's firehouse. They formed Terminal Operating Corporation and obtained a concession to operate a food stand on the shore of the Hudson.

One of the most important moments in dad's life occurred as he was working at his refreshment stand on the Hudson when the fleet was in. Robert Moses, the Commissioner of Parks, happened to walk by. The stories vary somewhat. As Moses approached dad's location, dad was either outside the stand picking up garbage or behind the counter handing out free water. Whatever it was, Moses saw it and told dad, "Young man, we need people like you running our food concessions in the City's parks. I want you to contact my office about operating some food concessions in our parks." As a result of this fortunate moment when he came to Mr. Moses's attention, dad ended up operating food concessions in several city parks including Prospect Park, Red Hook Park, Sunset Park, Alley Pond Park and Rockaway. His operation of these concessions made such a favorable impression on Mr. Moses that in 1941 Mr. Moses, who was also the New York State Parks Commissioner, asked dad to take over the operation of the Bear Mountain Inn. The Inn is located in a 50,000 acre park about 40 miles north of New York City overlooking the Hudson. Prior to the time that dad took over the Inn, it had been operated by the state and was a money-losing proposition. In the 25 years he operated the Inn, dad made it well known nationally and generated a profit for him and the state.

The Bear Mountain Inn is a four-story building with a basement for equipment and storage, a cafeteria on the first floor, a large combination dining and banquet room, a bar and the hotel lobby on the second and 15 guestrooms and several more rooms for the help on the third. Behind the Inn was a lodge with 16 bedrooms. About a half-mile away across a lake there were four cabins, each with four bedrooms. But the operation that my father took over was more than just the Inn, it also involved operating six refreshment stands located throughout the park as well as maintaining vending machines at various locations.

Taking over the operations at Bear Mountain was a big change both from how the Inn had been operated in the past and from the type of business my father had operated. While I was too young to understand these changes, it must've been difficult for my father to assume command of employees who were accustomed to government service jobs and subject them to the discipline of a private company that had to make money to survive. How he did it, I do not know, but he ended up running a successful business with a dedicated staff that admired and respected him. Running the Bear Mountain Inn and its related operations would have been a challenge for Harvard Business School graduate, never mind a high school dropout.

One of the challenges of running the Inn and the related operations arose from the fact that dad had to maintain a sufficient staff to support an operation that was busy in the summer when people flocked to the Inn and refreshment stands but was very slow from September through May. Although business was helped during the fall by football games at West Point, which is 5 miles away, and in the winter by ski jumps that drew large crowds on many weekends, on weekdays the staff had little to do.

The operation of this complex facility must have posed a daunting challenge for dad. While he ultimately overcame the challenges that the operation of the Bear Mountain Inn and its related facilities presented, his initial concern about the ultimate success of the venture was evident from the fact that while he took over the operation in April 1941, he did not move his family from Brooklyn until February 1943.

While dad was facing these challenges, we were living blissfully in Brooklyn. The family consisted of my parents, my sister Terry who is two years older, my brother Mike born in 1939, and my brother Bill who was born in December 1942 just before we moved permanently to Bear Mountain.

A Life Begun on Third Base

One of the major boosts to the Inn's success came in 1943 when the Brooklyn Dodger baseball team selected Bear Mountain as its spring training site. In 1942, the then Baseball Commissioner, Judge Landis, announced that the major league teams would no longer be permitted to travel to Florida for spring training- - the stated reason being that the railroads should be saved for the war effort and not to transport baseball teams - - although others have speculated that Judge Landis was concerned about the image of baseball if young ballplayers were photographed frolicking on the beach in Florida while other men of their age were dying fighting in Europe and Asia. When dad heard this news, he had a brilliant idea.

Bear Mountain had large fields that could be used as baseball fields, but the problem was that the weather in March and early April would make it difficult to train out doors. However, Bear Mountain was only 5 miles from the United States Military Academy at West Point, which had a large fieldhouse that was big enough to allow baseball practice indoors. Dad, who was friendly with a number of people in West Point's athletic department, persuaded them to agree that, if a major-league team was training at Bear Mountain and there was inclement weather, the team could use the West Point Fieldhouse while the cadets were in class.

I have been told that my dad presented this idea to the three major-league baseball teams then playing in New York City - the Yankees, the Giants and the Dodgers. Branch Rickey, then the general manager of the Dodgers liked the idea, and the Dodgers trained at Bear Mountain in 1943, 44 and 45.

The Dodgers training at Bear Mountain generated a huge amount of publicity for the Inn and its operations, which led to a number of sports teams staying at the Inn and using the park's facilities. The New York football Giants trained at Bear Mountain from the late 40s through the early 60s. The New York Knicks trained there for several years in the 50s. Most college football teams that came into New York to play Army, including Notre Dame, would stay there prior to the game. Also, in the 50s and early 60s, NFL teams from the West Coast who were coming East to play the Giants would usually have another game scheduled in the East within a week and they would spend that week training at Bear Mountain. The New York Golden Glove fighters also trained at Bear Mountain, as did a number of heavyweight contenders.

One of the most memorable of those was a man named Bruce Woodcock, who at the time was a heavyweight champion of England. Bear Mountain was the scene of several Revolutionary war battles that were commemorated on plaques at various places throughout the park. Having run by these plaques during his work out, Woodcock finally said to my dad, "John, isn't there at least one place where we gave them a bloody go?"

Although he had no training in public relations, dad recognized the value of publicity and, as a result, a sportswriter rarely paid for a drink at the Bear Mountain Inn. Consequently, it was not unusual to pick up a newspaper and read a story referring to John, or sometimes Jack Martin of the Bear Mountain Inn. Dad became a great friend of the leading sportswriters of the day, including the legendary Red Smith, Arthur Daley, Dick Young and, Jimmy Powers. He was so popular with the sportswriters that they honored him at an annual dinner they held in New York City. It was a casual affair paid for by the proceeds of a more formal dinner at which they honored luminaries of the baseball world.

I remember two things from that dinner particularly. One, the Toastmaster for the evening, Red Smith began by saying, "I've been asked to serve as Toastmaster because I am a good friend of your guest of honor and I remember at a time like this that a friend in need is a pain in the ass." Second was one of the best extemporaneous comebacks I have ever seen – – there was no formal program and Red Smith simply called on people at random. One of the people he called on was Stanley Woodward, the sports editor of the New York Herald Tribune. Stanley, who had consumed quite a bit of the free liquor said simply, "in the past you have honored a lot of pricks. It's nice to see you finally are honoring a non-prick." After Stanley sat down Red called on Bob Faischal, the director of public relations for the New York

Yankees. Bob started by saying, "Stanley I'm glad to see that you remember that I was honored here last year."

Dad's good relations with the sportswriters led him to play a minor but significant role in the founding of the New York Mets. When the Brooklyn Dodgers and New York Giants left for the West Coast in 1958, sports fans in New York were in an uproar. One of those people was George V McLaughlin, a friend of dad's who was a prominent banker, a former Police Commissioner of the City of New York, and a former Superintendent of Banks for the state. McLaughlin, as a banker, had financed Walter O'Malley's original purchase of his interest in the Dodgers. O'Malley was the man who moved the Dodgers to Los Angeles.

Sometime around the time of the move, McLaughlin, who drove with his wife to the Inn for brunch almost every Sunday, told my father that he and several wealthy friends around the country wanted to announce that they were going to form a new baseball major league—the Continental League. This was at a time before the development of major public relations firms, so McLaughlin said to dad, "John, I know that you know all of the major New York sportswriters. Do you think you could get them all together at some location where I can make this announcement? We are hoping that by announcing that we are ready to launch a new league we can generate enough pressure to get the Major Leagues to give us a new franchise."

Dad rented a suite at the Waldorf Astoria, set up a bar and invited all the leading sportswriters, most of whom attended. Mr. McLaughlin, made his announcement and said, "I do not want to be out front on this so it will all be handled by my lawyer, Bill Shea." Mr. McLaughlin's gambit was successful, the Mets franchise was created and its original stadium was named after Bill Shea.

Dad's personality was such that he had many close friends and people whose lives he impacted. Years after he left Bear Mountain, family members would run into people who had worked for dad who would talk glowingly about Mr. Martin. In many cases they would mention some specific act of thoughtfulness or generosity. While he was a tough boss, he appreciated the people who worked for him and looked for ways to show his appreciation. One winter, he hired a bus and took some of his key employees to Florida for a vacation.

One of my father's sayings that I have tried to live by is "never resist a generous impulse." It is one that he put into practice regularly. One incident that comes to mind was when a Capuchin priest, Father Finnian Sullivan, came to dad and said that his order, which had a monastery nearby, was having a major anniversary which they wanted to celebrate by inviting a number of nuns from each of the Catholic schools in New York City on a boat trip to Bear Mountain. Father Sullivan wanted to know what it would cost to feed the nuns at the Inn. I am not sure, but I think the answer was nothing. In any event, the response was so low that Father Sullivan was extremely grateful.

One of the results was that several years later Father Sullivan learned that mom and dad were planning a trip to Rome. He gave dad a letter of introduction to a Capuchin priest who was then Secretary of State of the Vatican. As a result, my parents had a private audience with Pope Pius XII. For mom, a devoted Catholic, it was one of the greatest moments of her life.

Another example of my father's generous nature is evidenced by a framed memento hanging in my apartment, which consists of a copy of an obituary of dad by Red Barber, the longtime Brooklyn Dodger announcer, and a gold-plated lifetime pass Ebbets Field that Branch Rickey gave to dad in the spring of 1945. The obituary recounts a dinner Mr. Ricky gave to honor my father for all that he did for the team during their stays at Bear Mountain. In his remarks that evening Mr. Rickey stated that when his daughter reached marriageable age, he and his wife discussed the quality they would most like to find in a son-in-law. He said they determined the quality they would like most was "infinite kindness." He concluded by saying "John, throughout our stay here, you have shown us infinite kindness."

Dad made close friends of many of the leading sports personalities of the time. People like Leo Durocher, the manager of the Dodgers, Joe Lapchik, the coach of the New York Knicks, Steve Owen, the Giants' head coach and Vince Lombardi, who dad met when he was the line coach at West Point and who later served as the Offensive Coordinator for the Giants and went on to legendary fame as the Head Coach the Green Bay Packers.

I remember one night I was invited to join mom and dad for dinner with Lombardi and his wife at Toots Shor's restaurant. After several drinks and a discussion of how lucky we were that our families had come to the United States, dad asked Toots to call and get a Carey limousine and put some champagne in the trunk. We then all traveled to the foot of Manhattan to drink a toast to those ancestors at Castle Gardens, the site of the original immigration center.

As noted earlier, the seasonal nature of the business made operating the Bear Mountain Inn and related facilities a challenge. But dad was an innovator— he studied what he could about corporate training and he worked to persuade major corporations to hold training conferences at the Inn. Dad was a creative thinker, as is demonstrated by the fact that in the early 1960s, he built a closed-circuit TV studio in the Inn so that it could be used in corporate training. Dad's efforts were successful, and several corporations such as New York Telephone did use the facility to hold training sessions. However, the Inn had so few decent hotel rooms that it could only accommodate small groups.

Dad operated the Inn under a series of five-year contracts, pursuant to which he paid a portion of his gross income to the state. When he received the proposed contract for the five year period that would commence in 1965, he told A.K. Morgan, the General Manager of the Park, that he would only renew the contract if the Park Commission agreed to build a new building with additional guestrooms. Mr. Morgan refused and dad decided to leave Bear Mountain and build his own hotel on a piece of property in Nyack New York. Dad died before the hotel could be built.

One of the ironies of life is that many years later after both dad and Mr. Morgan were dead, the Park Commission decided to build a new lodge with additional rooms which they named the A.K. Morgan Lodge.

My mother died having a minor operation in 1965. While I knew her death would cause dad grief, I did not anticipate that it would have too serious impact on him since he had spent so much time at work that he and mom had not spent a lot of time together. However, dad was really devastated by her death and spent the remaining three years of his life regretting the fact that he had not spent more time with her when he had the chance. This was a lesson for me and, after I married Peggy, I made every effort to spend as much time with her as possible and appreciate what a wonderful wife I had.

In 1968, dad was admitted to the hospital for what we thought was a relatively minor heart problem. I think he would have survived several years had he been willing to take care of himself. However, as a result of mom's death, he lost the will to live. He died of a heart attack on June 28, 1968.

A sign of how highly dad was regarded by his friends is that, after his death three of his friends, Walter Kennedy, then the Commissioner of the NBA, Dick Young, a leading sports columnist for the New York Daily News, and Joe Cahill, a former head of public relations for the Army Athletic Association and then a successful businessman, raised a fund to create a memorial in dad's honor. While dad was not a skier, Bear Mountain was known for its ski jump. They chose as the memorial, the establishment of a fund to finance the John Martin Award to be given to the outstanding skier at West Point. To this day, the award is presented as part of the prize day ceremonies during West Point graduation week.

THREE

Early Life

I was born on May 31, 1935 in Brooklyn, New York, and we lived in Brooklyn until we moved to Bear Mountain in February 1943. We lived at 815 Foster Avenue, and my grandparents lived across the street, about a block below us at 726 Foster Ave. When we wanted to visit my grandmother, we would walk down our side of the street then stand and scream at the top of our voices, "Nana!" If that didn't work we would look for a passing stranger and, using the lexicon of the city kid, say "Cross me, Mister." My own kids laughed when my wife and I told them that "Cross me Mister" was part of everyday life in New York City.

While I'm sure my parents struggled financially in the early days when Dad was running the diner and operating concessions in the city parks, their children never had a financial concern. Indeed, while we were never rich by modern standards, we were never denied anything on the grounds that we could not afford it. All of us went to Catholic grammar and high schools, college and two of us to graduate school—me to law school and my brother Mike to the to the Tuck School of Business at Dartmouth, with my father paying all of the tuitions. I did not realize at the time how fortunate I was to graduate from law school without the burden of student loans. Fortunately I was able to do the same for my children.

We moved to Bear Mountain in early 1943, and growing up there had its pluses and minuses. On the minus side, we were the only family living in the park so we had no neighbors. We went to grammar school in the town of Highland Falls, which is about 5 miles away.

Although we were fairly isolated for most of the year, there were many compensating features to our lives. The fact that we had few nearby neighbors made us much closer as a family. We depended upon each other for company. Even though there was a fairly large age range from Terry, the oldest, who was three years older than me and then the other three boys each about four years apart with Susie youngest being 17 years younger than Terry, we spent a lot of our social life together.

As I was growing up, the Brooklyn Dodgers, the New York football Giants, the New York Knickerbockers and various other professional sports teams spent time at the Inn. Thus I got to meet and interact with some of the leading sports figures of my youth. We became particularly close to many of the people in the Dodger organization, some of whom became friends for life. This included the family of Harold Parrott, who was the traveling secretary and later business manager of the team, and the Mulvey family, whose matriarch owned 25% of the team.

In 1946, Leo Durocher, then the manager of the Dodgers, asked my dad if I would like to make a trip with the team. As a result, I traveled with the Dodgers on what was then considered a Western swing: Pittsburgh, Cincinnati, St. Louis, and Chicago. Today the idea of a man in his 40s taking an 11-year-old boy on a trip as his roommate would raise considerable concern. However, Leo was a well-known heterosexual and I doubt, in that era, that anyone gave a second thought to my sharing a room with him.

The trip was extraordinary. Harold Parrott brought his two sons who were only slightly younger than I, and the three of us had great times together. We each had our own Dodger uniform and every day we

A Life Begun on Third Base

would travel with the team to the ballpark, run around in the outfield during batting practice, and sit on the bench with the players during the game. Although not quite the team of the "Boys of Summer," I got to know many of the legendary Dodgers, including Pee Wee Reese, Carl Erskine, Duke Schneider, Dixie Walker, Whitlow Wyatt, and Ralph Branca. While to the normal fan these men were on a pedestal, once you got to know them they seemed like everybody else. One incident demonstrating this occurred during that same season when I was attending a game at Ebbets Field. I was in locker room and I said hello to Dixie Walker. He said "John, I just got a new glove but my old one is still in pretty good shape—would you like it?" I replied, "Thanks, Dixie but I couldn't use it - - you're right-handed and I'm left-handed." Later that day at my grandmother's house, when I told the story to two of my uncles, they couldn't believe that I had turned down the opportunity to have Dixie Walker's glove.

While Leo had a reputation as being a tough guy and sometimes nasty, he could not have been kinder to me. When the word of my trip reached my relatives several of them gave me some spending money. My folks told me not to carry it myself but to give it to Leo and let him dole it out to me as needed. I did this and, as we were returning to Penn Station at the end of the trip, Leo said, "Here is your money." As I was putting it in my pocket he said, "Don't you want to count it?" I said, "No, I trust you," and he said, "Count it." I recall I started with about $33 and although I had spent almost all of it, Leo had handed me $33.

I went on a similar road trip in 1947, but not with Leo. Leo had been suspended from baseball for the year by the Commissioner, Happy Chandler. The Commissioner said it was because he hung around with some undesirable people, including the actor George Raft and friends of his who were said to be involved in organized crime. Since Leo could not take me, Harold Parrott asked my dad if I would like to make the trip with him and his sons Todd and Lynn, with whom I had traveled in 1946. The major difference between the two trips, other than the absence of Leo, was that 1947 was the year that Jackie Robinson became the first African-American to play in the big leagues.

The thing I remember most is how crowds of African-Americans would surround the team bus after games just so they could get a look at Jackie Robinson. I don't think I fully appreciated the history I was watching.

Although I did not travel with any of the other teams that stayed at Bear Mountain, I did get to meet and spend time around many of the players. I remember watching the Knicks' practices on the outdoor basketball court. Carl Braun, who was then their outstanding player, would stay on the court after practice throwing up shots and I would run and retrieve the balls that bounded away from the basket. This helped me understand a saying of Mr. Rickey: "Luck is the residue of hard work." Even though you have some degree of talent, if you want to be the best you still have to work hard.

We had a good life while living at Bear Mountain. Although Dad worked hard, we lived where he worked. I went to the Sacred Heart Grammar School in Highland Falls and to St. Patrick's High School in Newburgh. At the time, St. Patrick's was the only Catholic high school in a 50-mile radius, and the students it attracted were those whose parents were particularly motivated to see that they got a good education. It therefore produced a number of successful graduates, including Jay Oliva, who went on to be the President of NYU, the author James Patterson, and Richard Dillon, a classmate whom I still see often, who, as a secular priest, went on to become the head of the Theology Department at Fordham University, a Jesuit school.

One of the lasting benefits of having attended St. Patrick's High School was that I met Brother Cassian Gregory, who would become a major inspiration for my family. Although Greg taught in the grammar school, he was the athletic director and coach of the high school teams. While I was not much of an athlete, I did play JV basketball and served as the manager of the varsity team. Greg was an extraordinary individual. As my classmate Father Dillon said years later at Greg's funeral, "One of the amazing things about Greg is that everyone he met felt that they were his best friend."

He had an incredible ability to make friends across the generations. We were close friends, but he also had a special relationship with my mother, my wife, and all of my children. For example, years later when my daughters Anne and Meg were in England, they made a special trip to Dublin because Greg was there on a visit. Similarly, as an adult, my daughter Kate who was visiting from her home in Chicago for a few days, made a three hour round-trip on two of those days to visit Greg in Redbank New Jersey during his final illness. My son John and his wife, Christy, named their first child Gregory in his honor. A year and a half later when they named their second son John, I asked Christy, "If you were going to name one of your children after your husband, why did you not name your first son John?" Her response was, "We wanted to name a child for Greg while he was still alive." Greg was thrilled by his namesake, and I was impressed by the wisdom of Christy and John.

One of the most important things about my life at Bear Mountain was that Dad was a believer that we should learn to work. So, starting when I was about 14, I would work every summer at one of the refreshment stands or as a sweeper picking up cigarette butts outside the Inn. Dad would also insist that I work on many weekends during the school year, if the Inn was particularly busy. While at the time I somewhat resented the fact that I was working when my friends were not, I think I learned an important lesson about the value of work.

After graduating from high school, I attended Manhattan College in Riverdale, New York, which was run by the same Christian Brothers who taught at St. Patrick's. In those days, it was highly unusual for the graduate of any Catholic high school to attend anything other than a Catholic college. My years at Manhattan were enjoyable but not remarkable. I was a relatively good student but by no means at the top of my class. I was active in some campus organizations and served as the president of the Arts and Sciences Association and of my fraternity, Phi Beta Kappa. There were no fraternity houses but we got together for lunch and had a number of parties during the year. It was when I pledged for the fraternity that I met Otto G. Obermaier, who later served with me in the United States Attorney's office and with whom I started law a firm that continues to this day.

When I graduated from college, I was convinced that I wanted to spend my life working with my dad in the hotel and restaurant business, and I did that for one year. I found, however, that my father had the only good job in the place; the business did not need more than one senior executive. As a result, I spent a good deal of my time washing windows and scrubbing floors. After about nine months of this I came to realize that I should perhaps look for another line of work. I decided to go to law school.

One significant event during my year working with Dad was that I received an induction notice to report for service in the Army. For me, this was a somewhat startling event, since when I was in my first year of college I had lung surgery to remove a benign cyst, which had involved taking out a third of one of the lobes of my left lung. As a result, I assumed that I would be classified by the selective service system as 4F, unfit for military service. Thus, when I received a notice to report for a pre-induction physical, I assumed that I would take the physical and then get a notice that I was 4F. Instead, I got a notice that I was "physically acceptable for service." Not wanting to serve as an enlisted man, I hastened to find an officers candidate program. However, since I have poor vision in one eye as a result of having a lazy eye, I flunked the physical for officer candidate training. In approximately March of 1958, I received a notice to report for induction at the local selective service office in Nyack.

The Saturday night before I was to report for induction, my parents threw a going away party for me, at which a number of my relatives and friends gave me some money to supplement the meager pay I would draw as an enlisted man. My brother Mike drove me from Bear Mountain to Nyack in my car, which he then drove to Manhattan College, which he was attending. I was given a bus ticket to the induction center on Whitehall Street in lower Manhattan. I went from room to room, standing in line to take various tests, and at the end of the process carried my papers to a desk where an enlisted man was stamping something on the papers and telling people to report for induction in an adjoining room. After reviewing my papers he stamped them and said to me, "Go around the corner to the mess and have lunch and then come back to see me and I will arrange for your transportation home." I was shocked and wanted to be sure I had heard him correctly so I said, "What did you say?" He replied, "Go have lunch." Not wanting to rock the boat, I went and got lunch in the cafeteria. I ate very little and hurried back to the desk where I patiently waited as the clerk made out vouchers that would entitle me to subway fare to get me to the bus terminal and a voucher for a bus trip to Nyack. I then left the building and immediately hailed a cab to take me to Manhattan College where I got the car for my brother and headed back home. The shortest military service in history. I did not return the gifts.

FOUR

Peggy Conroy and Our Family

In March 1968, I was in Washington DC as an Assistant to the Solicitor General of the United States. I had only recently broken up with a woman I had been seeing who was the secretary to a second level assistant in the White House.

For years I had gone with my father to the annual dinner of the Society of the Friendly Sons of St. Patrick, and I made the trip back to New York to attend the 1968 dinner, which I believe was held that year on Monday, March 18th. The dinner was preceded by lengthy cocktail party and accompanied by copious amounts of wine. Despite the abundance of liquid refreshment, I thought it appropriate to stop with some of my friends for one more drink at Toots Shor's, a well known watering hole for politicians and sports figures.

To my great good fortune, one of my former colleagues from the United States Attorney's office, Ed Cunniffe had also decided that a nightcap at Shor's would provide a proper ending to the night. He asked what I was doing and, when I told him I was working in Washington, he said, "I know a girl in Washington you should look up. Her name is Margaret Conroy."

I cannot recall whether Ed gave me her phone number, but when I returned to Washington, I called her. I needed a date for a party the following Saturday, and since I had only recently broken up with the woman mentioned above, I thought I should try this friend of Ed's. Peggy later told me that as soon as she hung up after accepting my invitation, she called her sister Grace and said, "I have just done the dumbest thing, I said I would go out Saturday night with some friend of Ed Cunniffe."

I had no idea how much my life was about to change as I climbed the stairs of the lovely house in Foggy Bottom where Peggy had her apartment. I cannot say it was love at first sight for either of us. We spent the night at a party given by a colleague from the Solicitor General's office.

Our romance developed rapidly. We went out to dinner the next two weekends and then began seeing each other often. During this period Lyndon Johnson announced that he would not seek reelection and on April 4 1968, Martin Luther King Jr. was shot. I recall Peggy and I watching Bobby Kennedy coming out to try to calm the crowd

The riots sparked by Dr. King's death continued for several days and a curfew was imposed in DC. Although I did not know it at the time, the curfew helped advance my cause with Peggy because I ran the curfew to see her which the other man who she was dating at the time did not. I have to confess that my decision to run the curfew was aided by the fact that I carried Department of Justice credentials, which I could use if stopped.

I got a hint that Peggy also thought that this was a serious relationship when she invited me to have Easter dinner at the home of her sister Grace and her husband Donald Mulvihill. It was a wonderful occasion and was when I first met Peg's mother. After we left, Grace turned to her husband and mother and said, "I think this is serious, he's the first one she has brought here that she hasn't corrected."

I think that from that moment on both of us knew where we were headed but were not ready to talk about it. However, our swiftly developing romance took a slight detour, shortly thereafter. In late

A Life Begun on Third Base

April 1968, Columbia students protesting over various issues took over some of the campus buildings. After several days, Columbia brought in the New York City Police Department to clear the buildings and a melee erupted. People were injured and the campus was in turmoil. The University decided that it had to act and it appointed a special commission of prominent individuals to look into the conduct of the administration leading up to the protests and its decision to bring in the police. The Chair of the Commission was Archibald Cox, a Harvard law professor who would later become famous as the first Watergate special prosecutor and victim of the Saturday night Massacre. Shortly after the Commission was announced, I received a call from Michael Sovern, the Dean of Columbia's law school and a former professor of mine, who asked me to serve as the chief counsel for the commission. I discussed the matter with Erwin Griswold, the Solicitor General, who urged me to do it. At the time, the project appeared to have more public importance than it does looking back many years later.

While I was excited by the new challenge, I was not happy with the impact that it would have on my rapidly advancing romance. I talked to Peggy about it and, as she would often in the future when opportunities for public service were presented to me, she urged me to do it. This would mean we would be separated during the week but we agreed that we would see each other often on weekends.

I left for New York in early May, where I would live with my father in our house in Nyack. I did not realize it when I arrived but my detour back to New York was a blessing. My father was to die on June 28 and I am glad that I had the time we were able to spend together after my return from Washington.

Up to this point, Peggy had not met any of my family. She came to New York on the weekend of May 18 and we were to get together with my family for dinner at our home in Nyack on that Sunday. Peggy and I had dinner alone that Saturday night and as we sat in her mother's apartment in the early hours of Sunday morning I asked her to marry me and she did not hesitate to say yes. She then said that she would like me not to tell my family that we were engaged until after our dinner with them because she did not want her first meeting with them to be complicated by the news of our engagement.

Dinner with the family was a big success. I believe that all of my brothers and sisters and spouses gathered and as usual it was a lively conversation. After I took Peggy home that night I returned and sought each of them out to tell them the good news of our engagement. They were all delighted for me and much taken with Peggy. When my sister Terry met Peggy next she said, "Peggy, we really like you, but we were hoping for listener."

The time between our engagement and wedding is a bit of a blur. My work on the Cox commission ran into August and Peggy and I traded trips back and forth to Washington. On one of my early returns to Washington, I called Justice Thurgood Marshall, whom I had gotten to know when serving as a law clerk to Judge Leonard Moore after graduating from law school. I told him I had recently become engaged. I could hear him shout to his wife, "Hey Cissy we have got to call Leonard Moore and tell him that we got John Martin married!" He then invited Peggy and I to dinner at his home. It was originally just the four of us but later in the evening Roy Wilkins Junior, the son of the longtime president of the NAACP, joined us. Not surprisingly, Thurgood took an immediate liking to Peggy and I think his affection for her was in large measure responsible for the fact that he invited us often to join him and Cissy at the Second Circuit Judicial Conference.

When our wedding day finally arrived, September 14, 1968, it was a beautiful day. The wedding took place at Saint Philip Neri Church, which was across the street from Peg's mother's apartment. We were married by my mother's cousin, Edward Head, who was then in charge of Catholic Charities in New York and who would later be the Bishop of Buffalo. The reception was at the Larchmont Shore Club, a beautiful venue on Long Island sound.

We spent our wedding night at the Plaza Hotel and flew the next day to the Virgin Islands, where we spent our honeymoon on St. Croix and St. John's. One of the notable events of our honeymoon was the sunset cruise we took on a sailboat that was staffed by a crew from the hotel. The boat usually carried six passengers but it turned out that Peggy and I were the only passengers that evening. Undaunted we consumed all of the rum punch that had been prepared for six. Needless to say, we went right to bed.

We returned straight to Washington from the Virgin Islands to begin our married life in a small house we rented at 636 Independence Ave., S.E. The love we shared was particularly intense at the outset of our marriage as we delighted in the pleasure of being together all the time. If you look at our wedding album you can see how taken we were with each other. Years later we regretted that our album did not contain more pictures of our friends who were there. However, as we picked out the pictures to go in the album we were so enamored of each other that we focused on the pictures reflecting the love and happiness between us.

Our time to simply enjoy ourselves with our friends was short-lived because not long after we came back from our honeymoon Peggy realized she was pregnant. We were married on September 14 and John was born on June 23 so we were not a carefree married couple for long.

The news that Peggy was pregnant was exciting and to celebrate we decided to have dinner at Chez François, then one of the best restaurants in Washington. As we walked into the restaurant, standing there waiting for a table was my old boss, Bob Morgenthau, and his law school classmate Byron White, then a justice of the Supreme Court. In his earlier life White had been an all American football player, better known as Whizzer White, who was drafted number four in the 1938 NFL draft by the Pittsburgh Steelers and led the NFL in rushing yards in his first season. Bob introduced us to the Justice, but since we hadn't yet told our family Peggy was pregnant, we said nothing about the reason we were there.

It was approximately 7 a.m. on June 23, 1969 that I walked into a room in Georgetown Hospital and saw my wife in the bed holding John, our first born. As I have said to many people, no one can tell you before you have your first child what that child will mean for you.

Your love of a child is unique— in part because it does not depend on your being loved in return. If you are lucky, a child may begin to return your love as he or she matures but at the outset it is very much a one-way street. At that moment, I knew that I loved that little thing completely and sharing his life and that of his siblings was the best thing that happened to Peggy and me.

I can remember the joy of calling family and friends and telling them the good news. I do not recall if I engaged in the then prevalent practice of distributing cigars, but I am sure I bored all of my friends with descriptions of the beautiful my child was.

By the time John was born I had just about finished two years in the Solicitor Generals office and it was time to get back to New York. Our lease was expiring in September so we set that as a departure date. Peggy and I thought we would like to try living in Manhattan where I was scheduled to open a one man practice as a tenant in law offices of a friend. However, my father's home on the river in Nyack had been vacant since his death and we thought having people living there might make it easier to sell.

We moved back in early September and it took us almost a year to get the house sold. We never did move to Manhattan since Peggy was soon pregnant with Kate.

We finally got dad's house sold in August 1970 and moved to an apartment house on the river in Nyack. Shortly after we arrived at our new address, Kate arrived. Since Kate was due in early September and we spent the month of August at Peg's mother's house in Laurel Beach, we had found a doctor who would deliver our child at United Hospital in Port Chester New York and convenient to both Laurel Beach and Nyack.

I was in my office on the Friday of Labor Day weekend, September 4, 1970, when Peg called early in the afternoon to tell me that things were starting. As I recall, she said do not rush home but I said I would be on the next train. I don't recall how it was arranged, but when I arrived in Tarrytown on the train, Peggy was there with my sister Susan who had driven her. We immediately rushed to United Hospital where Kate was born about an hour and a half after we arrived. This time Peggy was allowed to have natural childbirth and I was present for the delivery. It was an exciting moment. Before Kate emerged, the doctor, who was a bit of a misogynist, said something like, "the hand is coming out first like a grabby woman so it must be a girl." It was then that it became clear to me that you could love a second child as much as the first, without diminishing your love for either of them.

Life in the apartment was no particular problem for me but a hassle for Peggy. In addition to all of the normal tasks of a wife and mother, she had to corral the kids into the elevator to bring our laundry to the machines in the basement. The apartment, which had a small terrace and overlooked the Hudson, was pleasant enough but we soon exceeded its capacity.

Meg arrived on September 15, 1971. Peg woke me in the middle of the night to say that we had to be on the way. I think it was my sister Susan who we called to take care of the two kids when we went to United Hospital. Once again I was thrilled to be present when the miracle occurred.

Our final child, Anne, was not born until five years later. Anne was due around Christmas day, and Peggy was faced with the possibility that on Christmas she would be in the hospital having a new baby. She dutifully did all her shopping and preparation for Christmas dinner and then prepared an elaborate set of instructions for those who would be in charge if she was in the hospital on Christmas Day

Fortunately, Christmas came and went without a baby but shortly after midnight on December 26, Peggy woke me and we were off to the hospital where Anne was born in the early morning hours. Once again Peggy decided against any type of injections and I had the privilege of being present at the birth.

Anne's birth provided two memorable stories. The first involves my daughter Kate, who was then a first grade student at the Purchase grammar school, which had a significant Jewish contingent. The children had just gone through the holiday play with Jewish and Christian songs. Shortly before Peggy gave birth, Kate looked her in the stomach and said, "mommy when the baby comes out how do you know whether it is Christian or Jewish." A great question.

The second incident is funny only in hindsight. When Anne was born she took Meg's place as the baby of the family. Meg was not happy about this and it was to infect their relationship for many years. Not long after Anne was born Meg's kindergarten teacher told Peggy that they should talk. She recounted an exercise in which the children were asked to draw a series of pictures that told a story. When Meg got to the front of the class to discuss her drawings the teacher noted that the first two drawings were obviously a woman with a baby in her stomach and the woman with the baby in her arms. The third picture was a rectangle and when she asked Meg in front of the class and what is this rectangle, Meg replied "it's a coffin." The teacher tried to soften the situation by saying, "oh Meg you have drawn the full cycle of life from the time that the baby is in the mommy's tummy, then it is born and then years later when it dies." Meg replied, "Some babies die soon." I am happy to be able to report that today Meg and Anne are as close as two sisters could be, taking turns babysitting each others children.

After Anne started school, Peggy was able to find a way to balance being a mother with a new professional career. The Columbia School of Social Work offered an MS program in which most of the courses could be taken at SUNY Purchase, which was only 10 minutes from our home. As would be expected, she successfully completed the program and began her career as a therapist. She worked first at the New York Psychiatric Hospital in White Plains, known as Bloomingdale's, the street on which it was located. After about three years there, she joined the Samaritan Counseling Center in Rye New York, an organization designed to provide mental health counseling at a reasonable rate for those who could not otherwise afford it.

After several years, Samaritan closed because of lack of funding and Peggy set up her own office in space she rented in Port Chester New York. Over the course of her years, I know she helped many patients who were grateful for her efforts. The work was difficult but it gave her a sense of fulfillment and, since she was always working close to home, she could still be there for her children. She retired about six years before she died because of the problems caused by our being in Florida for substantial periods of time. She also found the work very stressful—a number of her patients were suicidal, so often a patient's life was in her hands.

As was her career in government service prior to our marriage, Peggy's choice of her career as a therapist was consistent with her core value, which was that she was here to try to make the world a better place

Raising our four children was the most important thing Peggy and I did in our lives. For her, it wasn't always easy. She had become accustomed to serving as an executive in important positions that gave her professional fulfillment. The day-to-day tasks of being a mother were not the things of which dreams are made. Peggy sacrificed her career to do them because she felt it was necessary. The wisdom of her choice is evidenced by the fine people our children have become.

Although raising children is not an easy task, it is extremely rewarding and a source of great joy. We had many wonderful times with the children both at home and during the vacations we took.

Raising the children was filled with innumerable moments of joy. It was fun to watch them grow and develop and to share their every day experiences. Having children made all the holidays special, particularly Christmas. I remember saying at some point that it would be sad to have a Christmas when none of the children believed in Santa Claus. I was wrong. The first Christmas we had when none of the children believed in Santa Claus was probably the best ever. The joy came from seeing our children concerned as much about what they were giving to their parents and siblings as they were about what they were receiving.

It was great to share their achievements, whether it was academic success, a performance at a play, a recital or debate. It was rewarding to see the joy they took in each other's success

Since my work often caused me to be in the office in the evening or traveling overnight, I made a special effort to see that we always took time for vacations with the children. We had some wonderful trips including at least two trips to Europe.

We also rented a ski house for several winters in Stratton, Vermont. We were not up to a weekly 4 hour drive to the ski slope so we rented the house with two other couples, the Nussbaums and the Callagys. Skiing is a wonderful family activity because you are always with your children, either on the ski slope, at meals or in a ski house.

One of our most memorable experiences was a 6 1/2 week trip through the national parks in the West. We flew to Salt Lake City and rented a car which we drove to Yellowstone National Park and the Tetons where we rented cabins. The parks were rich in natural beauty and extraordinary wildlife. You might wake up in the morning to see a moose looking through your bedroom window.

When we left the parks, we drove back to Salt Lake City where we rented a motorhome and drove to the Grand Canyon, Bryce, Zion and Canyon de Chelly National Parks, Las Vegas and then over to San Diego, and up through Los Angeles and along the coast highway to San Luis Obispo where we visited the Hearst Castle. From there we traveled to Yosemite National Park, then back to Utah stopping in Reno Nevada.

The greatest joy of raising children comes from watching them develop from helpless creatures depending upon you for everything into self-sufficient adults who are kind and caring and whose company you enjoy.

I asked each of my children to share their recollection of growing up in our family. They provided the following, which are presented in the order in which each of them joined our family.

A Life Begun on Third Base

John Conroy Martin

In thinking about growing up in our family, I realize that most of my childhood memories are of spending time with our family. We obviously did other things and had other friends with whom we spent time—but I mostly remember our times together. Some of that was attributable to Kate, Meg, and I being so close in age—especially as young children, each always had the others around. I think some was also attributable to the house in which we grew up. It was located in a neighborhood without sidewalks, or a lot of young children, so of course we spent time together. Moreover, the house itself was large and rambling, with many add-ons to what I think was originally a colonial-era barn, resulting in lots of different levels and connected that provided ample room to chase each other around or play hide-and-go-seek.

But I think the biggest reason why I have so many childhood memories of my siblings and parents was that we all assumed the importance of family. Dad says that "raising our four children was the most important thing Peggy and I did in our lives"—and that, from my experience, was the way he and mom viewed it. When I was very young, Mom was always present – having chosen to raise us over pursuing a career in other areas. But Dad was hardly a distant figure himself. I seem to remember seeing him most evenings and weekends, and we were constantly doing things together. Mom and dad of course took time for one another (the wisdom of which I have come to appreciate as the father of four children myself), but also found lots of time to spend with all of us. We always vacationed together, would go play tennis (and later golf) together, and would go out to restaurants as a group. We still do—the annual trips we make to Florida, with our own spouses and children in tow, are just the latest outgrowth of the tradition I remember.

I've seen a lot of unhappy families in my life. I know many people who do not (or cannot) remain in touch with their parents or siblings. As a lawyer, I have handled more cases than I can count arising out of children estranged from each other or from their parents by money, maltreatment, or long-simmering resentments. While I am very sorry for those troubles, I have no understanding of them from experience. I know that I am not always the most attentive brother or son (or husband, or father), but I really do still enjoy spending time with my sisters and my dad and take genuine joy in their many accomplishments. That's the natural result of the parents who raised me and is a legacy I hope I can carry on with my own children.

Katharine Marie Martin

Many of my clearest memories of growing up Martin are set in Laurel Beach, at our Grandma Conroy's house. We spent two weeks every August in that house up until John went to college, if I remember correctly. I remember how impossibly long the drive seemed to get there when I was a kid. It actually took an hour, maybe an hour and fifteen minutes if there was traffic. Our longing to get there made every minute in the car seem like an eternity.

Grandma's house was at One Seaview Avenue in Milford, CT, right on the boardwalk overlooking the beach and Long Island Sound. There were big paw prints painted onto the boardwalk, which made it feel like a direct road into adventure. We used to love to walk down to the gate at the end of our section of the boardwalk in the early evening and then turn around and come home. I remember smelling people's grills and hearing their TVs and catching sight of families through the screened porches of the houses that lined the boardwalk. I remember looking forward to getting home to have dinner with our own family, which at the beach included the six of us, Grandma and mom's brother Uncle John. I most definitely remember Grandma's chocolate cake, made from scratch (the icing too), which was even better after it sat for a day or two and the icing hardened. I remember playing a ton of cards.

Meg, John, Anne and I spent hours climbing on the rock jetty that extended from the beach right in front of the house out into the water. We'd jump off into the Sound on the deep side if we were feeling brave. We scanned the water for jellyfish before entering—all of us got stung and we used to debate whether the purple or the red jellyfish stings were worse. JAWS came out in 1975 and we watched it at our friend Sarah Nalawack's house on video a few years afterwards (despite mom forbidding it). After that, the Long Island Sound was also filled with giant sharks, at least in my mind. It didn't keep us out of the water. We actually found a dead shark on the beach one day (it was probably a dog fish, and probably 4-feet long at the most.). It was THRILLING.

Laurel Beach had a magical quality about it, like Narnia. It was a total break from our regular lives, and featured a different cast of colorful characters. The Hoags lived across the street from Grandma. Mr. Hoag looked a lot like Santa Claus, and used to tease Grandma, and mock-argue with Uncle John, which was delightful. I don't remember Mrs. Hoag at all - maybe Mr. Hoag was a widower? She was probably just quiet. Mr. Hoag was not ... he was very memorable. There were the Nalawacks, our neighbors up the street who had a daughter our age. The Nalawacks had a big, wooden playset in their backyard - it had swings and ladders and ropes. It also had earwigs, which was repulsive but made playing on it that much more dangerous and therefore exciting.

There was Uncle John, who we didn't see that much of during the year, since he lived in DC, but who was a fixture at Laurel Beach in August. Uncle John was a larger than life Irishman with a boat called The Gael Wind and a snore like an dying engine. He filled the house with energy and took particular delight in teasing Grandma about everything. He was the one who caught the big swordfish that hung over Grandma's mantle in the living room. There were our Mulivihill cousins, who we overlapped with for a few days each summer, and our Aunt Grace and Uncle Donald. I don't know how we fit when everyone was there, and it must have been cacophony for the adults, but those were great days for us as kids. A house full to bursting.

One of the best things about Laurel Beach was that it was a time to do not much of anything but hang out with our family. Dad worked a lot during the year, so at home we'd generally see him at nights and on the weekends, but at Laurel Beach we got to see him during the day. He brought us donuts and corn muffins from beloved Dunkin' Donuts for breakfast. He and mom would dress up in their all white outfits and head off to play tennis at the local courts, and sometimes we got to join them. Dad took us fishing and did the hard stuff, like baiting the hooks and waiving away the bees. Mom did the harder stuff of cleaning the fish that we brought home and cooking them.

We kids spent our days on the beach, building elaborate castles on the sand bars at low tide and then standing on them as the tide came in to see whose would last the longest. I don't remember having many plans. Laurel Beach wasn't about plans. It was about being together. It was about knowing that after you walked down to the end of the boardwalk with the paws painted on it and then turned around to come home, everyone you loved most would be waiting for you in the house on One Seaview Avenue.

I like to think of Baboo's house in Florida as the Laurel Beach of my siblings' children's lives. I hope my nine nieces and nephews remember it throughout their lives as we remember Laurel Beach—as a place of respite, adventure, and profound security—but most importantly as a place where you know you can find the people you love most.

In other words, home.

Margaret Ann Martin Ables

When I talk about "growing up Martin," I have come to appreciate that on Puritan Road, myself and my siblings were members of an extraordinary ordinary family.

The house itself was a large white colonial complete with small sections of picket-adjacent fencing, an ordinary suburban cliche. But walk inside and the place was a twisting fun house of random staircases, pass-through bedrooms, hidden crawlspaces, a closet with raised Zebra wallpaper and, yes, a full replica mini-pub with service bar and booth. It was, as it turns out, an extraordinary place.

A Life Begun on Third Base

My life inside this home was ordinary in its own way. There were family meals, siblings who loved and fought and played, and a mom and dad who loved each other and their kids. It wasn't until I got to college that I realized how out-of-the-ordinary this reality seemed to many of my peers. My friends came from backgrounds that lacked not just the comforts of privilege and wealth but the solid foundation of a family whose members loved and respected each other and—gasp—even enjoyed spending time together.

I remember a night spent trading childhood memories with my roommates. I described how on Friday nights we would have a babysitter and my siblings and I would be watching TV in the family room at the bottom of the stairs that lead down from my parents bedroom. I reveled in memories of those nights—we would be sitting, eating McDonalds and watching the Muppet Show as dad in a tux and mom in a beautiful dress trailing Joy perfume would wave goodbye to us as they headed off to some fancy event in the city.

My roommates all gasped at the image and told me it sounded like something out of a movie. It had never occurred to me before that there was anything extraordinary about those ordinary Friday nights.

We had some excellent events and some memorable vacations. Mom's seventieth birthday at the River Cafe was a wonderful night. Our trip to Prague was fun, silly, adventurous, and pretty much everything a trip should be. And, let's be honest, our summer in Honey was nothing if not memorable!

But our day-to-day was unexceptional. Our days were spent in the care of two parents with good values who practiced their faith and lived their marriage vows on good days and bad. In light of Dad's job, people often asked if there were famous people who came to the house when I was growing up, but the truth was that our lives were filled with ordinary people. These people (like Brother Greg, Sister Ranney, Father Dillon, and the Lanes) showed us the best kinds of lives were possible if one met the challenges that might come with extraordinary goodness.

When I talk to fellow parents in my current life as a podcaster, I often find myself returning to what I see as the misguided view of parenting that our jobs are to make our children's lives "special." I see many parents chasing the idea that there is some mythical camp, or some costly travel experience, or some high-end education that will "shape" a child and make them turn out "well".

I try in these moments to emphasize that, from my experience, kids are shaped not by their extraordinary experiences but by a million ordinary ones. There will be a thousand dinners, several hundred conflict-fueled car trips (some of which will involve vomiting), dozens of vacations that will turn out better than you could ever have expected (or maybe worse than you could have ever imagined), and a host of Sunday nights watching 'Murder She Wrote" together in the den and marveling at how Jessica's nephew Grady could find himself accused of murder YET AGAIN!

The simple truth is that, as the writer Annie Dillard says, "How we spend our days is how we spend our lives." How lucky I was to spend so many of those days in the company of my siblings and my parents in our extraordinarily ordinary home on Puritan Road.

Anne Elizabeth Martin Richards

As the youngest Martin sibling, it is no surprise that most of my memories of early childhood involve my big brother and sisters. Mom and Dad brought me home from the hospital to the house on Puritan Road that they, along with my older brother, John, and sisters, Kate and Meg, had already made "the Martin house," one that I would live in until I left for college. As a kid, I never knew our family any other way.

I was the youngest by five years, with my older siblings each only a year apart from one another. This meant they formed something of a cluster, so I was always trailing along, both metaphorically and literally, as fast as my little wobbling legs could carry me. And though there were times where they took issue with my very existence — Meg's grave proclamation to her kindergarten teacher that, "Some babies die soon," being a prime example—more often than not, they tolerated and even welcomed me into the big kid fold in a way that seems pretty generous in retrospect.

One of my earliest memories is of flying off of John's feet as he launched me from the couch across the living room in a game of "human cannonball" as the lightest—and therefore most suitable projectile—of any member of the family. Needless to say, Mom and Dad put an end to this game as soon as it came to light, but it was fun while it lasted.

I also remember what must have been one of the last Christmas Eves where I believed in Santa Claus. John, Kate, and Meg, who were at that point probably teenagers, spent hours with me at bedtime, winding me up with speculation about where Santa must be at that very moment—and were those reindeer hooves they heard on the roof? It was only later that I realized that the whole show had been for me.

As I got older, of course I began to idolize them and watch greedily as they passed through milestones that I yearned to experience myself. Whether it was seeing my brother heading off to high school in the magical and mysterious world of New York City, or watching my sisters in the Holy Child high school musical and thinking, "How could anyone be that cool?," I was always peeking ahead around the corner and wondering if I, too, would ever be that grown up and impressive. And then there were the awesome nights when they came to my own violin recitals and school plays and I could proudly point them out to my friends from behind the curtain.

When John, Kate, and Meg went off to college, they continued to invite me into their lives—asking me up to visit in their dorm rooms, see their improv performances, hang out with their friends (and yes, even John's "kinda sorta current girlfriend" who would eventually become my beloved sister-in-law). In retrospect, having a 12 year-old hanger on in your dorm room must not have been the pleasure for a college student that I imagined it to be at the time, but I knew that I was a member of a special club—the Martin siblings.

That time was also a very special one for me in my relationship with my parents, as it marked the beginning of a period where I lived with Mom and Dad on Puritan Road essentially as an only child. I have always felt so fortunate for having that time with them, just the three of us at home. It was also the time that I think of as marking the transition during which my siblings became more wholly my friends and peers, ones I have relied on throughout my adult life.

My father often says that one of the joys he and Mom experienced as parents was seeing their kids form our relationships to each other as adults. And I will always be grateful for John, Kate, and Meg for loving me as I am, as they have from the beginning. But as I get older and raise children of my own, I begin to see my parents in the background of these scenes of our childhood.

I see Mom and Dad encouraging the big kids to keep an eye out for their little sister and include her in their games. I see them gently reminding their teenagers that Anne still believes in Santa Claus. I see them calling their older kids at college and asking if they might invite their little sister up for a visit. I see them making space for us to explore and get into scrapes together—and even knock a lamp or two over playing human cannonball—and doing all this knowing how important the relationships we were building with each other would be in our adult lives.

However explicit or implicit this guidance was, what I am certain of is that Mom and Dad made our home on Puritan Road a place where we could be together as siblings that was warm, loving, silly, and fundamentally stable. They raised us with respect for one another as individuals and with a firm sense that we were a unit, regardless of age, or intermittent fights, or of temporary shifts in alliance. As I look to my own children, I can only hope that I can create as space for them to grow into themselves and to hold each other close half as well as Mom and Dad did for us.

A Life Begun on Third Base

AT THE TIME IT OCCURRED, ONE OF THE SADDEST MOMENTS of my life was when Peggy and I dropped our oldest, John, at college. I recognized that it was the end of the relationship we had for 18 years. What I failed to recognize was that our children's departure from our home for college was a critical step in their developing into a responsible adults with whom we would continue to have a loving relationship which would enrich our lives for years to come.

The saddest moment of my life actually occurred on August 10, 2017, the day Peggy died. She was the rock on which our family was built. Our son John gave the following eulogy at her funeral which beautifully captures the incredible woman she was:

> For my mom's eightieth birthday, we assembled a book of stories and photographs, containing remembrances from her friends and family—it's called "the Book of Mom." A copy is circulating around, and I recommend it because it provides a broader glimpse of my mom's life than I'm going to be able to provide today. In its spirit, however, I wanted to share with you two stories about Margaret Conroy Martin, also known as Peggy.
>
> The first story is about my mom's first meeting with my father's family. Back in 1968, my dad and mom had been dating a few weeks, and were already in love. Indeed, they were already engaged to be married, even though they hadn't told anyone yet. My dad therefore decided to bring Peggy home to meet his family. Obviously, meeting your future spouse's family is—under any circumstance—somewhat intimidating, and here there were some factors at play that increased the degree of difficulty. For those of you who do not know them, the Martin-O'Donohue clan has many fine qualities: they are passionate, they are opinionated and informed and they look out for their own. They are not, however, quiet, and a dinner conversation amongst them is best described as a free for all. It can be a tough place to make a first impression, or indeed any impression.
>
> In this particular instance, however, my father's family had no idea what they were getting into. Peggy Conroy was the middle child between a sister, Grace, and her late brother John, the daughter of two

educators, born in the Bronx to an Irish Catholic family. And, for those of you who do not know them, the Conroy-Kelleher clan aren't shrinking violets. My mom came to the meeting with a wealth of accomplishments. She had been educated at Smith College, and had both worked and traveled in Europe. She had then worked in nonprofits and on Capitol Hill where she became, in my brother-in-law David's words, "A DC mover-and-shaker in an age when women were rarely found in such places", including working for the longtime Democratic House Leader John Brademas and serving as the head of talent search for the Peace Corps, in charge of seeking out and hiring the talented people who would serve as its global administrators. She was, in short, more than prepared for whatever my dad's family could bring to the table, and no doubt leapt into the conversational fray with both feet and standard flying high. And, at the end of the evening, my aunt Terry delivered to her the family's verdict: "You know, we really like you, but we were hoping for a listener."

I've always liked that line, but as I said a minute ago, my father's family in fact had no idea what they were getting when Peggy Conroy Martin joined their family. As I think most of you know, my mom in fact was a great listener—one of the best I've ever known. Throughout my lifetime, my mother was a person to whom I turned, and to whom I knew people turned, with problems. In the span of the decade that followed that meeting, she went from being a DC mover and shaker to being a wife and mother of 4 children. I don't know how she felt about that—because it is not a topic she would have ever have brought up. She was too busy dealing with the crises we brought her on a daily basis—from skinned knees to how to handle our schoolwork to what jobs we should pursue to what people we should marry to how to handle her shrieking grandchildren. To her credit, as my wife has pointed out, my Mom usually offered advice only when asked, rather than offering it whenever she felt things might be going wrong and, in responding to those, my mom didn't waste time on platitudes—her reply was not going to be a mere "there there, it will be alright" or a general reminder of the powers of God or positive thinking. If you had shared your problems with her, she took them seriously and you'd get full the benefit of her thoughts and experience. Accordingly, when you spoke to her she'd listen—carefully and quietly. Then, she'd think. Then, after the thought, she'd tell you how she might approach the situation, or how others she knew had previously addressed it. The advice was usually direct and to the point—the morning after my mom's death, we found that the materials on her reading table included a copy of Strunk and White's *The Elements of Style*; while the copy belonged to my sister Kate, my mom's conversational style often followed William Strunk's famous dictum: "omit needless words." When she spoke was gentle, but she did not lie. She would tell you, as my cousin Grace remembers, that sometimes the best results that could be expected were "kind of a mixed bag." As my brother in law Matt has pointed out, Peggy might address a particularly long-winded, but not necessarily well-thought out plan with a simple "And how would that work, exactly." But because it was honest, and because she really listened to what the problem was, the advice she gave was almost always spot-on and wise. My sister Anne tells the story of repeatedly sharing mom's insights with her friends. Ultimately, when Anne's friends came to her with their problems, they would listen to what Anne had to say, but would then get to their real question: "Well, what does your mom think?"

The second story I wanted to share comes from the house in which my mom raised her four children. For those of you who may not remember it, it was this big sprawling house on the corner of Puritan Road and Purchase street, built in pieces over nearly two hundred years without clear architectural rhyme or reason, with the result that there were at least three main entrances. The one that got the greatest use went into my mom's domain – the kitchen - and for many years, entering that room, your eyes would be immediately drawn to a poster that my mom had framed and hung on the wall. It showed an emperor penguin, looking very much like a diplomat in a tuxedo, and beneath him the caption read: "I cried because I had no shoes, until I met a man who had no class."

My mom believed in, and valued, class. I don't of course mean economic class, or to suggest for a second that she believed in classes of people who could be ranked or valued differently. To the contrary, my mom reserved her most withering insult for those who thought that their wealth or background entitled them to special deference, or afforded them license to treat others badly. Those people, my mom would tell us, were "tacky."

Class, to my mom, involved handling oneself with dignity. On perhaps its most obvious level, her belief in class meant that it was important to look your best, and dress appropriately for the situation. My sister Meg, in her book of mom essay, talks about her childhood memories of my mom's elegance—of her "coming down the stairs with a whiff of joy perfume"—and my mom certainly embodied elegance. Indeed, I should tell you that the last trip I took with my mom was to visit her longtime stylist, John, because—even if my mom was having problems getting enough oxygen to stay alive, that was no excuse not to look her best. My mom also had fairly detailed rules respecting one's appearance, rules that included "one piercing per ear, please" "adorn not thyself with tattoos" and "are you really sure you want to wear that?" In honoring my mother's honesty, I'm not going to tell you that my mom didn't take those appearance rules seriously – because she did. But I will note that my mom's application of them was at least tempered by her sense of humor. Meg at some point accused my mom of being the "taste police" and my mom, to her credit, was able to laugh at that. Indeed, within a few years my mom, having caught herself spending a little more energy on some minor infraction of the appearance rules would punctuate her sentence with "I know... Taste Police... wrah wrah wrah wrah wrah."

But "class" to my mom was about more than appearances. If you had to boil it down to a single commandment, it might be "Don't spend too much time on your own troubles, because other people require your attention." That commandment was not intended to dismiss one's difficulties, but sprang from an unflinching recognition of what people could do if they set their minds to it. My sister Kate tells the story of my parents coming to see her do a mile-long ocean swim. My dad, having remarked that it seemed like an awfully long way, wanted to wait for Kate at the half mile mark then walk along the rest of the course as she went by, so that if she couldn't complete the race, they would be there to greet her. My mom agreed that they should meet Kate—and promptly proceeded to the finish line because that's where Kate was going to end up. My mom understood that things could be hard, and that it could be tempting to dwell on obstacle. But class, to my mom, demanded that one avoid the temptation to dwell on one's own sufferings, or allow them to distract from the real task at hand. And the real task at hand, for my mother, was always the same: it was serving God by loving other people. My mom had any number of events in her life that other people might have treated as requiring a detour—from mastectomy and open heart surgeries to the losses of her mother, brother, and countless friends, to life's daily disappointments and reversals. They all caused my mom pain, no doubt, but never distraction —she had children to raise, in-laws to welcome into the family, friends and relatives to advise and enjoy, and above all a husband with whom she could share the love and affection for all that God had given her.

JOHN S. MARTIN JR.

Peggy at her 70th Birthday Party

FIVE

Mentors

Before turning to the description of my professional career, it is important to acknowledge the debt of gratitude I owe to the people for whom I worked and who by their advice and example guided me throughout my career. In the early part of my career, I was fortunate to work for some outstanding lawyers and public servants: Judge Leonard P Moore of the United States Court of Appeals for the Second Circuit; Robert M. Morgenthau, then United States Attorney for the Southern District of New York and later the District Attorney of New York County; Thurgood Marshall, who in his career served as Chief Counsel of the NAACP Legal Defense Fund, a Judge of the United States Court of Appeals for the Second Circuit, Solicitor General of the United States and as a Justice of the Supreme Court of the United States; and Erwin N. Griswold, a former Dean of the Harvard Law School. Each of these men provided a great example of how to do your job and how to treat other people and each gave me valuable advice.

Judge Moore had been a Wall Street lawyer and served as the United States Attorney for the Eastern District of New York during the Eisenhower administration. Serving as his law clerk gave me a unique insight into how courts operate. He was also a wonderful example of how a judge should conduct himself. He was polite and courteous to all who appeared before him and generous in his assessment of others. I only heard him speak ill of an individual on one occasion; that person was Learned Hand, one of the most highly regarded judges to ever serve on the Second Circuit. What bothered Judge Moore was that Hand treated lawyers badly—he would sometimes yell at them or turn his back on them as they argued. This was antithetical to Leonard Moore, who believed that every lawyer should be treated with respect. One of the things Judge Moore told me, which guided me throughout my judicial career, was that it is important that all of the parties come away from their courtroom experience believing that they have had a fair trial and a reasonable opportunity to present their arguments. He said this was particularly important since 50% of litigants ended up on the losing side. Judge Moore's most direct impact on my career came from his advice that I should apply to the United States Attorney's office because that would give me valuable trial experience.

I took Judge Moore's advice and applied to the office of the United States Attorney for the Southern District of New York, then headed by Robert M Morgenthau. Bob was from a distinguished family. His grandfather had been the United States Ambassador to the Ottoman Empire and his father served as Secretary of the Treasury under Franklin Roosevelt. Bob had been a supporter and friend of John F. Kennedy and his brother Robert. He had a distinguished war record and, although he had no prosecutorial experience, was appointed by Kennedy in 1961.

Bob did not try cases himself, but took an active interest in the more significant investigations in the office. He hired and promoted people on merit and never took political affiliation into consideration. The worst thing that the subject of a criminal investigation could do was to have some politically connected friend call Bob Morgenthau on his behalf. Bob's response would be to call the Assistant handling the investigation into his office to tell him to make sure that this individual was thoroughly investigated. Bob promoted me twice during my tenure in the office and never asked my political affiliation until the meeting at which I told him I was going to leave the office to practice in Nyack, New York. He then raised the question of my political affiliation because it could be important in developing a law practice in smaller community.

I was in my law office in Nyack when I received a call from Thurgood Marshall, then the Solicitor General of the United States. I had first met Thurgood shortly after I started clerking for Judge Moore when Thurgood was appointed as a judge of the Second Circuit. Thurgood had spent his life representing victims of discrimination and he treated everybody the same regardless of their place in the judicial hierarchy. If you walked into Judge Marshall's chambers at 10:15 in the morning, the door to his office would be open and he could be seen sitting at the end of a conference table having coffee with his law clerk Ralph Winter—later the Chief Judge of the Second Circuit. Thurgood would look up and invite you to join him. The next 20 minutes would be spent listening to his stories, a combination of jokes and true stories of his experience as a civil rights lawyer in the South where he often had to be smuggled out of town because someone wanted to kill him. After 20 minutes had passed, his secretary would appear and tell us: "you have to get out of here, the judge has to go back to work."

In April 1967 Judge Marshall hired me to serve as an Assistant to the Solicitor General. When we discussed a starting date, I said that I had to close up my practice and planed to attend the wedding of a friend in Geneva. I asked if I could delay my start until early July. He agreed. It was on my way to that wedding in Geneva that I stepped off a plane in Berlin and learned from a headline in the Paris Herald Tribune that Thurgood Marshall was being appointed to the Supreme Court. As a result, my service with him in the Solicitor General's office was very brief and during most of my tenure Erwin Griswold served as the as the Solicitor General.

Griswold, who had for years been the Dean of the Harvard Law School, was someone for whom I would develop great affection. However, he had an unusual personality and the ability to say the wrong thing on almost any occasion. For example, at the end of a luncheon that he hosted for all of the staff at a fancy private club shortly after he took office, he went around the table asking the members of the staff where they had gone to law school. The last person who would respond was Louis Claiborne, a graduate of Tulane Law School. Before Louis could speak, the Dean said, "well Louis that leaves you and me, Harvard and Tulane, kind of the Alpha and Omega." Apparently immediately recognizing his faux pas he added, "of course I'm not saying what order."

About nine months into my service in the Solicitor General's office, the Dean of Columbia Law School, Mike Sovern, called and asked me to serve as chief counsel to a commission being established to look into a student uprising at the University. When I asked Dean Griswold what to do, he immediately said I could have a leave of absence and urged me to take the job. Shortly after I went back to New York, my father died and I received a three-page handwritten note from Dean Griswold offering his condolences. He was a very decent man. Many years later I attended a small dinner for Justice Marshall to celebrate his 80th birthday. I was surprised to see Dean Griswold there because he and the Justice had strikingly different personalities. However, when it became time for Marshall to respond to various toasts, he noted that he was particularly pleased that Erwin Griswold was there because, in the early 50s, Griswold had gone to Texas to testify for Marshall in the case challenging the exclusion of African-Americans from the Texas law school. Griswold had been an early supporter of civil rights and Marshall did not forget a friend who came to his aid.

SIX

My Introduction to the Law

The Bear Mountain Inn dining room had roughly 300 feet of casement windows, each of which had eight individual pains, and a floor that was approximately 3500 square feet. The job of washing those windows and waxing the floors had a lot to do with my decision to go to law school.

I think it was in July 1958 that I decided to apply to law school. Dad's brother Bill was a successful lawyer and, in my senior year of college, I had taken the Law School Admissions Test. By this time the normal admission process for the September class was long over and I recognized that my best chance of getting into Columbia Law school would be if my uncle could help. I called him and he arranged an interview with the Dean of Admissions. What I remember best about the interview was the Dean asking me how I had done on the law school admission test. I recall that I was in the top 80% of those who had taken the test and I thought this was quite good since I knew only one or two people at Manhattan who had done better. Thus, when the Dean asked the question I thought I would seal my admission by impressing him with my score. When I told him I was in the 80th percentile, he paused and said, "Well, you will be in the bottom third of the class but if you work hard you can probably get through." I was suitably deflated, but I was admitted. A year later, I saw the same Dean as I arrived for the prize day ceremony where I would receive a certificate as a Harlan Fiske Stone scholar attesting to the fact that I was in the top 10% of my class. When I saw the Dean he said, "What are you doing here?" He was shocked when I told him I was a Stone scholar.

I was taken with the law immediately. The first week of law school for first year students was devoted to a course called Legal Method. Its purpose was to educate the students in how to read cases and statutes to extract the governing principles from them. Our system of law is based on the Common Law developed in England. The Common Law is simply the accumulation of governing legal principles that have evolved over years as individual cases that have been decided by judges, tested on appeal and then applied to future cases of a similar nature. What the student has to learn is how to focus on the particular facts that are significant to the decision and to separate gratuitous remarks of the court (in legal jargon "dictum") from "the holding," which is the legal principle that controls the disposition of the case. It turned out that I had a facility for appreciating which of the facts were central to a decision and, therefore, what legal principle was being applied.

After one week of Legal Method, the law student had the feeling of being a lawyer and the rest of the time was spent reading cases to understand the principles that made up the body of particulars field of law. Law school was based on the Socratic Method in which the teacher engages in a dialogue with the students concerning the critical facts of the case and the legal principle to be derived from them.

During the first semester of law school there were a number of students who seemed eager to raise their hand so they could be recognized to demonstrate their recognition of the significant facts of the case and its holding. Once the first semester grades came out, a substantial number of this group stopped trying to dominate the discussion.

A Life Begun on Third Base

One of the most vivid recollections I have of my first year involved a class in contracts with Prof. William Young. For there to be a contract there has to be 1) an offer (someone has to propose the terms of the contract), 2) an acceptance (someone must accept the terms of the contract that has been offered), and 3) consideration, (something of value given or promised by each side). For example, if I say, "I will give you $100 next week," and you reply, "terrific," I am not obligated by contract to give you $100 because you were not giving me anything in exchange. With this background I return to Prof. Young's memorable class. I forget what particular area of contract law we were discussing but the professor, a Texan, asked, "what one word describes this case?" Any number of eager hands went up with students yelling "offer," "acceptance," "consideration," or other contract principles. Finally, Prof. Young interrupted, "no, one word describes this case: Hogwash." That's when I learned judges are not always right.

Law school was my first exposure to anything other than a Catholic school education. Among my group of first-year friends were a variety of people of different faiths, although I would say the majority of the class was either Catholic or Jewish. I remember one of my Jewish friends, Lenny Rubin, saying to another friend, David Patterson, who was the consummate WASP, "You know, David, Columbia has a lot of scholarships for members of minorities and, as a WASP, you clearly qualify."

I distinctly remember Ash Wednesday of my first year. I had gone to church before heading to school and during the course of the day several people said to me, "You have some dirt on your forehead." When I said it was Ash Wednesday the typical response was," Oh it is that time of year." However, when I told one of my classmates it was Ash Wednesday he said, "What is that?" He was clearly not from New York.

Although I made several friends during my first year, my closest friends from law school would be people I met on the *Columbia Law Review*. The *Law Review* is a journal with articles on various aspects of the law, some written by students and others by practicing lawyers or law professors. It was staffed by approximately 25 students from each of the second and third years. The second-year students wrote shorter articles for the *Review* and spent a lot of their time cite checking the articles to be published. Each case is cited by reference to a volume and page number for the reported case together with the date of publication, some description of the court, and any subsequent appellate history. For example, a case from the Southern District of New York might be cited as 321 F. Supp 2d 286 (S.D.N.Y. 2002), *aff'd* 401 F.3d 743 (2d Cir. 2003). The *Law Review* prided themselves on the accuracy of their citations and therefore student editors spent a lot of time checking volume and page numbers and ensuring that the citations to the courts or other authorities were done in the proper form.

The management of the *Review* was done by the Administrative Board, in our case six third-year students, each assigned a particular responsibility. During my years at Columbia, the top 10% of the first-year class were selected to serve on the *Review*. The six members of the Administrative Board were selected by the vote of the outgoing members of the *Review* at the end of their third year. The administrative board consisted of an editor-in-chief, an articles editor, two notes and comments editors, a decision editor, and a managing editor. At the end of my second year I was selected as the managing editor. Harris Weinstein, who would become a lifetime friend, was the editor-in-chief and, while I cannot remember the particular positions, the remaining members of the board were Richard Sobol, Martin Balsam, Malvina Halberstam, and Peter Greunberger.

My job as managing editor was to assign the second year students to the various cite checking tasks and review each of the articles to ensure that the citations were in the proper format. I think one of the consequences of having to spend so much time proofreading articles for minor typos is that in the years that followed I became very poor at picking up typos in any work.

Part of the education I received Columbia resulted from the fact that I was the only one on the administrative board in our year who was not Jewish. Malvina and Marty Balsam were fairly Orthodox and were the only other single people on the board. Thus, when Harris, Dick and Peter went home at night for dinner with their wives Marty, Malvina and I would often end up going out to a kosher restaurant. As a result I learned a lot about Jewish food, customs and holidays.

One of the things I learned was that the Orthodox Jewish woman is not supposed to be touched before she is married—it is offensive even to take her arm to help her up the steps. I learned this when Malvina was bending over to put something on lower shelf and one of the Jewish men gave her a slap on the butt. She turned and let him have it in no uncertain terms. After they both left, Harris Weinstein explained the tradition. Several months later a group of us were out at a bar and Dick Sobol, who had a fairly good quantity to drink and was not particularly Orthodox, was slapping Malvina on the back telling her what a wonderful person she was. When Malvina went to the bathroom, I reminded Dick that she might not be happy with all the touching. He raised his hand stared at it and said, "what do I do now, boil it."

In the late winter or early spring I came into the *Law Review* office to find everyone sharing a bottle of wine. It turned out it was the Jewish feast of Purim and I was invited to share a drink. About a week later it was St. Patrick's Day and I came in to find a bottle of Irish whiskey on my desk with a card that said, on the first page, "On this St. Patrick's Day" and then, on the inside "all best wishes for the Passover season." The group had taken two cards and made them into one.

Being on the *Law Review*, and particularly the administrative board, involved a lot of work and as a result we missed a lot of classes. However, there were shared class notes and other things that helped us keep up. Thus, despite the fact that I missed several classes, my third-year grades were the best of any year. Mike Mitchell, a classmate who I would not get to know well until we served together in the US attorney's office, later told me that he was annoyed that I got a better grade than he did in labor law because he thought the teacher was favoring me because I was on the *Law Review* and gave me a good grade even though I missed many of the classes.

As I mentioned earlier, I worked as a summer associate at a law firm between my second and third year of law school. Insofar as my legal career is concerned, it was probably the most important job I had because it was there I met and became friends with Chet Straub. During his legal career, Chet became active in politics and served in the New York State legislature. More important, he became close to Senator Moynihan and served as his campaign manager. He then served on the Senator's judicial selection committee, which also made recommendations with respect to United States Attorneys. It was Chet who suggested I submit an application when the committee was interviewing candidates to become United States Attorney for the Southern District of New York. He would later talk to Senator Moynihan about my desire to become a judge.

When law school ended, I took a major part of the summer off and traveled for the first time to Europe. I went with my brothers Mike and Bill and our friend Tod Parrott. We sailed to Europe on the S.S. United States. Although we went tourist class, dad knew some people at the shipping line and we ended up in first class cabins. Thus, our cabin tended to be a gathering spot for nightly parties after dinner. We arrived at Le Havre and, when we went to Hertz to pick up our car, it was not ready. To make up for the fact that the car was late, the local manager took us on a tour of the Normandy beaches where the allies landed during the second world war.

We traveled through France and Belgium, into Germany and down through the Alps to Austria and Italy, then back to France for a flight home.

By the time I got back it was time for me to start my clerkship with Judge Moore. I have described the judge earlier and noted his impact on my career. Serving as a law clerk to an appellate judge was interesting because you got to know not only how your particular judge went about deciding cases but also about the interactions of the judges. The Second Circuit at the time had nine active judges and several senior judges—judges who had reached retirement age but continued to sit on a more limited schedule.

When I was clerking, judges sat for a week about once a month. After hearing oral argument, each judge wrote a brief memo to his colleagues on that particular panel indicating his views on the merits of the case. On the Friday of the week following the argument week, the three judges would meet for a conference and decide the cases. The law clerks would help draft pre-conference memos and would assist in drafting any opinion that had been assigned to the judge. Once an opinion was drafted, it was circulated and the other judges would comment and suggest changes. As a result of these procedures the law clerks got a good view of how each of the judges on the court approached the job of decision-making and on the most effective way to write something designed to persuade someone else. You also got an education in the broad areas of the law that came before the court.

The hardest part of the job of a law clerk came when you had to tell the judge that, in your opinion, the results he wanted to reach was wrong and not supported by existing case law. Fortunately for me, Judge Moore never reacted strongly and was prepared to be persuaded by a good argument that drew his attention to the relevant cases. No one could have been more pleasant.

I viewed my clerkship as part of my education and the law and I felt ready to take on responsibility for cases of my own, which I would do in the US Attorney's office

SEVEN

Assistant United States Attorney

I was sworn in as an Assistant United States Attorney on the day after Labor Day 1962 by Robert Morgenthau, the U.S. attorney. That afternoon Bob resigned to run for governor of New York. He lost badly to Nelson Rockefeller and returned to the office shortly after the election.

I was one of three assistants sworn in that day, the others being Charlie Fanning and Michael F. Armstrong. We would join a group of outstanding young lawyers, many of whom would become lifelong friends. At the time, I did not realize how truly special this group of lawyers was, but over the years it became obvious as our alumni became leaders of the profession. Among the people with whom I served were Franklin Thomas, later president of the Ford foundation, Bob McGuire, Mayor Koch's first Police Commissioner, Bernie Nussbaum, Bill Clinton's first White House Counsel, as well as future circuit and district judges and prominent partners of major law firms. At the time, however, we were just a group of young lawyers having fun, doing what we thought was important work, in a totally noncompetitive environment. Although I had several important positions thereafter, none was more enjoyable.

JOHN S. MARTIN JR.

My Swearing-In as an Assistant United States Attorney

US v. Bidwell

At the time I was hired, I was one of only two Assistants who had clerked above the District Court, so I was viewed as a "law man," someone who would be particularly adept at research and brief writing. As result, the day I was sworn in I was assigned as the third and junior lawyer on a major tax evasion case. The defendant, Truman Bidwell, a former chairman of the New York Stock Exchange, was represented by former federal judge Simon Rifkind, one of the leading lawyers in New York. The case would go to trial the following week before the Hon. Thomas F. Murphy, one of the truly great trial judges in the country, who would serve as a model for me some 30 years later when I became a federal judge. The two other Assistants on the case were Stephen Kaufman, then the Assistant Chief of the Criminal Division, and Arnie Enker, a fairly Orthodox Jew, who was the Chief Appellate Attorney.

We had a pretrial conference with Judge Murphy a few days before the trial. I remember two things about that conference. One: Judge Murphy said to Judge Rifkind, "While I have great respect for you, in front of the jury I will refer to you as Mr. Rifkind." The other had to do with the scheduling the following week, which included Rosh Hashanah. Judge Murphy asked what time we should break on the eve of the holiday. Although Steve and several of the defense lawyers were Jewish, they were uncertain and Enker was not present. Finally, Steve said, "Judge, I do not know but keep an eye on Mr. Enker. When the first ray of darkness comes through the window he will be off and you will know it is time to adjourn."

The trial was a great experience for a young lawyer because the lawyers on both sides were very good. Although Judge Murphy made an effort to keep the jurors from knowing that the defense lawyer was a former judge, Rifkind's trial team were constantly saying things like, "Judge Rifkind, this is the document you're looking for." Judge Murphy's wisdom became apparent after the case ended in a hung jury and one of the jurors who voted for acquittal gave as one of his reasons: "Well, that Judge Rifkind is a former federal judge and he said the man was not guilty."

The charges against Bidwell related to the fact that he claimed approximately $40,000 for deductions for things like entertainment, bonuses, business gifts and travel but an analysis of his bank accounts did not show any such payments. As the agent stated in accountantese: "We analyzed all of his accounts and he did not have $40,000 in cash available funds that could have been used for these expenses." The defense was particularly incredible given that Bidwell was the former Chairman of the New York Stock Exchange. He claimed that his wealthy stepgrandmother, Tekla Einstein, had given him numerous cash gifts for birthdays and Christmas, which he kept in a tin box in his closet and used for the payments at issue.

The trial ended in a hung jury and so we had a second trial a month or two later. For the second trial I had a slightly expanded role and examined my first witness in court. There was also a change in the judge and our trial team. Judge Murphy, having sat through one trial, apparently decided he did not want to sit through two, and the case was reassigned to Judge Croake. Since Judge Croake had only been appointed a year earlier, it was felt that the prosecution team should have a very senior lawyer, so Vincent Broderick, then the Chief Assistant U. S. Attorney, replaced Arnie Enker on the team.

In our last pretrial conference with Judge Croake, Steve Kaufman said to the judge, "It is not without great respect for Judge Rifkind that I will refer to him before the jury as Mr. Rifkind, as Judge Murphy did during the first trial." Although Judge Croake said nothing at the time, in fact he always spoke of Mr. Rifkind in the presence of the jury. However, that did not prevent the jury from learning that Rifkind was a former judge.

I had one witness at the trial, a bank official who was there to authenticate some of the defendant's bank records. After marking the exhibits for identification and asking the witness the formula of questions necessary to authenticate them, I proudly said, "Your Honor at this time the government offers government exhibits 13, 14 and 15 into evidence and may the record reflect that I'm showing them to Judge Rifkind." By the time I got back to my seat at the prosecution table, there was a note from Vin Broderick: "In view of your prejudicial reference to defense counsel, there is an opening for you in the civil division." Vin was not serious.

The second trial ended in a verdict of not guilty. While to us it seemed that the tin box defense was ludicrous, I think the verdict was not totally irrational. Bidwell had been audited by the IRS for five years prior to the one in question and it took the agent only three or four hours to uncover the fact that Bidwell did not have the cash to make the payments at issue. I think the jury thought Bidwell knew he would be audited and so when he prepared his returns he included some expenses he could compromise on to satisfy the agents. After the verdict came in, we spoke to Judge Rifkind, who said, "Do not be too distressed, boys, he has paid a heavy fine." I am sure that Rifkind's fee was a heavy fine.

In addition to the valuable experience I gained from my work on the Bidwell case, I also benefited from a lifetime friendship with Steve Kaufman and Vin Broderick, who would later be my colleagues on the District Court.

A Life Begun on Third Base

Learning the Ropes

Once I was finished with the Bidwell case, it was time for me to start handling my own cases. After sitting in and watching other Assistants handling routine matters, the first significant assignment for a new Assistant was handling the calendar in courtroom 318. At that time, all criminal matters were handled prior to trial in courtroom 318, referred to as Part 1. This involved things like setting bail, scheduling motions, and adjourning cases so that discovery and plea negotiations could take place. The Assistant assigned to the part might handle several cases for others who were on trial or otherwise not available. It was said that you came of age as an Assistant United States Attorney when Judge Weinfeld was in Part 1 and you had the calendar. Judge Weinfeld was one of the most highly respected judges in the country and he expected the Assistants to know the proper standards for bail and to be ready to answer any questions relevant to the matter before him. While he was forbidding on the bench, he was very pleasant when you met him on other occasions.

Another responsibility for relatively new Assistants was what was known as night duty. No federal law enforcement agent could have a person locked up without getting the approval of an Assistant United States Attorney. So, if an arrest was made after normal business hours, there had to be an Assistant available by phone to authorize the detention. You were given this assignment 4-6 months into the job. One of the more humorous incidents occurred when my friend Bob McGuire, who was at the time living with his parents, heard the phone ringing at 1 a.m. in the morning. He rushed to the phone not fully awake to hear the following: "Mr. McGuire, Lee Lowery FBI, I have a UFAP top 10." Confused and half-awake McGuire replied: "I have no [expletive deleted]ing idea what you're talking about." To this Lowery responded, "Unlawful flight to avoid prosecution, one of the 10 most wanted men in the country, can I lock him up?" Federal law made it a crime for anyone who had been charged with a crime in any state to flee to another state. This jurisdiction was used by the FBI to track down the most serious wanted criminals in the country. Every profession has its jargon and "UFAP top 10" was one that new Assistants had to learn.

The first case that I was to try myself involved a small grocery store owner on the Upper East side of Manhattan who was charged with knowingly cashing welfare checks that had been stolen from the mail. My two principal witnesses were drug addicts who would break into hallway letterboxes, steal the checks and then bring them to this grocer to get cash. The trial was before Judge Irving Ben Cooper, a former state criminal court judge who was known for his sometimes erratic behavior and quick temper. Although I always got along with him, during each of the trials of this case (just as in Bidwell the first trial ended in a hung jury), Judge Cooper stormed off the bench and called into his robing room the senior Assistant who was sitting in to supervise my work. Although the door to the robing room was closed, we could hear the judge screaming at the Assistant, apparently because the judge perceived him as having been making faces when the court ruled against the government.

I learned an important lesson from Judge Cooper during that trial. One of the benefits of being an Assistant U.S. Attorney is that, unlike state prosecutors who have an overwhelming caseload, we had the time to really prepare our cases for trial. Thus, I had spent a good deal of time with my two drug addicts getting them ready to testify. At the trial, I was partly through my examination of one of these addicts when I said, "Subsequent to that what occurred?" There was no response. Again, I said, "Subsequent to that what occurred?" When again there was no response from the witness, Judge Cooper looked down and said, "What happened next?" The witness immediately responded and I learned the valuable lesson that as a trial lawyer you have to ask questions in language that both the witness and the jurors will understand.

This lesson served me well over the years because lawyers can sometimes lose track of the fact that their job is to persuade the members of the jury and to do that you have to use language that they understand. In later years, when as a judge I spoke to young Assistants about trial presentation, I would often point out that they had a tendency to ask questions like "By whom are you employed?" and "In what capacity are you employed?" I would note that at a cocktail party you would never ask for this information in that way; you would say, "Where do you work?" and "What do you do?"

US v. Nelson Cornelius Drummond

My case against the grocery store owner had the same results that we had in Bidwell: a hung jury followed by an acquittal at the second trial. As a result, when some of my friends would pass me in the hall they would grab their ties and pull the end up over the heads simulating a hanging. I was to have one more hung jury.

On September 28, 1962, Nelson Drummond, Navy yeoman, was serving at the Newport naval base as a clerk in the offices of Mobile Electronic Technical Unit 8 (METU 8), a Navy unit responsible for doing repairs on sophisticated electronic weapons that were beyond the capabilities of the ship's crew. As a result, Drummond had access to the technical manuals for some of the Navy's most sophisticated weapons.

Early on the evening of the 28th, when the office was closed, Drummond returned and removed from the files several highly classified documents. He then left the office, got in his car and started driving to New York. Unknown to him, while he was in the office, he was observed by an FBI agent hiding behind a bookshelf, who was watching through a bolthole on one of the support columns. He was also being observed on a closed-circuit television that was monitored by two additional agents. FBI agents also followed his car as he proceeded from Newport to a diner in Larchmont, New York. After he parked his car, he was approached by an individual known to the FBI as a Russian diplomat. As they conversed through the cars open window, they were surrounded by FBI agents and arrested.

I first heard of Nelson Drummond the following morning when I picked up a paper headlining the fact that the FBI had arrested a spy and a Russian agent at the Larchmont diner. At that time, I had nothing to do with the case which was being handled by my colleague

Richard Conway Casey. Fortunately for me, after it became clear that Drummond would go to trial, it was decided that this was an important case and I was assigned to assist Dick. This would be the beginning of another lifelong friendship and Dick would ultimately serve with me as a judge in the Southern District.

Over the years, J. Edgar Hoover, the first and longest serving Director of the FBI, has been criticized for a number of failings. However, when it came to the field of foreign intelligence, he assembled an outstanding group of talented agents and I was fortunate to get to know some of them. The principal case agent was Homer Boynton, who would later be promoted to the number three spot in the FBI. There were a number of talented and interesting people who worked with him.

One of the agents was Joseph Palguda, who was assigned the task of interviewing Drummond when he agreed to cooperate with the FBI after his arrest. Over the course of several meetings, Drummond gave Palguda a detailed account of his meetings with the Russians from 1957 until his arrest in 1962. His story included details of his meetings, the type of documents he regularly provided to the Russians, and descriptions of various espionage techniques, including the use of dead drops and intermediaries to set up his meetings.

Given the extent of his confessions, it was somewhat of a shock to the prosecution team when they learned that Drummond would not plead guilty but would go to trial. It was at that point I was assigned to the case, along with Vin Broderick. Since Vin was the Chief Assistant United States Attorney, he would have ultimate responsibility and authority, while the bulk of the trial work was handled by Dick Casey. The case for the prosecution was overwhelming. As noted above, Drummond had been observed taking classified documents and bringing them to a meeting with two Russian agents. In addition, he had confessed on several occasions after being fully informed of his constitutional rights.

Joseph Palguda's trial testimony was the most impressive I ever saw. He had what I recall as four lengthy meetings with Drummond at which he provided highly detailed accounts of his meetings with the Russians over five years. Drummond's recitation of the events was not always consistent, so Joe had to testify about inconsistent versions of the same events given by Drummond at different interviews. While Joe's version of what Drummond said on each occasion was set forth in detail in contemporaneous notes and memorandum, at trial he testified from memory and it was a tour de force of recollection. It confused the defense attorney, who tried to impeach Joe by arguing that he was inconsistent as to what he said about particular meetings between Drummond and the Russians. However, Joe would patiently respond that it was on a particular date that Drummond gave one account of that meeting and then on another particular date that Drummond gave an inconsistent account.

Given the strength of the prosecution's case, we were all wondering what Drummond could possibly say in defense. Drummond testified that yes, he had met with the Russians and yes, he had given them documents that had classified stamps on them. However, he claimed that he had been fooling the Russians for years by giving them old documents, which although still bearing the stamp, were not classified. Although he could not dispute the fact that at the time of his arrest he had in his car documents that were at the time highly classified, he had an explanation for this.

One of the items seized from Drummond's car at the time of his arrest was a pistol located under the front seat. This would be the heart of Drummond's defense. He testified that at the meeting he had with the Russians just prior to the meeting the night of the arrest, the Russians told him that they realized that he had been giving them documents that were not really classified. They threatened that, if he did not show up with documents that were genuinely classified, they would expose him to the FBI. The reason he brought the classified documents on the night of the arrest was that he intended to use them to lure the Russians into his car and then he would use his gun to kill them.

At some point after the trial began, we learned that Drummond had presented this defense to a jury of his peers—other prisoners being held in pretrial detention—and was convicted. However, our jury hung. We later interviewed some of the jurors and learned the reason. Drummond was an African-American, and the first African-American ever charged with espionage. There was one African-American on the jury and he would not vote for conviction.

As fate would have it, as we got down to the end of jury selection at the second trial, there was one African-American potential juror. To our shame, Dick and I said that, given the prior result, we should use one of the government's peremptory challenges to strike this juror. To his credit, Vin Broderick said that the United States of America was not going to strike a juror because of her race.

The evidence at the second trial was no different and we almost had the same result. Fortunately, the indictment had two counts. One was the substantive crime of engaging in espionage and the other charged a conspiracy to commit espionage. The jury convicted on the conspiracy count but hung on the espionage charge. For us it made no difference, since each count subjected the defendant to a sentence of death or of imprisonment up to life. Judge Murphy, who presided at the trial, did not make a lengthy sentencing speech. He said simply, "Mr. Drummond, it is only out of sympathy for your family that I will not impose the ultimate sentence. I therefore sentence you to the custody of the Bureau of Prisons for the term of your life."

Many years later I learned that Drummond had been released on parole after he had served the 10 years that made someone sentenced to life eligible for release. Although we would have been appalled at the time, there was probably no benefit to society from keeping him in jail for the rest of his life.

The Drummond case was great for me. It established my friendship with Casey and Broderick, Homer Boynton and other of the agents. It would also have an impact later on my work in the office of the Solicitor General.

I cannot leave the Drummond case without recounting one further incident. One of the best times of the trial is after the summation has been completed and the case is adjourned to the next day when the judge will charge the jury. As in most cases, its work completed, the prosecution team adjourned to one of our regular hangouts, a bar and restaurant named Gassner's. There were the three of us, five or six FBI agents, and a Navy Captain, who had testified about the classified nature of the documents in Drummond's car on the night of the arrest. We probably arrived at 5:30 and Gassner's normally closed about seven. At seven, Jack Gassner, the owner, said, "I am leaving, when you leave put whatever money you owe me on the bar and lock the door on your way out." I think it was after eight when we left, all of us feeling the effects of the night's drinking. The Navy Captain who had been sitting drinking one martini after the other, stood up, straightened up his uniform, and walked out as sober as a judge. An FBI agent who had been sitting next to the captain and matching him martini for martini was basically carried out by a couple of his colleagues. The Captain was obviously a man of some experience.

The next morning, Vin Broderick's wife Sally was in the courtroom. We asked Vin if Sally was refusing to let him out of her sight after his performance the night before? It had been a grand evening.

US vs. Bujese and Hutchins

On October 22, 1963, Jeffrey Bujese and Brian T. Hutchins, armed with guns, entered the Tappan, New York, Branch of the First National Bank of Spring Valley and robbed it of several thousand dollars. It was the second time they had robbed this bank and they had also robbed a bank just across the state border in Old Tappan, New Jersey.

Several weeks later a woman who had been Hutchins' girlfriend at the time but whom Hutchins had recently ditched, told the FBI that she had been with Bujese and Hutchins on the morning of the robbery and when they returned with the money. She said she would have gone with them on the robbery, but Bujese was superstitious about having a woman on the job. Based on this information, the FBI got warrants and arrested the two of them. Hutchins, who was arrested in Florida, immediately confessed and a written statement was taken.

Ultimately, the case was brought to our office and I was assigned to handle the prosecution. Immediately after the defendants were arraigned in the Southern District, I had Hutchins brought to my office by the agents. I told Hutchins I understood that he had confessed to the robbery and asked if he would be willing to testify. He said that he would and told us that, in addition to the one robbery on which he had been arrested, he and Bujese had robbed the same bank on another occasion, as well as a bank just across the state line in Old Tappan, New Jersey. I said the agents would want to take statements about those robberies, which they did later in the day.

When the case was assigned to Judge Canella for trial, I had Hutchins brought to my office so that I could prepare him to testify. At that time, he said he was willing to plead guilty but he was not going to testify. I told him we could do it the easy way or the hard. Either he could cooperate fully and get the benefit of that when he was sentenced or, if he pled guilty, he would no longer have a Fifth Amendment privilege and I could compel him to testify under pain of contempt. He said if that was the case he would go to trial, and go to trial we did.

As I recall our case was overwhelming. We had Hutchins' ex-girlfriend, who had actually gone with them when they cased the bank. She described the events of the day, when they left armed to go to the bank and when they returned with the cash. In addition, people in the bank at the time of the robbery were able to identify the defendants. I also introduced Hutchins' confession, although the jury was instructed that it could not be considered as evidence against Bujese. So up to the end of the case, it was a very routine and solid prosecution.

The case got interesting when the defense started. After Bujese's sister testified that he was with her throughout the morning of the robbery, Hutchins testified in his own defense and swore that he had never been in the bank, denied confessing and swore that it was not his signature on the confession I had introduced into evidence.

A Life Begun on Third Base

This was no surprise, in a motion to suppress the confession made prior to trial, Hutchins testified that he had not signed the confession. Unfortunately for me, in a somewhat unusual situation for the FBI, only a single agent from Miami had witnessed the confession. Since I did not want it to be a swearing contest with only one witness on each side, I had a handwriting expert prepared to testify that the signature Brian T. Hutchins that appeared on the two additional confessions Hutchins signed on the day of his arraignment in New York was the same as the one signed in Miami. I would, therefore, the able to call the two FBI agents from New York to say that Hutchins signed those two confessions.

The cross of Hutchins was like shooting fish in a barrel. I was able to take him line by line through the confession that he signed detailing the events of the day of the robbery, pointing out there were details that only a participant in the robbery could know. I then turned to what I thought would be the end of my cross-examination. What occurred next was so dramatic I think I can recall it word for word:

Q: Mr. Hutchins, I place before you Government's Exhibit 13 (the original confession). Did you sign that document?

A: No.

Q: I am now placing before you what have been marked Government's Exhibits 14 and 15. Would you look at the last page of each of those documents and tell me if the signature that appears thereon, Brian T. Hutchins, is your signature?

A: I refuse to answer that question on the grounds that it may tend to incriminate me.

[From Judge Cannella, a powerful looking 6 foot 4 man, who was one of the seven blocks of granite at Fordham, in a booming voice:] I direct you to answer the question.

A: All right, I admit it, I am guilty of the robbery and of the conspiracy but don't ask me any more questions about anybody else.

It was my Perry Mason moment, but I was so shocked that all I could think of to say was, "So you admit that is your signature."

At that point Judge Cannella sent the jury back to the jury room and began the inquiry to determine whether to accept a plea of guilty from Hutchins. However, when the Judge asked the question had anybody threatened him in order to induce him to plead guilty, Hutchins replied "Well, Mr. Martin threatened that, if I pleaded guilty, he would force me to testify against my codefendant." Once Judge Cannella heard Hutchins say he had been threatened, he said he would not take the plea and he would let the case go to the jury. The judge then said he would take a recess to allow the defendant Bujese to consider whether he wanted to call Hutchins as his witness.

After the recess, the defendants announced that Bujese would call Hutchins as his witness. Hutchins took the stand and testified that on the morning of the robbery, he left Bujese with his sister and drove into Greenwich Village where he went to a bar. At the bar he met another individual and after some discussion they decided to go to Tappan to rob the bank. After the robbery he went back to Greenwich Village dropped off this other individual and then rejoined Bujese and his girlfriend in New Jersey.

Cross-examination was even more fun. One of the problems with the story that Hutchins told was that there was not sufficient time between the time Hutchins left his girlfriend in the morning and when he returned with the loot for him to have driven into Greenwich Village, had a few drinks, driven to Tappan, New York, some 20 miles away, and then go back to New York and return to New Jersey. I also had the details from the earlier confession and the fact that he signed 2 other confessions. As I was ending my cross-examination, I asked Hutchins what the name of this other individual was. After pausing to think for a few seconds, he said, "I think his name was Griffin, yeah, Tommy Griffin from Miami."

After the cross-examination, the Judge adjourned the case until the next morning and I went back to my office. The agent from Miami who took the original confession had been excluded from the trial as a witness, so I started to tell him what happened in court that day. After telling him about the confession and Hutchins testimony that it was not Bujese but someone he met in Greenwich Village, the agent asked, "Did he give you a name?" I replied, "I think he said someone named Griffin, Tommy Griffin from Miami." With that the agent almost came out of his chair, "One-eyed Tommy Griffin from Miami? I was in Miami two months before this robbery when they fished Tommy Griffin's body out of the canal. He had been in the water so long, that you could only identify it by the glass eye rolling around in his skull."

I gave some thought to calling the agent in rebuttal, but that would have delayed the case because we would need to call the medical examiner from Florida who identified Griffin's body by comparison to known dental records. I concluded that our case was so strong, there was no reason for delay. I was right. It did not take the jury long to convict and Judge Cannella ultimately sentenced each of the defendants to 20 years in jail.

There is an epilogue to this story. It was probably sometime in the mid-70s that I was approached by someone I did not recognize as I was crossing Follet Square in front of the courthouse. He said, "Hi, Mr. Martin, you probably don't recognize me, I am Billy Bujese. I am on parole and am down here to see my parole officer. I just want you to know, no hard feelings."

US v. Frances Kahn

Frances Kahn was something unusual at the time, a woman criminal defense lawyer. She was also crippled by polio and appeared at trial in a wheelchair. Among her clients was an individual named Charlie Hedges, a drug dealer who had been convicted in the District Court in Connecticut in early 1961. In 1962, while his appeal was pending, Hedges agreed to cooperate with the government and testify against some of his former associates, principally his supplier Vincent Pacelli.

While Hedges was in jail, Pacelli approached his wife and gave her $500 after learning that Hedges needed additional money for bail. The next character to arrive on the scene was Israel Schwartzberg, a convicted felon who while in prison developed a reputation as a "law man." Upon his release from prison, he approached Kahn and told her that he would try to steer some of his former prison inmate clients to her if she would agree to certify to the New York courts that Schwartzberg was working in her office while attempting to qualify for admission to the bar. In New York at the time, as in many states, you did not have to go to law school to become a lawyer; you could "read law," i.e. work under a practicing lawyer for several years.

In January 1963, Schwartzberg contacted Hedges' wife and told her that the Pacelli would give them as much money as they needed to go away and that "he [Pacelli] just doesn't want Charlie to do anything against him." Shortly thereafter, Francis Kahn visited Hedges in prison and asked him what he intended to do. Hedges replied, "Tell them to run because I am through with them." She replied "I don't think that's like you. You wouldn't do anything like that." Kahn also told Hedges Pacelli would lend him $25,000 if he did not testify. In another meeting, Kahn told Hedges that, if he were called before the grand jury, he should push back the dates of his narcotics dealings so any prosecution would be barred by the statute of limitations.

I had nothing to do with the Kahn case prior to the indictment. However, shortly thereafter, I was told by either Bob Morgenthau or Steve Kaufman, then the head of the Criminal Division, that in view of the significance of a case in which we were prosecuting a defense lawyer, I was being asked to take over primary responsibility, working with the Assistant who had been handling it until then.

It was very unusual for an Assistant handling a case to have the responsibility assigned to someone else. It was, therefore, a somewhat uncomfortable situation but, fortunately for me, the Assistant involved handled it well and there was no friction between us.

The case was assigned for trial to Judge Edward McLean, the former head of the firm of Debevoise Plimpton & McLean and a leader of the bar. Francis Kahn was represented by William Kuntzler, who would later become prominent as a defender of radical defendants and liberal causes. Vincent Pacelli was represented by Al Krieger, an experienced criminal defense counsel, and Israel Schwartzberg represented himself—a moment of glory that he cherished.

The trial was straightforward. We had the testimony of Hedges and his wife as well as records corroborating the visits to him. The most memorable moment of the trial was when Israel Schwartzberg made a motion to have his bail limits extended to allow him to go to Connecticut to give a speech on his experience reading law to gain admission to the bar to the Connecticut Young Lawyers Association. Judge McLean quickly denied the application and called me later to direct me to call the Connecticut lawyers to expresses his dismay that someone like Schwartzberg would be invited to address them.

The defendants were convicted on all counts. Like the other defendants, Israel Schwartzberg went to jail and he was never to become admitted to the New York bar. However, I still remember one of the lines of his summation in which he said:

> "Ladies and gentlemen, years ago in the courts of the Kings there was a Jester who sang a song: 'Whose bread I eat, whose wine I drink, his song I sing.' Ladies and gentlemen, you have heard from Charlie Hedges. He has eaten the government bread, he has drunk the government's wine, but you do not have to dance to his tune."

Not a bad argument.

This is one of the few cases I had where I thought a defendant might have been acquitted with a better defense lawyer. The defense that Kunstler asserted was that the United States Attorney's office did not like people who represented criminal defendants and, therefore, set out to frame Francis Kahn. On my cross-examination of her, I went one by one through approximately a dozen appeals that she had argued and she had to admit that the government prevailed in every case. More important, I was able to argue to the jury, "Ladies and gentlemen, if you think for a moment that I and my colleagues set out to frame Francis Kahn, you should not hesitate to acquit her. If on the other hand, you find that the government's overwhelming evidence shows that she knowingly attempted to bribe Charlie Hedges, you should convict."

In New York in the mid-60s, it was a mistake to put the government on trial. I have often wondered what the outcome would have been if Kuntzler had argued:

> "Ladies and gentlemen, what you have here is an embittered client, Charlie Hedges. Despite her best efforts, Francis Kahn lost his case and he was angry. Hedges therefore decided to place her in the middle of a conspiracy to obstruct justice. Are you going to take the word of this drug dealer against that of this woman lawyer, a trailblazer in the criminal defense field?"

US v. Bottone

This was another case that I was asked to take over after the indictment. In this instance the senior Assistant in charge of the case had left the office after the indictment was filed and the decision was made to add someone to the case more senior to Dan Murdoch, the Assistant who had been working on the case for some time. While I'm sure that he was disappointed not to have been allowed to have sole responsibility for the case, we worked well together and there was never any hostility.

The case involved several scientists who worked at American Cyanamid's Lederle Laboratories in Rockland County, New York. At the time Lederle was producing three widely used drugs: aureomycin, achromycin and declomycin. The production of these antibiotics involved a patented process in which microorganisms that created the antibiotics as a byproduct of their growth were run through a fermentation process to extract commercially reasonable amounts of the antibiotic. The process was complex and was detailed in highly confidential standard operating procedure manuals. The process required developing strains of the microorganisms that would produce a sufficient amount of the antibiotic to make the process commercially viable. The microorganisms that were developed in the laboratory were frozen and stored for production.

Recognizing the value of this process, three Lederle employees, Sidney Fox, John Cancelarich, and Leonard Fine, engaged in a conspiracy to steal samples of the microorganisms and to photocopy the standard operating procedures. They then sold the cultures and the manuals through a series of intermediaries to a company that would attempt to set up production in Italy, where there were no pharmaceutical patents.

At some point American Cyanamid became aware of what their former employees had done and brought a lawsuit in New York State courts against Fox, seeking to compel him to return all of the documents that had been taken. After spending some time in jail for contempt of court for not complying with a turnover order, Fox agreed to cooperate with American Cyanamid's lawyers. Cancelarich and Fine followed suit. Ultimately, Walter Mansfield, the senior partner of Donovan & Leisure handling the case for Americans Cyanamide, turned all of the information he had developed over to the United States Attorney's Office and indictment was obtained.

One of the interesting things about being a lawyer is that, to present a case effectively, you often have to learn about a business about which you knew nothing. That was the case here. The defendants were charged with transporting, in interstate and foreign commerce, stolen goods and merchandise having a value of more than $5000. A principal defense at the trial would be that the material at issue was not worth $5000 because, in filing its patent application, American Cyanamid had to disclose the process for extracting the antibiotic and had to deposit with the Patent Office a strain of the microorganism that would produce the desired antibody. The fallacy of that argument was that the patents only described a very basic means of producing the antibody. To produce the antibody in commercially reasonable amounts, the manufacturer had to take the microorganism through an extensive series of mutations that were induced by exposure to various chemicals and radiation with the hope of eventually developing a strain that would produce commercially viable amounts. Thus, the cultures and processes that the defendant stole were much more sophisticated then the information available in the Patent Office. To learn enough to present evidence to counter the defendants' arguments, I had to spend a day at Lederle Laboratories viewing and learning about the fermentation process.

The trial of the case was made easier by the fact that Walter Mansfield and his associates had already prepared the case for their civil trial and that gave us a good roadmap. The defendants who went to trial were Seymour Salb and Nathan Sharp, owners of a company called Biorganic Laboratories, to whom the Lederle employees originally brought the stolen material, and Caesar Bottone, who acted as an intermediary with those in Italy who were to manufacture the drugs. The principal witnesses for the prosecution were John Cancelarich and Lenny Fine.

John and Lenny were a contrast as witnesses. John had one of the sharpest recollections I have ever seen and Lenny, though always positive about his recollection, often got things wrong. In order to avoid a defense argument that the government witnesses concocted a story, we never interviewed John and Lenny together. In our prep sessions, I would ask Lenny something like, "When was the first meeting at Biorganic laboratories?" Lenny might answer, "June 1960, I'm sure it was June of that year." We would then go to another room where John was being interviewed. Asked the same question, John might say "August 1960." When asked if he was sure that it was not June 1960, John might say something like, "It could not have been June 1960 because Lenny was on his honeymoon and he would not of been available." We would go back to Lenny and ask, "Are you sure that meeting was in June; weren't you on your honeymoon in June?" To which Lenny replied, "That's right, it couldn't have been in June, it was in July. I am positive it was July." Lenny was invariably wrong and positive and John's memory was always spot on.

John's memory of events was so detailed that I sometimes worried that he might be making it up. A prosecutor dealing with a cooperating defendant always worries that the witness may make up details to enhance his story and thus the value of his cooperation. My concerns about John were alleviated one day when I was preparing him for trial.

A Life Begun on Third Base

One of my colleagues in the office, Jerry Walpin, stuck his head into my office about 12:30 and asked if I wanted to go to lunch. I invited John to join us. Although John had testified before the grand jury at least two years earlier, he said to Jerry, "I think you and I had lunch when I was down to testify before the grand jury. Remember we went to that Italian restaurant and you had the eggplant Parmesan and I had the sausage and peppers." John simply had phenomenal memory.

There were two things of note that occurred during the prosecution. One night as Dan and I were working together to prepare for the trial, the lights in our office went out. As we sat waiting for them to come on, someone with a radio came by and told us the power was out all over the city. It was the night of New York City's major electrical blackout. Since I had driven to work, Dan and I went to my car so I could drive him home. We drove up through Midtown and on the way we picked up any number of people, dropping one off and picking up another, all the way up through Manhattan.

The other memorable event occurred when Dan and I were sitting in my office just after the judge had charged the jury and they had commenced deliberations. My secretary buzzed me and said, "There is a Mr. Mansfield here and he would like to see you." It was Walter's case that we had tried. When Walter came in he said, "As you know I have not come to court because I knew the defendants would try to make this a case about American Cyanamid trying to punish a competitor. I have, however, been reading the transcript of the trial every day, and before the jury came in, I wanted you to know what a great job I thought the two of you did." This was class. He was saying it doesn't matter whether you win or lose, you did a good job.

Promotions

It was a general rule that the Assistant who tried the case would handle the appeal. All briefs were edited by a second Assistant and finally reviewed by the Chief Appellate Attorney. Since I had experience as a clerk to a Circuit Court Judge, during my first two years in the office I was often assigned to edit an appellate brief. Near the end of my second year, Bob asked me to take over as Chief Appellate Attorney when my predecessor left the office. It was an interesting job and it gave me the opportunity to work closely with many of my colleagues in the course of reviewing their briefs. I also got the opportunity to argue a number of cases that had been handled by people who had left the office after the trial.

As I was ending my third year in the office, Vin Broderick left the office to become the New York City Police Commissioner and the Chief of the Criminal Division was promoted to take his place. Steve Kaufman took his place and Bob asked me to serve as the Assistant Chief of the Criminal Division. This job was probably the best experience I could have had to prepare me for being a judge. I spent my day in meetings or on telephone calls with federal agents discussing the facts of their investigations and deciding whether to issue a grand jury subpoena, get an arrest warrant, or take some additional investigative step. Each decision had to be made on the spot and had consequences. If you did not arrest a subject might flee. If you arrested too early, the case might be thrown out. You had to decide and move on. There were judges who had trouble making decisions but, with the experience I had had, I was never one of them.

The United States Attorney's Office was not a place where you generally spent your career. So, during my fourth year I began to think about what I would do next. I may have been influenced by my mother's death one year earlier, but for some reason I decided to forgo big firm practice in New York City and to go into practice in Nyack, New York with my brother-in-law Jack Hekker and his partner Jerry Johnson.

Bob Morgenthau hired me and promoted me twice. But the first time he asked me about my politics was when I told him I was considering leaving to open a practice in Nyack, New York. He asked me about my politics because he said he thought it could be important to someone practicing in that community. It was simply another example of the fact that Bob Morgenthau ran a totally politics free office.

EIGHT

Country Lawyer

I resigned from the United States Attorney's Office in August 1966 and began practicing law with Jack Hekker and his partner, Jerry Johnson, in the firm of Johnson, Hekker & Martin. Physically, I had the best office I would ever have in my life. Jerry owned the building at 53 Burd Street in Nyack. It was a white clapboard two-story structure. My office was in what had been the library—with bookshelves lining the walls and a working fireplace.

Five years earlier, when I was going through the process for admission to the bar, one of the requirements was an interview with a local lawyer who was on the admissions committee. I do not recall his name but he was in the very office in the building at 53 Burd. When I returned home from the interview, I told my mother, "I have just been in an office which I would love to have if I ever practice privately." And there I was.

There was not a great deal that was memorable about my practice in Rockland County. One of the first cases that came to me was referred by some former colleagues from the U.S. Attorney's office. My clients, several individuals who had formed their own business selling cleaning supplies to schools, had been sued by their former employer, who claimed that they had stolen its trade secrets and used its copyrighted sales literature. By the time they were referred to me, my clients had been served with an order to show cause why they should not be enjoined from soliciting clients of their former employer and copying its sales literature.

Johnson, Hekker and Martin

The case looked bleak. The plaintiff's motion papers attached copies of various pieces of sales literature of the plaintiff and almost identical copies with the only change being the use of the name of the defendant's company. To my surprise, I learned that we had a good defense. It seems that the plaintiff had started its business in the same way. It had been formed by employees of a prior company selling cleaning chemicals to schools and its founders had copied all of the sales literature of their former employer. Apparently the industry was full of similar stories. Since the plaintiff could not prove that the defendants misappropriated anything in which the plaintiff had a unique interest, the case was dismissed.

The only other case that I remember was an action in which Mike Wallace, a major CBS News personality and father of the current Fox News anchor Chris Wallace, was sued by his former agent. Mike had

A Life Begun on Third Base

been a client of Jerry Johnson for years, going back to the time when Wallace was a newscaster in Chicago. The reason Jerry had come to New York was so that he could continue representing Mike. There was little memorable about the case. The contract with the agent had an arbitration clause and this was the first arbitration for me. Mike was very pleasant and it was an easy representation. My recollection is that we settled at some point.

The only other memorable event in my brief practice as a country lawyer was the result, in part, of my kosher dinners with Marty and Malvina during my Columbia days. In the fall of 1966, Jack Hekker asked me to cover for him at a local zoning board hearing, which would only involve seeking an adjournment. After I made my application, the Chairman suggested a date in the future. The lawyer for the other party responded, "I am not terribly religious but my wife is and I think that is a Jewish holiday, I think Purim." I responded, "It couldn't be Purim, Purim is in the spring. It must be Sukkot." I am sure that there were many present who wondering how this goy knew one Jewish holiday from another.

The most memorable event occurred in April 1967 when my secretary said there is a Judge Marshall on the phone. I am sure she had no idea that she was talking about the most famous civil rights lawyer in the country and the current Solicitor General of the United States. The first words I heard from Thurgood were, "Are you tired of being a country lawyer?" He explained that Nate Lewin, one of his assistants who was handling most of the criminal cases, was leaving the office and he wanted me to take his place. I told him I appreciated the offer but I did not think it was fair for me to leave a firm I had only recently joined and I was living at home with my father who was still suffering the effects of my mother's death. He said he understood and that appeared to be the end of the matter.

When I discussed the call with Jack and Jerry, and later my father, they all agreed that this was a unique opportunity and urged me to take it. I then called Thurgood back a few days later. He said the position was still open and the job was mine, if I wanted it. We discussed the timing and I told him that it would take me a few weeks to close up my practice and a friend was getting married in Geneva in June and I intended to go to the wedding. I asked if I could start in early July and he said that was no problem.

I closed up my practice and in early June headed to Geneva for Steve Kaufman's wedding. My first stop was Berlin and when I got off the plane I saw the headline in the Paris Herald Tribune "Thurgood Marshall appointed to the Supreme Court." I was not particularly concerned because I knew the nature of the job was not political so I would probably be able to start as planned.

Steve's wedding was a unique experience. His bride Marina Pinto was from a wealthy family. Her father was an international tea merchant and his brothers were international investment bankers. I arrived in Geneva on a Saturday but the wedding was not until Wednesday. We spent every day going to beautiful homes on Lake Geneva for lunch and dinner, toasting the bride and groom.

Two of my friends from the U.S. Attorney's office, Bob McGuire and Andy Lawler, were at the wedding. Bob had a car and after the wedding we drove through the Alps to Italy and ultimately France. One thing I remember from the trip was that, as we were driving through the Alps, we picked up a young good-looking woman who was hitchhiking. I was in the backseat and she joined me there. About an hour or so later we stopped for gas and I asked Andy, who considered himself somewhat of a ladies' man, if he would like to switch places with me. After we resumed our trip Andy realized what I had: that the woman had not bathed in several days. I'm not sure he ever forgave me.

NINE

Supreme Court Advocate

The Solicitor General is responsible for representing the United States in Supreme Court. He and his staff argue most of the government's cases before the Court. Since the Solicitor General will ultimately have to support the result in any case the Government appeals to a Circuit Court, he must approve all government appeals to Circuit Courts.

When I joined the staff in July, 1967, there were ten Assistants to the Solicitor General, seven line Assistants and three Supervisors. The majority of the work involved reviewing briefs in opposition to applications asking the Supreme Court to hear a case. As a general rule, the Supreme Court has the discretion to decide which of the many cases lawyers wish to appeal should be granted argument. There are thousands of cases filed in the Court every year but less than 100 are granted argument. Thus, "briefs in opp" were the daily grind and briefs in cases in which oral argument was granted were the highlight. Since the Solicitor had to approve any appeal by the government, we also spent time reviewing memoranda by various Justice Division lawyers seeking approval of an appeal.

While the justices and their staffs are busy all year reviewing the thousands of applications seeking review by the Court, arguments begin in October and usually ended in May. By tradition, the court generally issues the last of its opinions on the cases argued by late June or very early July. The Court's year, known as its Term, begins in October. I served in the Solicitor General's office during two Terms of the Court, 1967–1968 and 1968–1969.

The 1967-68 Term

During my first Term, I argued five cases before the Court, an unusually high number for a junior member of the staff. The fact that I got to argue so many cases was not some recognition that I was one of the better advocates – it was simply because nobody was anxious to argue a clear loser, so I got those cases.

The first case I argued was *Katz v. United States*. The fact that a case was a clear loser did not necessarily mean that it was insignificant. Although I got to argue *Katz* because it was a loser, it turned out to be one of the most significant constitutional decisions that year.

Charlie Katz was a professional gambler who was living in an apartment in Los Angeles and using a public telephone booth to place calls to bookmakers in Las Vegas. It was a crime to use the facilities of interstate commerce, such as the telephone, to gamble. The FBI learned of Katz's activities and placed a microphone on the top of the booth he regularly used. The microphone was activated when Mr. Katz was observed leaving his apartment and heading towards the booth. It was turned off immediately after he left the booth. Using this technique, the FBI recorded a number of incriminating conversations in which he placed bets. They then obtained a search warrant for his apartment where they seized approximately 120 pages of yellow foolscap containing his analysis of the strengths and weaknesses of various college teams. Apparently when two of his teams played, he would use this analysis to determine where to bet.

The significant constitutional issue the Supreme Court was to decide was the legality of wiretapping and other forms of electronic surveillance. The existing case law made it clear that this was a loser for the government. In fact, the leading Supreme Court case on the issue, *Berger v. New York*, contained broad language suggesting that wiretapping might never be constitutional because it involved a general search, i.e., a search not directed to specific items of evidence or contraband.

On October 17, 1967, I stood at the lectern in the Supreme Court and uttered my first words to that august body, "Mr. Chief Justice and may it please the court." The lectern is close to the bench and I could hear Justice White whispering to Mr. Justice Stewart, "He worked for Bob Morgenthau in the U.S. Attorney's office." Apparently, the justices are as curious as everyone else when someone new appears on the scene.

My argument was based on the line of cases in the Supreme Court that drew a distinction in the requirements for a constitutional search based on the nature of the premises involved. While generally agents would need to obtain a court authorized search warrant to conduct a search of a home, an automobile could be searched without a warrant, if the agents had probable cause to believe that it contained contraband or evidence of a crime. In *Katz*, I argued that a telephone booth was more like an automobile than a home and, therefore, since the agents had ample probable cause to believe that Katz was using it to make illegal bets, they could conduct the search without a warrant. As I was making this argument, Mr. Justice Black looked down and said, "I take it, Mr. Martin, what you are saying is that a man's phone booth is not his castle." His was the only vote I got.

Although the *Katz* case was technically a loss for the government because his conviction was reversed, it was in fact a major victory for law enforcement. In his decision for the Court reversing the conviction, Justice Stewart wrote that everything the FBI did in this case would have been constitutional had the agents obtained a warrant from a judicial officer. Within six months of the *Katz* decision, Congress had passed and the President had signed legislation authorizing judges to issue warrants authorizing wiretapping and other forms of electronic surveillance.

Thus, a clear loser became a historically significant Supreme Court precedent. Approximately 50 years later my grandson Johnny would visit a museum in Philadelphia containing a display relating to significant Supreme Court cases. He ended up listening to a recording of his grandfather's argument before the Supreme Court in *Katz*.

None of the other cases I argued in the 1967–68 Term were of major constitutional significance. However, the second case I argued, *Schneider v. Smith*, may have involved one of the more bizarre incidents in Supreme Court history. The case involved a federal law that required anyone who served in the merchant marine to sign a loyalty affidavit. A seaman who had been denied a necessary federal certificate to serve in the merchant marine brought an action claiming the loyalty oath requirement was unconstitutional but he lost in the lower court. As with *Katz*, a clear loser. The government had the usual one hour allotted for its argument. On December 12, 1967, as I got up to begin my argument, Justice William O. Douglas got up and disappeared through the curtains behind the bench. One hour later Justice Douglas returned. Unfortunately for him, because of questions from other justices, he had to listen to five minutes of argument from me, although my time had officially expired. Approximately one month later, the Supreme Court unanimously found the statute unconstitutional, with Justice Douglas writing the opinion. Obviously, Justice Douglas knew from the outset that he would vote to reverse and that nothing I could say would possibly change his mind—so why waste his time listening to my argument.

My next argument would be my only win. Neiffert-White was a company that had submitted a false application under a government loan program. Upon discovery of the fraud, the government brought a successful action to obtain a statutory penalty for filing a false claim with the government. The Ninth Circuit reversed the government's award, holding that the False Claims Act did not apply to applications for loans. The Supreme Court then granted the government's application for review. This was the least enjoyable of all of my arguments before the Supreme Court. Even though I was usually arguing a loser, as in *Katz*, how the decision would ultimately be written was important, and the arguments were hot and heavy as I fielded questions from the Justices. As I argued in *Neiffert-White*, it became clear that the Court had taken this case to reverse and the Justices did not need the benefit of argument. I do not recall being asked a single question and I simply droned on with the argument I have prepared, feeling like a comedian whose audience was not responding to his jokes. The opinion of the court reversing was unanimous.

On March 25, 1968, two days after I met Peggy Conroy, I argued for the United States in the case of the *Puyallup Tribe v. The Department of Game of the State of Washington*. The United States was not a party to this case, which arose in the state courts of Washington. The case involved the application of state conservation laws to fishing rights that had been granted to the Indians in the 1854 Treaty of Medicine Creek. In cases in which a statute or treaty of the United State is involved, it is not unusual for the government to ask for the right to present its views on the merits of the case as *amicus curiae*, or friend of the court. In this case, the State of Washington had very detailed rules about where and how people could fish for certain varieties of salmon and trout. The question presented was to what extent these laws could be applied to Indians who had been guaranteed the right to fish by the United States in a treaty.

The position we took was that there had to be a balance between the conservation needs of the state and the treaty rights of the Indians. We proposed a standard that would require the state to show that the need for conservation arose as a result of the fishing practices of the Indians, and not from some commercial fishing by others in other parts of the state. While I made this argument, it did not get careful consideration by the Court because the lawyer for the tribe, himself a member of the tribe, stated in argument that the tribe had an absolute right to fish as it wanted and that the state could not regulate it in any way. I recall him being asked, if the tribe was taking every last fish out of the waters of the state, was the state was powerless to stop it. His answer was yes. I knew we were in trouble. The Supreme Court did not reach a final result but sent the case back to the state court for consideration of various issues. The issue would again arise when the case came back up to the state court system, but by that time I was out of government.

My final argument for the 1967 Term took place on May 2, 1968. By this time, Peggy and I were in a serious relationship and I believe she came to the argument. The case, *Sabbath v. United States*, involved a question of the procedures law enforcement agents are required to use when entering an apartment or house for the purpose of making an arrest. In prior cases the court had held that before agents could break open the door to conduct a search or make an arrest, they had to knock and announce their purpose. Here, agents, who had an informant who had entered an apartment to deliver drugs, approached the door which was closed but unlocked and opened the door and went in with guns drawn. We argued that because the door was not locked there was no need for the agents to knock and announce their purpose. We were not surprised when the Supreme Court rejected that argument 8 to 1 in an opinion by Justice Marshall.

It was shortly after my argument in *Sabbath*, that I took a leave of absence to go to New York and serve as Counsel to the Committee Investigating the Disturbances at Columbia University. I would not return until mid-August.

The 1968-69 Term

In my final year in the Solicitor General's office I would argue only three cases but would also take on one of the most interesting assignments in my legal career.

Kaufman v. United States, which I argued on November 19, 1968, involved the question whether a convicted defendant could obtain habeas corpus relief based on a claim of illegal search and seizure that had not been raised on appeal. Habeas corpus literally means have the body of a prisoner brought before the court in order to determine the legality of his imprisonment. Traditionally it had been used to raise issues that could not reasonably have been raised on appeal. For example, a prisoner who had been represented at trial and on appeal by the same lawyer could file a habeas corpus petition alleging that his right to the effective assistance of counsel was violated because he had incompetent counsel.

In *Kaufman*, the defendant had been convicted of bank robbery after a trial in which his sole defense was insanity. On appeal he did not raise a claim that evidence used against him had been the result of an unconstitutional search and seizure. When he thereafter sought habeas corpus relief, it was denied on the ground that the claim was waived because he had not asserted it on appeal. I argued before the Supreme Court that there was a need for finality in the adjudication of guilt and a defendant should not be able to appeal a guilty verdict but withhold a constitutional claim for subsequent habeas corpus review. The court rejected my argument by a vote of 5 to 3, Justice Marshall not participating, apparently because of prior association with the case as Solicitor General.

Leary v. United States, which I argued on December 12, 1968, generated a good deal of publicity, not because of the constitutional issue involved but rather because of the notorious defendant. Timothy Leary, who had been a member of the Harvard faculty and who was fired in 1963, was an outspoken advocate for, and user of, psychedelic drugs. He was somewhat of a pop culture hero. Leary had been arrested in Texas when law enforcement officials searched the car in which he was driving and found marijuana. He was prosecuted under two different statutes, one which imposed a tax on marijuana and the other which made it a crime to possess marijuana that had been illegally imported. Leary challenged the constitutionality of both statutes.

With respect to the tax act, the Supreme Court had recently held unconstitutional a federal law requiring people who engaged in the gambling business to register, saying it violated the Fifth Amendment right not to incriminate yourself. Since gambling was illegal in most states, the Court found those who registered would be providing local officials with evidence that they had been violating the law and thus be witnesses against themselves. In *Leary*, the Supreme Court held that the Marijuana Tax Act was similarly unconstitutional, since by paying the tax and filing the forms an individual would be admitting violating laws in almost every state.

The charge against Leary for possessing illegally imported marijuana was based on a statute that provided that, if someone was found in possession of a drug that was illegal under federal law, it could be presumed that the drug had been illegally imported. The statute was framed this way because, in the early 20th century when the narcotics laws were originally enacted, the power of Congress under the commerce clause, i.e. its right to regulate issues affecting interstate commerce, was not as clear as its right to regulate foreign commerce. The rationale of the presumption was that since it was illegal to manufacture certain drugs in United States, it was rational to presume that any drugs found in this country were in fact imported.

Leary contended that the presumption violated his Fifth Amendment right not to be compelled to be a witness against himself, because in order to rebut the presumption he would have to testify to establish that the marijuana was not illegally imported. The fallacy of the government's rationale was amply demonstrated by the most difficult question I was ever asked in the Supreme Court. As I tried to argue that the presumption was reasonable, Chief Justice Warren interrupted: "Mr. Martin, are you trying to tell this court that, if a man is arrested in a field in Missouri where he is growing marijuana, we have to presume that it is illegally imported?" It was clear, as I knew before I started my argument, that the government was not going to win this case. Just for the record, I thought I gave a pretty good answer: "Mr. Chief Justice, it is only a presumption and, of course, it can yield to the actual facts of the case."

The final case that I would argue for the government in the Supreme Court was one of those rare cases that I did not lose. *Du Vernay v. United States*, which was argued February 27, 1969, involved a 22-year-old African-American who had been convicted for refusing to be inducted into the Army after having been drafted. At trial and on appeal he contended that the indictment should have been dismissed because

African-Americans had systematically been excluded from his local draft board. His appeal was rejected by the Circuit Court on the ground that any challenge to the racial composition of the draft board

A Life Begun on Third Base

should have been raised through an appeal from his selective service classification during the administration process. About a month after the case had been argued, the Court issued a one line order saying the conviction was affirmed by an equally divided court. Justice Fortas, who was then under an ethics violation investigation and would resign the following May, had apparently recused himself and did not participate. Technically, I could claim this as a win since the conviction was affirmed. However, since there was no decision on the merits, it would be inappropriate to claim that my argument had prevailed.

A Unique Assignment

Although there was no federal law authorizing wiretapping until after the Supreme Court decided *Katz*, the FBI had been conducting wiretaps for years under authorizations from the Attorney General. Originally targeting organized crime and foreign espionage, the wiretaps were extended to controversial organizations including the Communist Party, the Socialist Workers Party, and individuals such as Dr. Martin Luther King, Jr. This was all done under the rubric of "national security."

After Ramsey Clark became the Attorney General in March 1967, the Justice Department adopted a policy of informing the Supreme Court of any instance in which someone who was seeking Supreme Court review of a conviction had been subject to electronic surveillance. This was generally done in a footnote in the brief in opposition to the defendant's petition for review. The surveillance was disclosed and the government asked that the case be remanded to the trial court so that it could prove that none of the evidence used at the trial had come from the electronic surveillance.

My first involvement of substance with this issue came when I was routinely assigned a brief in opp in the case of *Ivanov v. United States*. Ivanoff was a Russian spy whose cover was as an employee of Amtorg, a Russian trade organization. On October 29, 1963, Ivanoff was arrested by the FBI as he was meeting with John Butenko, an employee of a military contractor who had access to highly sensitive documents relating to the Strategic Air Command systems. I was very familiar with the case because on the afternoon of October 29, 1963, I had received a call from Homer Boynton, the case agent in charge of the case. Homer wanted to know where I was going to be that night because his squad was going out that evening to make an arrest in an espionage case that was centered in New Jersey. If they could get the defendants into New York before the arrest, the case would be mine – Dick Casey had previously left the office. The arrest was made in New Jersey and I had no role in the prosecution.

As I read through the brief in opposition in the *Ivanov* case, I saw a familiar footnote advising the court that Ivanov had been the subject of electronic surveillance and asking the Court to remand the case to the trial court for a hearing at which the government would prove that the evidence used against Ivanov had not been derived from information obtained through electronic surveillance.

I immediately went to see the Solicitor General, Erwin Griswold, to tell him we could not follow the normal course in the *Ivanov* case. I explained that, as Assistant United States Attorney, I had worked with the agents involved in the Ivanov matter and, since Ivanov was employed by Amtorg, I was certain that electronic surveillance had been used in the course of the investigation.

This resulted in a series of meetings to determine how we should handle the issue of Attorney General-authorized wiretapping for foreign intelligence purposes. The decision was made to advise the Court of the nature of the electronic surveillance in this case and to seek a ruling that electronic surveillance authorized by the Attorney General for national security purposes was constitutionally permissible.

The Supreme Court rejected our request that it rule on the constitutionality of such wiretapping and remanded the case to the trial court for a hearing to determine whether unconstitutionally obtained evidence had been used in obtaining the conviction. However, Justice Stewart filed a concurring opinion in which he noted that the Supreme Court had never ruled on the constitutionality of electronic surveillance authorized by the Attorney General for foreign intelligence purposes and that would have to be the first question addressed by the trial court.

Shortly after the remand order I received a phone call from Beatrice Rosenberg, an outstanding lawyer and, I believe, the first woman ever mentioned as a serious candidate for the Supreme Court. Bea was the highly respected Chief of Appeals of the Criminal Division. She said there were several cases in the division involving electronic surveillance that had been authorized by the Attorney General in the interest of national security that would have to be litigated in the District Courts. She thought it made sense for all of these cases to be handled by one person and, since I had experience as an Assistant United States Attorney and the cases would be coming back for Supreme Court review, I should handle the cases in the District Court. I told Erwin Griswold and he agreed.

One of the first things we had to decide is where we should draw the line with respect to the Attorney General's authority to authorize electronic surveillance. Justice Stewart's concurring opinion focused on foreign intelligence gathering, in its discussion of the legality issue, although it did contain a reference to "national security." National security had been the justification for organized crime wiretaps, as well as for surveillance of suspected subversive organizations and individuals.

There were a series of meetings to discuss where we would draw the line, with the Attorney General, senior officials from the Criminal Division and Internal Security Division, and members of the Attorney General's staff in attendance. I expressed the view that maintaining the authority to authorize electronic surveillance for foreign intelligence purposes was most important and that we risked jeopardizing that case if we argued for the authority to authorize electronic surveillance of organized crime or of individuals or groups whom someone might consider subversive.

The Attorney General at the time was John N. Mitchell, a former municipal bond lawyer, who had been a partner and was a close friend of President Nixon. I recall that at the end of one of these discussions he said to me, "I understand the argument you are making but I am reluctant to say that something that one of my predecessors approved was unconstitutional." Thus, we would attempt to defend some of the "national security" orders, although not all of them.

At the outset, I faced two challenges: 1) Where do I find precedent to sustain our position; and 2) What procedure can we use that will prevent our having to disclose where the electronic surveillance took place? We could not go into court and publicly announce that we were wiretapping some foreign government.

As I started my research, I was given access to all of the Justice Department's files with respect to all of the authorization that had taken place in the past. In those files, I found a memorandum by a criminal division attorney stating, in effect, "It's important for the public safety that we do this, but, if we ever have to justify it in court, I don't know how we can do it." Well that was what I was being asked to do. Ultimately I was able to find a number of cases discussing the President's primary role with respect to foreign affairs and the need of the government to protect national security, and I was able to write a reasonable brief.

The question of procedure was particularly important because the government could not walk into open court and identify the foreign countries, not all of them enemies, which had been the subject of electronic surveillance. Ultimately, the procedure adopted involved filing an affidavit from the Attorney General of the United States stating that the particular defendant had been overheard on electronic surveillance authorized by the then Attorney General, The affidavit attached two exhibits: a description of the premises that had been the subject of the electronic surveillance and transcripts of the overheard conversations. It would then be up to the District Court Judge to determine whether any of the material should be disclosed to the defendant.

Ironically, one case I did not handle in the District Court was *Ivanov* because the Internal Security Division was jealous of its prerogative and did not want outside help. While we used the procedure I devised in several cases, there was only one case in which the trial court ordered a hearing. The title of the case was *United States v. Cassius Marcellus Clay, Jr.*, but he was better known at the time as Muhammad Ali.

Clay, who had been convicted for refusing to report for induction, had been overheard on a foreign intelligence wiretap when he sought a visa to visit a foreign country. He'd also been overheard on wiretaps the FBI had placed on the phones of Elijah Muhammad, the leader of the Nation of Islam, and Martin Luther King, Jr. While there had been widespread reports that the FBI had tapped Dr. King's phones, I was the first government official to ever acknowledge that fact publicly.

Although Attorney General Mitchell had refused to give up all claims to a right to authorize electronic surveillance for "national security" purposes, the decision was made that we would not try to sustain the validity of the Elijah Muhammad and Dr. King taps.

The District Court accepted our argument that the foreign intelligence surveillance was constitutional and that no evidence from the Muhammad and King taps had been used at Clay's trial. The Fifth Circuit affirmed. Ali's conviction was ultimately set aside on other grounds.

Shortly after the Fifth Circuit decision, Congress enacted the Foreign Intelligence Surveillance Act, which established a special court to review applications for warrants in foreign intelligence matters. The FISA court would ultimately become well-known in connection with the investigation of possible links between the Trump campaign and Russia.

When I first started preparing individual cases that had to be litigated, I would have the Attorney General's Executive Assistant set up a time for me to bring the affidavit to the Attorney General for execution. After the first few cases, I would simply leave the affidavit with the Executive Assistant, who would get it signed and returned to me. Shortly before I was to leave the Department of Justice for private practice, I brought one of these affidavits to the Executive Assistant and told him I would be leaving the following week. He said that he would set up a meeting for me with the Attorney General so that I could say goodbye.

Attorney General John N. Mitchell had been portrayed in the press as ruthless and not a particularly pleasant individual. I did not get that impression from the larger meetings I had attended with him but I did not really know him. I arrived at the meeting and gave my prepared statement, "Mr. Attorney General, I am leaving the Department of Justice today and I just wanted to say goodbye." I assumed that he would say thank you for your service, goodbye and good luck. Instead he said, "I heard about that and thought maybe I could talk you out of it, sit down." He then spent 15 or 20 minutes with me in a most pleasant conversation. He said he would not try to talk me out leaving because he too wanted to return to private practice, but the President had asked him to stay until after the election. It was a delightful conversation with a very pleasant man. When Mitchell was later indicted and convicted in connection with the Watergate affair, I thought back on that conversation and how much better off Mitchell would have been had he left the Department of Justice earlier.

A Final Supreme Court Argument

I was sitting in my law office in New York in July 1974 when once again a secretary said: "Justice Marshall is calling." He told me that he would like to assign me to represent an indigent defendant whose case the Supreme Court had taken for review. He explained that two defendants, Tony Wilson and Bobby Bryan, had been convicted of contempt of court for refusing to testify after a grant of immunity. On appeal the Second Circuit reversed the convictions on the ground that the defendants were not given a hearing before they were found in contempt by the trial judge. The government then filed a petition with the Supreme Court seeking review of the Second Circuit's ruling. Wilson, represented by the Legal Aid Society, had filed an opposition brief, but Bryan's counsel did nothing. Ultimately the clerk of the Court had to call him to tell him the Court wanted to him to file something in opposition. The lawyer then filed a brief stating that he relied on the arguments made by the Legal Aid Society.

When the Supreme Court granted the government's petition for review, the same lawyer filed an application to be appointed to represent Bryan in the Supreme Court. Justice Marshall, as Circuit Justice for the Second Circuit was the one to decide such matters. Justice Marshall told me he was prepared to grant the application to the extent that it requested the appointment of counsel to represent the defendant, but he was not going to appoint this lawyer. He asked if I would take the appointment and I, of course, said yes.

The following September, Peggy and I attended the Second Circuit Judicial Conference as guests of Justice Marshall. When I saw him, I told him how excited I was about the opportunity to argue again before the Supreme Court. The first words out of his mouth were, "You know you're going to lose—they didn't take that case to affirm." This was something that should've been obvious to anyone, although in my excitement I had overlooked it. It was the government's appeal and the fact that four justices had to vote to grant the petition was strong evidence that they did not take the case to affirm.

Despite the likely result, one that would not be new to me as a Supreme Court advocate, I was anxious to prepare the brief and argue it. Wilson was represented by Sheila Ginsberg of the Legal Aid Society, whom I had known for some time, and we worked well together.

The case was not terribly complicated. After they had been called as witnesses at a criminal trial and granted immunity, each of the defendants refused to testify and the court immediately said that they were guilty of contempt of court. They were later sentenced to 60 days imprisonment in addition to the criminal sentences they were then serving.

The question for the Supreme Court arose from the fact that the Federal Rules of Criminal Procedure provided two different methods for a contempt finding. Contempt committed in the presence of the court could be punished summarily by the presiding judge. However, contempt committed outside the court's presence, for example, the refusal to testify before a grand jury, required a hearing at which the defendant would be represented by counsel. In this case, the defendants had refused to testify in the presence of the trial judge and he found no need for any further hearing with respect to the contempt. A majority of the Supreme Court agreed and reversed the Second Circuit's ruling that a hearing was required. Sheila and I did get three votes, from Justices Marshall, Brennan and Douglas.

One final word on my argument in *United States v. Bryan*. The case was set for argument on December 17, 1974, a Tuesday, and Peggy and I decided to use the occasion to visit her family in Washington and to bring the kids. John was five at the time and we thought he was the only one of the children who might be able to sit through a Supreme Court argument. Fortunately, Justice Marshall arranged for Peggy and John to sit in a special section reserved for friends and family of the justices and Cissy Marshall joined them there. As the cases before mine droned on, Cissy took John back to the Justices' chambers and then brought him back for my argument. That night, as we were driving with the kids back to New York, we overheard John saying from the backseat, "Kate, you would not have liked the Supreme Court. It was very boring, except when Daddy talked." I may have lost the case but it is a wonderful memory.

When Thurgood called the in April 1967 and offered me a job, I could never have anticipated how important my decision would be. I arrived in Washington as a bachelor. In slightly less than a year, I had found the woman I would love for the rest of her life and we got started on a wonderful family. The experience of arguing at the Supreme Court was exciting and very helpful on my resume but the family I began was my greatest reward.

TEN

Private Practice

As I came to the end my second year in the Solicitor General's office, I began to think about the next phase of my career. I doubt that I ever considered staying longer than two years in the SG's office—the experience was unique but after two years there was not much more to learn and the $15,000 a year salary was less than lawyers were making in private practice.

I was convinced I wanted to begin as a sole practitioner. Looking back, it seemed very risky to start out in practice with no guaranteed clients while having to support a wife and child. However, several of my colleagues from the United States Attorney's Office had opened up either alone or in small firms and seemed to be prospering. My reaction was, if they can do it, so can I.

The first question was where to start the practice. Peggy and I both loved living in Washington and her brother and sister were there. However, my potential sources of business, my former colleagues in the US Attorney's office and friends from law school, were centered in New York, so we decided to move back home.

The lease of our apartment at 666 Independence Ave. SE would expire in early September 1969, so we set that as a target date for our move.

At the time, my father's house in Nyack was fully furnished but empty as we were making efforts to sell it, so we decided to move there until it got sold.

The next question was where I would take space for my law office. In seeking advice about establishing an individual practice, I spoke to a number of my former colleagues, including Sheldon Elsen, who had left the office to establish a small firm with friends, Orans, Elsen & Polstein. We met early in the summer of 1969 when Peggy and I were up visiting the family. In the course of that conversation, Sheldon said that his firm had an extra office that they would be happy to sublet to me. Although at that time I had not fixed a definite date to open my office, we agreed that I would take the space and inform him later of my start date.

After I returned to Washington and began to focus on the date, we decided to make the move just as our lease was expiring, and that the day I would open my practice would be September 13, 1969. I then wrote Sheldon to give him the date. Sometime later, I returned to New York to start ordering all that I would need to open my own office. Sheldon and I had lunch at the Harvard Club to discuss the final arrangements. In the beginning of our conversation Sheldon asked, "Do you know what September 13 is?" I responded, "I did not realize it at the time I selected it, but I now know that it is Rosh Hashanah." Sheldon replied, "Well, Jerry Orans said, 'He did not have to make it so obvious.'"

I do not recall a lot of the detail of my first few months in private practice. I know that I took out a $10,000 line of credit to carry me through the first few months. My recollection is that I only drew down about $3000 of this and that from there on I was able to support myself with the income I was making.

Chalmers Impey

The first major case I had was a securities fraud case, *Leasco v. Maxwell*. Leasco was a company run by Saul Steinberg that had purchased stock in a British company, Pergaman Press, which was controlled by British businessman Robert Maxwell. The claim was that the financial statements of Pergaman Press that Maxwell had provided to Steinberg were false and fraudulent. The complaint that Leasco filed also named as a defendant Chalmers Impey, an English firm of Chartered Accountants, which had performed the audit of those financial statements.

My friend and former colleague Peter Leisure represented Maxwell and he recommended me to Chalmers Impey. They turned out to be one of the nicest clients I ever represented. Every time I would send them a brief for their comments as the case progressed, I would receive a note thanking me for the wonderful brief that I was filing on their behalf. The case also involved at least one and possibly more trips to Europe.

I was retained in late 1969 and charged an initial retainer of $10,000. Sometime early in my practice, I told Peggy that the first time I received a retainer of at least $10,000, we would go to a fancy restaurant to celebrate. We had a marvelous meal at one of the top restaurants in New York at the time, La Cote Basque.

I went to London to meet with my clients, a small firm with fewer than the hundred professionals. I had the unhappy task of explaining to them the scope of the liability they were facing under the United States securities laws. Even though they had received only a modest fee for reporting on the financial statements of Pergaman, they could theoretically be held liable for the full amount of $22 million that Leasco had paid for the stock. This was well beyond any liability they might have under English law.

The first major thing to be done was to prepare a motion to dismiss the complaint. There were two main arguments: 1) we claimed that the US securities law could not be applied to a transaction that was centered in London—in legal terms, we claimed that the United States did not have subject matter jurisdiction, i.e., it could not apply its law to a transaction centered in a foreign jurisdiction; and 2) we argued that the partners in Chalmers Impey had not performed any acts in the United States that related to the claim at issue and, therefore, the courts of the United States did not have jurisdiction over them—in legal terms, the United States did not have personal jurisdiction over the defendants.

Although the District Court rejected our claims, the Second Circuit found in our favor on the personal jurisdiction issue. The court found that there was subject matter jurisdiction but, based on well-established precedent, our courts could not exercise jurisdiction over people who did nothing here and, who, at the time they acted, had no reason to anticipate that the financial statements they audited would later be provided to a United States purchaser.

One of the things I learned from this case was the importance of getting the right facts in the affidavits filed in connection with the motion. In preparing the affidavit for the partner who had done the work on the Pergaman account, I included the statement that the first time he heard of the Leasco transaction was when he read about it in the newspaper. This statement was specifically mentioned in the opinion of the Second Circuit ordering the dismissal of the complaint against my clients.

Zafe Zafer

My first major criminal case involved a client with the improbable name of Zafe Zafer, a stockbroker working for a small firm in Chicago. He was one of 14 people charged with participating in a scheme to fraudulently promote the stock of a company called Hercules Galion. Stockbrokers were paid to recommend the stock to their clients in order to drive its price up.

Eight defendants went to trial before Judge Lasker in the Southern District. The trial began in late February 1971 and ended on June 7, 1971 with a guilty verdict as to Zafe and four other defendants, the acquittal of two and a hung jury as to one. While there was nothing particularly remarkable about the scheme, the trial was a great experience for me as a fledgling defense lawyer.

As a prosecutor, my demeanor was low-key. I did not get angry or raise my voice, I simply methodically presented the facts on direct and cross-examination. I thought that a good defense lawyer had to be mean and nasty in cross-examining codefendants who were testifying for the government. Fortunately for me, in this trial the defendants were represented by a cross-section of able defense lawyers.

One of them was Arnold Bauman, who would later become a federal judge and appoint me to represent Stephen Buzzie, about whom there will be more later. Arnold could do mean and nasty as well as anyone I would ever see. However, the most effective of the defense lawyers was George Collins from Chicago. George never raised his voice and was never nasty. However, he figuratively picked the pockets of the government witnesses. With a smile on his face he would lull the witness into making damaging admissions that contradicted the direct testimony. After one cooperating witness testified for hours about his participation in the scheme with various of the defendants, George closed his cross-examination by asking, "Sir, at the time you did these things with the people on trial here that you have testified about, you weren't trying to cheat or defraud anybody were you?" The witness replied, "No sir." You could not ask for more on cross-examination.

With my first few witnesses, I tried the mean and nasty with disastrous consequences. As I concentrated on remembering to be mean and nasty, I lost track of the theme I was trying to develop through the cross-examination. Fortunately, I learned quickly by watching George and the others that the best cross-examination style is the one with which you are comfortable and natural. For Arnold it was mean and nasty, but for me I would do what came naturally and use the low-key approach that George had demonstrated to be so effective.

The highlight of the case for me was the cross-examination of one of the government's main cooperators, Burton Buddy Kozak. He was one of the stockbrokers who had taken money to promote the stock and work cooperatively with the others. He was also a friend of my client Zafe. After the indictment was filed, and, before I represented him, Zafe had become suspicious of Kozak and tape-recorded a long telephone conversation they had. In the conversation Kozak said many things that contradicted the testimony he gave at trial.

While the tape was valuable evidence for the defense, there was a major problem. In order to have the tape received in evidence there had to be a witness to authenticate it—someone to testify the tape-recorded conversation was what it purported to be. The problem was, given the evidence that had been introduced, I could not call Zafe as a witness to authenticate the tape. Fortunately, Judge Lasker went along with the solution I devised.

Even without authenticating the tape, I could use the transcript to ask questions of the witness. I therefore began my cross-examination with a series of questions to the effect, "Did you ever say the following to Zafe Zafer?" and then read something verbatim from the transcript. After only a few of such questions, the prosecutor, Gary Naftalis, a nice guy who would become a good friend, objected, saying, "Your Honor, given the detailed nature of these questions I would ask for an offer of proof." A lawyer is not permitted to ask questions that represent that certain facts occurred unless the lawyer has some reasonable basis for the facts.

When Gary made his statement in front of the jury, I quickly replied, "Your Honor, I am reading from a transcript of a telephone conversation that Mr. Zafer had with Mr. Kozak [giving the date]." At that point, the Judge sent the jury out of the courtroom and we began discussing how I could use the tape. One of the basic rules of evidence is you can use anything available to refresh a witness's recollection of an event. Normally it would be something like a memo written contemporaneously that you would show to the witness to refresh the witness's recollection about a long past event.

I told Judge Lasker that I would like to use the recording to refresh the witness's recollection about things he said to my client in this conversation. I had a tape recorder in the courtroom with headsets. I asked that I be permitted to give Mr. Kozak a headset and to make one available to Mr. Naftalis so he too could listen. Since this would permit the witness to listen to the recording without its contents being played for the jury, the judge agreed.

A Life Begun on Third Base

What followed was what Gary subsequently told me was one of the worst times he ever had in court. Kozak could not have done better for me if I had written him the script. I played the tape from the outset and from time to time would interrupt to ask if what he heard refreshed his recollection that he had this conversation with my client. His first response was, "Is that supposed to be me?" As we went further through the conversation, his reactions slowly changed and he responded things such as "That's possibly me," "Maybe that's me," or "I might have said that."

We then came to a part of the tape in which Kozak could be heard saying to his wife, "Honey, will you turn that down, I am talking to Zafe." On hearing that Kozak said, "Yeah, that's me." He then went on to admit saying everything on the tape, which I was then allowed to play for the jury. I had a field day pointing out all of the things he said that were inconsistent with his direct testimony. For example, he was a principal witness against a defendant named Weitz, a dentist. On the tape, Kozak states, "I do not understand how the government could have indicted Dr. Weitz."

Unfortunately for my client, the tape ultimately did him no good because there were too many other witnesses against him. However, two of the defendants against whom Kozak was the principal witness were acquitted and the jury could not reach an agreement on Dr. Weitz.

The cross-examination of Burton Buddy Kozak was the type of experience every lawyer dreams of. However, when I got up to begin my cross-examination I was worried because I had given all of my colleagues on the defense team copies of the transcript of the conversation. If I screwed it up, they would know it. Fortunately for me, Judge Lasker let me do what I had to do and Burton Buddy Kozak fell right into the trap.

One of the benefits of the trial was that it introduced me to Judge Lasker, one the most decent individuals to serve on the bench in the Southern District. Not long after the trial, he invited Peggy and me to be his guests at the Second Circuit Judicial Conference. For a young lawyer it was a marvelous experience, getting to know some of the judges on a more personal level.

ITT-Dita Beard

My next major case began about a month after the Zafer trial. I returned to our apartment at about 10 p.m., following a Bar Association meeting. Peggy said that Mike Mitchell, a friend and former AUSA colleague, had called and asked me to return his call as soon as possible. When I called, Mike asked if I was free to go with him to Washington, DC the next morning. He explained that Jack Anderson, a syndicated columnist, had published parts of a memorandum prepared by an ITT lobbyist named Dieter Beard, in which she claimed that a $400,000 contribution which she had persuaded ITT to make to the 1972 Republican National Convention was responsible for the fact that the Justice Department dropped an antitrust investigation of ITT. The next day, Anderson wrote that in response to his revelation, people in the Washington office of ITT had been observed shredding documents. Mike said that Congress had called for an investigation and it was obvious that the people who worked in ITT's Washington office would need a lawyer and asked if I would serve in that role. I said I would be happy to do so. He said a limousine would arrive at the apartment at 5:30 the next morning to take me to LaGuardia, where I would join him and others on an ITT plane to Washington.

Thus began three to four weeks in Washington with brief trips home on the weekends to see Peggy and our two children. While my absence was not easy for Peggy, I made enough from that representation that I could afford the down payment on our first house. I still remember returning to my hotel with Mike Mitchell at about 2:30 a.m. after the first day in Washington. Since my day had started when I got in the limousine at 5:30 a.m., I asked Mike, "How do you bill for day like today?" His response was, "For every hour." I do not remember my hourly rate at the time, but it turned out to be a substantial amount of money.

A Life Begun on Third Base

The first days in Washington were spent interviewing the people working in ITT's Washington office who had shredded files the day Anderson's first column came out. At that time, ITT was responding to an outstanding Justice Department subpoena and it was possible that shredding documents could be considered an obstruction of justice, if the intent was to destroy documents so they could not be produced pursuant to the subpoena.

Our interviews established that the people who shredded documents were not thinking about the Department of Justice subpoena. Their concern was that someone was giving Jack Anderson access to their files and they did not want to see more memos published in his columns.

The hearings were held in the Senate and went on for a couple of weeks. The highlight came for me late in the hearings, when Harold Geneen, the chief executive of ITT, testified. One of the Senators asked him about the shredding and he said counsel was looking into it. He was then asked if he was expecting a report from counsel and he said he was. He was asked if he thought he could get that report by the following day and he said yes.

As soon as we left the hearing, Howard Able, ITT's General Counsel, asked the three of us who had conducted the interviews, Mike Mitchell, Herb Teitelbaum and me, to draft the report. We worked late into the night and got it to the typists in the morning. At the morning's hearing, Mr. Geneen was asked when the report would be available and he said it would be ready in the afternoon.

That afternoon, Howard Able was sworn as a witness and sat next to Mr. Geneen and read the report to the Senators. After he finished reading, the Senators began to question him about the details of the investigation. Howard was asked to identify the lawyers who prepared the report and he named the three of us. Sometime thereafter, Howard made a major mistake in response to a question and I thought it had to be corrected. I was seated about a row behind him and I walked up and whispered in his ear. He then said, "Mr. Martin has advised me that there was something incorrect in my last answer that I would like to correct." With that one of the senators said, "Is that the Mr. Martin who worked on the report—why doesn't he come up here and testify?" With that I took the oath and sat down next to Howard and Mr. Geneen.

I testified for about an hour or an hour and a half. Given the political nature of the proceedings, the Republicans wanted to prove that absolutely nothing wrong had been done and the Democrats the opposite. For me, the more difficult questions came from Republicans. I remember being asked in substance, "Isn't it true that you conducted the most exhaustive investigation possible and you found that there was absolutely nothing wrong done?" I said we had done as thorough investigation as we could and we concluded that the people in Washington office had not intended to obstruct the Justice Department investigation.

This was an interesting experience with a substantial payday. One thing I learned is that a congressional investigation is not necessarily a search for the truth.

Martin, Obermaier & Morvillo

One of the nice things about practicing by yourself is all of the money you make is yours. However, the more successful you become, the more you need a bigger organization. As my practice grew, I began to think about forming a partnership. Otto Obermaier was a natural candidate. He and I had met when we both pledged the same fraternity at Manhattan College and we had been colleagues in the US Attorney's office.

Before we met, Otto had had a memorable experience with my father. The biggest event of the year at Bear Mountain was the annual Home Insurance outing, which involved a buffet lunch served outdoors and later a sit-down dinner for several hundred Home Insurance employees. To supplement the staff for the day, Dad called upon Leo Paquin, the football coach at Xavier High School, who worked as the refreshment stand manager for Dad in the summer. Otto was one of the Xavier high school students shipped on a bus to Bear Mountain,

A Life Begun on Third Base

where he was assigned to dish out potato salad. As he was doing this job, a man he later identified as my father came by and said, "Hey kid, will you cut down the amount of potato salad you're giving out?" Not long after that, he passed by Otto's line again and said, "Hey kid, what do I have to do, kick you in the balls to get you to stop giving away all of my potato salad?" Otto remembered my father.

Otto and I had served as law clerks in the US Courthouse at the same time and then in the US Attorney's office. After leaving the office and spending a short time in private practice, Otto became the Chief Trial Counsel in the SEC's New York office. About six months after I started my practice, Otto also opened an office as a sole practitioner.

Our offices were fairly near each other and we regularly had lunch. I think from very early on we each thought about forming a partnership, but we both wanted to be sure that we would be successful enough that we could form an equal partnership without either one of us being more responsible for generating business. We finally decided to do it and on August 1, 1972 we started Martin & Obermaier—two lawyers, no waiting. In the time since I began my private practice, Orans Elsen had moved to Rockefeller Center and they had excess office space that we could use.

In case we thought we were two hotshot lawyers, in one of the first cases referred to us, the client asked if he could pay with American Express money orders—no wire transfers for Martin Obermaier. Not long after we started, we hired our first associate, Betty Santangelo, and the following spring began talking to Bob Morvillo about joining us. Bob had served with us in the US Attorney's office and he and Otto had become close friends. Bob was then serving as the Chief of the Criminal Division in the Southern District.

Bob joined us in May 1973 and we planned a celebratory dinner with our wives. The dinner was for a Friday night in late May and early that week Bob got a call from Jim Vorenberg, a Harvard law professor who was helping the newly appointed Watergate Special Prosecutor, Archibald Cox, to set up the office to investigate President Nixon. Bob flew to Washington on the day of our planned dinner to meet with

Cox and Vorenberg. When he returned that afternoon, he said that he been offered the job of Chief Assistant to Cox and he wanted to take it. We agreed it was the right thing for him but we went ahead with our celebratory dinner that evening. I told Bob at the dinner that we had planned to get him a gold watch to celebrate his time with the firm but we could not find one with only a second hand.

In the end, Bob did not take the job. When he called Jim Vorenberg on the Saturday after our dinner to tell them he would accept the job, he said he had two conditions: 1) he wanted a commitment that if there was a major indictment and Cox was not going to try it, then he would get to try the case, and 2) he said he had talked to several top Assistants from the Southern District who would be willing to join the staff and he wanted a commitment that they would be hired. He later received a call saying they agreed he could try the major case but they would not commit to hiring any of the people he wanted—Cox wanted to have a national staff. Bob was concerned that without a staff ready to go, in six months he would end up before Congress being asked why the office had not done anything. So he turned down the job. It was our gain.

Martin, Obermaier, and Morvillo would ultimately add several wonderful lawyers, including Marty Perschetz and Betty Santangelo. We also decided to bring in a younger lawyer as a junior partner. Since Bob had recently served as the Chief of the Criminal Division, we asked him who we should interview. He said there were only two people he would suggest—Tom Fitzpatrick and Rudy Giuliani. We picked Fitzpatrick. Many years later, I told Tom that if we had made the other choice he might've been mayor of the City of New York.

Tony Natelli

The first major case I had after forming Martin & Obermaier taught me one of the most painful lessons I learned in my career—the criminal justice system is not infallible. I represented Tony Natelli, who was convicted of stock fraud, and I will go to my grave convinced that he was innocent.

Tony was the partner in charge of the Washington office of Peat, Marwick, & Mitchell, and in charge of the audit of National Student Marketing. This was a company that developed marketing programs directed to college students. It received a fee for the services that covered several years of work. The accounting issue involved determining what year to recognize the income derived from these contracts. If payment was not made until year three but the work was done in years one, two and three and the company waited until year three to record the income, the company would appear unprofitable in years one and two and then very profitable in year three. This was an issue that came up in in long-term construction contracts and accountants used a percentage of completion method to record the income, i.e., if the contract was for three years for $300,000 and one third of the work was done each of those years, the company would report income of $100,000 in each year, even though the payment was not made until year three.

Whether it was appropriate to use this method for a company like National Student Marketing was an issue on which reasonable people could differ and there was no question that Tony was called to make some difficult decisions. Unfortunately, the company was a fraud and what we represented to him to have been valid contracts turned out to be unenforceable. While looking back and rereading the Second Circuit opinion affirming his conviction, I can understand why the court ruled as it did. Knowing Tony as well as I got to know him, I knew that he just made the best judgment he could in a difficult situation. In its opinion the Second Circuit noted:

"When we deal with a defendant who is a professional accountant, it is [hard] to distinguish between simple errors of judgment and errors made with sufficient criminal intent to support a conviction, particularly when there is no financial gain to the accountant other than his legitimate fee."

I cried when the jury announced its verdict of guilty and felt outraged when the trial judge sentenced Tony to 60 days in prison. However, the experience made me a better United States Attorney and Judge.

Tony never blamed me for the result and, although we lost regular contact, we never ceased being friends. At some point, Peg's brother John, who lived in Washington and had met Tony, told me he had heard that Tony was living in a mansion on the ninth hole of the Avenel golf course. I knew that Tony, who had been forced to leave the accounting profession because of his conviction, had gone into real estate. With a group of his former partners, they purchased a large parcel of land in Potomac Maryland and gave the core of it to the PGA for construction of the Avenel golf course. They subdivided the rest of the land into building lots, which turned out to be very valuable when the course was completed.

After I talked to John Conroy, I called Tony and said, "I hear you're living in a mansion on the golf course." Tony replied, "John, it is only a small mansion." He then went on to say that, on reflection, his conviction may have had a positive impact on his life. Obviously, he had done well financially, but more important, because he was not practicing as an accountant, he had more time to spend with his family and develop a wonderful relationship with his children. Tony's reflection on his trial and conviction simply demonstrate what a wonderful individual he was.

The final irony in Tony's conviction became known to me many years later when I was serving as a judge. One of my cases involved the criminal prosecution of Con Ed and two of its executives on charges that they had failed to disclose the dispersal of asbestos as a result of an explosion in the power lines near Gramercy Park in New York. One of the executives was represented by Rusty Wing, a friend and partner at Weil Gotshal, and his associate Eve Burton. The trial ended with guilty pleas to misdemeanors by the executives and a felony plea by the Corporation.

A year or two after the Con Ed case, I was at a cocktail party with Eve Burton, then the general counsel of the Daily News. At some point she said, "You know, Judge, that case I tried before you with Rusty was one of the reasons I left private practice." I replied, "Did I treat you that badly, Eve?" She said no, that it was she was so convinced of her client's innocence that she never wanted to have that type of pressure again. I said I understood because when I was in private practice I represented somebody who was convicted and I would go to my grave convinced he was innocent. She asked who that was and I said, "He was an accountant convicted in the 70s in a securities case." I was shocked when she said "Natelli." I said, "How do you know about Tony Natelli?" She replied, "My father was also convinced he was innocent." It turned out she was the daughter of Sandy Burton, who had been the Chief Accountant of the SEC at the time Tony was indicted. An accountant could understand errors of judgment with respect to difficult accounting issues, but the lawyers of the US Attorney's office saw fraud.

John Peter Galanis

In the fall of 1976, the US Attorney's office in Connecticut obtained an order to arrest John Peter Galanis so that he could be extradited to Canada where criminal charges had been filed against him. John had years earlier pleaded guilty to securities fraud in the Southern District and had become a major cooperator. The extradition proceeding was commenced not long after John testified in the last of the criminal cases arising from his cooperation.

From the outset of his criminal problems, John had been represented by Paul Grand, a former colleague in the US Attorney's office who had been on the Columbia Law Review in the class ahead of me. Paul called and told me that John's employer told John that to handle the extradition case he needed a constitutional lawyer. Although John was happy with Paul, he wanted to please his employer. Paul explained that since I had been in the Solicitor General's office and had argued in the Supreme Court, he thought I could be passed off as a constitutional lawyer and I was retained.

While we constructed a number of defenses to the extradition request, the one that was ultimately successful involved a provision in the existing extradition treaty that provided, if the person whose extradition was sought had been "proceeded against and punished" in the country where the extradition request had been filed, he could not be extradited. The concept was similar to the well-recognized principle of double jeopardy that prevents the government from twice prosecuting someone for the same crime.

Although John had not been charged with the crime that was set forth in the extradition request, it was among the many crimes that he had disclosed to the Southern District prosecutors in connection with his cooperation and for which he was granted immunity. The decision as to which of the crimes John disclosed would be the subject of the criminal charges to which he pleaded guilty was made by the Southern District prosecutors who wanted him to plead to charges in a case or cases in which he would be testifying.

We argued that in practical terms John had been proceeded against and punished in the United States. He had disclosed the crime, it had been included within the immunity the prosecutors had conferred upon him, and all of his criminal conduct was considered by the judge who sentenced him. The argument was creative but far from a sure winner. He had not, in fact, been prosecuted for the Canadian crime in the United States and the minimal sentence he received as a cooperator could be attributed to the crimes to which he pleaded guilty. Fortunately for us, the prosecutors from Connecticut never made that argument.

The United States extradition treaty with Canada containing the "proceeded against and punished" provision had been adopted after the crimes for which extradition was being sought and the earlier treaty did not have a comparable provision. Without boring you with the details, there were two separate District Court proceedings and an ultimate appeal to the Second Circuit of the final order of extradition. As we briefed the argument in the various courts, the pattern was the same. We would make the "proceeded against and punished" argument, the prosecutor would simply reply that this provision did not apply in cases where the crime had been committed before the treaty was amended. We would then file a brief stating that the prosecutor apparently conceded that if the new treaty applied, John could not be extradited.

We lost the case before both of the District Judges who had to rule on the request. However, on appeal, Judge Friendly began his discussion of the legal issues by saying that apparently the government does not challenge the factual assertion that Galanis had been "proceeded against and punished." He then went on to find that there was no reason not to apply the new treaty retroactively. John could not be extradited.

John Galanis was one of the most intriguing people I ever represented. He would become a friend and, unfortunately, a recurring violator. Early in his career, John had been considered one of the boy wonders of Wall Street, extremely successful at picking stock winners. However, when the market turned south, he and his partner engaged in a series of frauds to keep their business afloat. That led to his cooperation with the Southern District.

John was in ways a financial genius, but he had no ability to perceive the difference between a great idea and a fraud. The first check John gave me when he retained me bounced. He was in desperate financial straits, but as the extradition case dragged on for a couple of years, he achieved great financial success. To celebrate the victory after the Court of Appeals threw out the extradition request, John took Peggy and me and the Grands out on his 65 foot sailboat with a crew of four.

John loved all that money could buy, particularly good food and drink. After a day in court, we would likely find ourselves in one of the better restaurants in the area with John ordering the food and wine. Another celebration of our victory in the extradition case involved John taking everyone who worked on the case and their significant others to what was then the most expensive restaurant in New York. There were 12 of us. We started with martinis and, over the course of several hours, finished 14 bottles of wine. The dinner ended with everyone but one of the women smoking cigars dipped in brandy and drinking cognac.

When we staggered out to find our cars, John had a row of limousines waiting to take us home. We picked up our cars the next day.

Unfortunately, John could not see the fraud in many of the deals in which he became involved and he would spend the better part of his remaining years in jail, where he is today. Judge Brieant summed things up very well when, in sentencing John to 23 years in jail in 1988, he said, "I received a lot of letters from people who know the defendant. Mr. Galanis seems to be a very nice man, when he's not committing crimes."

The 1988 case had one interesting epilogue. I had not represented John at the trial of that case, but I agreed to handle the appeal and John asked me to be present at the sentencing. The sentence was set for a day when Peggy and I were scheduled to be in Kiawah, South Carolina, celebrating our 20th anniversary. I called Vincent Brecetti, the Assistant handling John's case and explained the situation and asked him to agree to put the sentencing over for two weeks so that I could attend. He refused. I was angry, but I submitted an application for an adjournment, which Judge Brient granted, and we went to Kiawah.

Years later when I was on the court, Brecetti was the defense lawyer in a criminal case that I dismissed at the end of the government's evidence because I found the government failed to prove an essential element. Later that afternoon, as I was sitting in my office, Brecetti came to thank me for granting the motion to dismiss which was very rare in a criminal case. I said, "Vince, I did no more than the law required me to do but it does show one thing—I do not hold a grudge." He had no idea what I was talking about and I reminded him of his refusal to consent to an adjournment so I could celebrate my anniversary.

Jerry Lee Brammer

Jerry Lee Brammer got away with $1 million fraud — that is, until he got caught. Brammer, a lawyer working for Champion International, embezzled just over a million dollars from his employer and then retired in 1975. Prior to his departure, the accounts from which he had embezzled the funds were audited and no irregularity was detected.

Brammer's scheme was ingenious. One of Brammer's responsibilities was to oversee the settlement of consumer claims against the company, which could run into hundreds of thousands of dollars. Brammer's embezzlement scheme involved his creation of phony claims using the name of a person from whom he desired to make a purchase.

For example, one of his purchases was of a house in the Hamptons. After agreeing to a price at or near the asking price, Brammer explained to the owner that his family were major owners of Champion International and that, to purchase the house, he was going to have to sell some of his stock back to the company. He told the owner that the company was reluctant to disclose that a major owner was selling the stock and therefore preferred to issue a check directly to the seller. Brammer then set up a fictitious claim in the name of the person from whom he was purchasing the house. He then settled the claim and had a check issued to the owner. The purchase of the house went through with no questions asked.

Brammer used this basic scheme to also purchase an apartment at UN Plaza, luxury cars, artwork, and, finally, a restaurant he would operate in retirement. To purchase the restaurant, Brammer set up a corporation, Sustain Enterprises, and established a fraudulent claim in its name. A check was issued and the funds used to purchase a restaurant called Katja.

Although Brammer had been retired for about two years and Champion International was totally unaware of this fraud, the roof fell in on Brammer in 1977, when he made the mistake of firing the maître d', whom he had hired when he was setting up Katja. At the time he hired the maître d', Brammer told him the same story about the selling of his Champion International stock. Apparently, the maître d' did not believe the story, but thought that Champion was the hidden owner of the restaurant. When Brammer fired the maître d', he wrote to Champion telling them how Brammer was mismanaging their restaurant. As a result of this letter, Champion re-examined Brammer's files and discovered the fraud. Brammer was arrested in March 1997.

It was clear from the outset that Brammer was guilty and the evidence against him was overwhelming. Therefore, the only thing to be done was to work out a plea agreement with the District Attorney's Office. It was finally agreed that, in exchange for his plea of guilty, the District Attorney would agree to a sentence of two years in prison.

That would have been the end of the story, were it not for a very successful criminal defense representation by my friend Bernie Nussbaum. At the same time Brammer's case was going through the courts, Bernie was representing Joel Dolkart, a lawyer who was charged with embezzling over $2.5 million from his employer Gulf and Western Industries. After his arrest, Dolkart cooperated with the SEC and the District Attorney's Office by providing them with evidence of corporate wrongdoing by his employer. As a result of this cooperation, the District Attorney's Office agreed to a sentence of probation. Although the sentencing judge originally refused to go along with the plea agreement and sentenced Dolkart to three years in jail, the appellate court reversed and ordered that the court impose the agreed-upon sentence of probation.

The controversy concerning the Dolkart sentence had received substantial publicity just prior to the sentencing of Jerry Brammer. When Jerry was asked by the sentencing judge if there was anything he wanted to say before sentence was imposed, Jerry replied, "The only difference between Mr. Dolkart and me is that I worked for an honest company and so had no information to give up."

Until then, I had never thought of how a criminal defendant may perceive that he is being treated unfairly by a system that sends him to jail but allows another equally culpable individual to go free simply because he can provide useful information to a prosecutor.

A Life Begun on Third Base

Chemical Bank

In April 1977, I pleaded guilty in United States District Court for the Southern District of New York to 422 violations of the Bank Secrecy Act. Fortunately, I was not admitting that I had personally committed any crime, but as a lawyer I was entering a guilty plea for my client, Chemical Bank. A corporation may have either an executive or its attorney enter a plea on its behalf and no corporate officer was anxious to plead guilty in federal court. One of the amusing aspects was that the judge, following the usual ritual for accepting the plea, said "Mr. Martin, I know this sounds silly, but you know that the bank has a right to be represented by counsel."

This was the first major internal investigation I conducted for a corporate client. Sometime in 1975, a friend who was a partner in Cravath Swain & Moore recommended me to John Wynne, the General Counsel of the bank. The bank had been informed by the United States Attorney that it was conducting a criminal inquiry into money laundering at certain of the bank's branches in Manhattan and the Bronx. The bank needed someone to conduct an internal investigation to determine if there was any truth to these allegations and, if so, to identify the responsible employees.

I spent several weeks interviewing employees at the bank branches the government had identified as being involved. Employees were told that they were expected to cooperate with my investigation and testify truthfully. The employees were told that, if they did not cooperate or lied in the course of the investigation, they would be fired.

The investigation revealed that employees in several of the branches had been exchanging large denomination bills for small bills for some of their customers and not reporting to the government transactions of more than $10,000, which they were required to do by the Bank Secrecy Act. These activities were vital to narcotics distributors who would receive small bills from the customers but needed large denomination bills to make purchases from their suppliers. They could not pay a supplier $20,000 in five-dollar bills. Although to an objective observer it was obvious that these employees were facilitating the operation of drug dealers, all of the employees involved claimed that they thought the money came from gamblers.

As a result of this investigation and my recommendation, approximately 25 bank employees were fired, including a regional vice president who was not a participant in the scheme but became aware of it and took no action. Even though we told this individual when he was fired that we had strong evidence of his awareness of the scheme, he thereafter testified before a federal grand jury that he had not been aware of it. He was indicted and convicted of perjury.

One of the benefits of the case was that I got to know John Wynne, who was a marvelous person with a good sense of humor. John and his wife Sally lived in Greenwich not far from us and, for a period of time, Peggy and I saw them socially.

One incident with John that I remember occurred when I was down at the bank's corporate headquarters shortly after I had sent what I thought was a large bill for a month of work. As we walked out of John's office into a large reception area, a new carpet was being installed. John delighted in pointing out that the new carpet cost more than my bill.

Stephen Buzzie

Stephen Buzzie was one of three people arrested by the FBI in New York where they were trying to sell various pieces of art stolen from a museum at Wellesley College. Upon their arrest, Steven's codefendants began cooperating with the government. Stephen was indicted and the case assigned to Judge Bauman, my former colleague on the Zafer trial. Arnold called and asked if I would accept an assignment to represent Buzzie and I agreed.

The case was a typical criminal case. The two codefendants testified that they committed the crime and that my client was with them. Often, when potential defendants would come to me about possibly representing them, they would be anxious to know whether I had tried cases involving the exact same criminal violation. My answer was always the same, "I will answer that question but first I will tell you it makes no difference. All criminal trials are basically the same, whether they be securities fraud, narcotics or murder. You end up at a trial with one or more people testifying for the prosecution that they committed the crime and that the defendant on trial was with them."

As I prepared for trial, I thought there was little chance of success and I searched unsuccessfully through the documents the government had supplied in discovery looking for a defense. I do not recall which of the cooperators was testifying or whether it was on direct or cross-examination that one of them testified, after planning the crime, they had to find a car to use and they borrowed a Volkswagen belonging to a friend. I had my defense.

The evidence was that the defendants had stolen a number of pieces of art including paintings, a triptych, and several pieces of sculpture. I never mentioned the Volkswagen during the presentation of the evidence. However, I spent most of my summation talking to the jury about how impossible it would have been to have Buzzie and the two cooperators in a little Volkswagen with all of this art.

The jury began its deliberations in the morning, and I thought I had accomplished a great deal when they failed to reach a verdict by the end of the day. With two cooperators testifying against him, there appeared little chance my client would be acquitted.

When I arrived at court the next morning, I was told the judge wanted to see us in the robing room. Judge Bauman told us one of the jurors had a heart attack during the night and could not continue to serve. He asked me if my client would take a verdict from a jury of 11.

I spent a long time discussing the question with my client. For me personally, I had no desire to try this case a second time. However, the prevailing wisdom was that a criminal defendant would always rather have a mistrial than consent to a jury of 11. I explained to my client, however, that this was a unique case. The best thing he had going for him was the Volkswagen defense. If we refused to consent and a mistrial was declared, he could expect that at the second trial it would be either a Volkswagen bus or there would be FBI sketches showing how the three defendants and the stolen art fit comfortably in the Volkswagen.

My client ultimately decided that he would take the risk and consent to a jury of 11. About three hours later, the jury found him not guilty.

A verdict of acquittal is a rare experience for a criminal defense lawyer in the federal courts. I enjoyed this one particularly since the prosecutor Peter Putzel was a friend who I would kid about my victory often over the years.

Several years later when I was US Attorney, the chief of the securities fraud unit sent me a draft press release relating to an indictment for the fraudulent sale of gold futures contracts. Although I had been aware of the investigation, I did not know the name of all of the potential defendants but there was a name I recognized—Steve Buzzie. The indictment was filed and the following day, as I was conducting a meeting with some of the staff, my secretary buzzed to say, "There is a Mr. Buzzie calling you." My reaction was that it was Peter Putzel, who had a reputation as a practical joker. I told those present that it was probably Putzel and I picked up the phone only to hear the distinctive Boston accent of Stephen Buzzie, "Mr. Martin I don't know if you remember me but you represented me." I quickly told him I could not talk to him about the case and hung up. The last time I saw Stephen he was standing before Judge Milton Pollock, one of the toughest sentencers on the court, telling Judge Pollock, who had presided over the trial at which he was convicted, "Your Honor, if I knew my employer was not buying gold to back up the contracts I sold, I would've turned him into the FBI myself." Not a good tactic before Judge Pollock, who then sentenced him to 12 years in jail.

Norton-Ali at Yankee Stadium

When I picked up the paper on May 15 and read that it had been announced that Muhammad Ali would fight Ken Norton at Yankee Stadium in September, I did not realize a new case was coming my way. Not long after the fight was announced, Don King, a well-known boxing promoter, brought a lawsuit against Norton. He claimed that he had a contract with Norton that gave him the exclusive right to promote any fight in which Norton participated and asked the court to enjoin the scheduled fight at Yankee Stadium.

After the lawsuit was filed, I received a phone call from Bob Arum, a former colleague at the US Attorney's office. As an Assistant, Bob had handled a tax investigation arising from the Floyd Patterson-Ingemar Johansson title fight. As a result of the connections he made through that investigation, Bob became a fight promoter after he left the office.

Bob asked me if I would represent Norton in the suit to enjoin the fight. It turned out to be a fascinating case, in large part because of the people involved. Don King was a larger-than-life character who, at one point in his career, served a jail sentence for manslaughter because he beat someone to death. Ken Norton had been a Marine with an impressive amateur record. When he was leaving the Marines, a group of wealthy San Diego businessmen put up some money to sponsor him and, at the time I represented him, his manager was a former senior executive from General Dynamics — far from your typical fight manager.

In order to prove his right to stop Norton from fighting Muhammad Ali, King had to prove that he had a valid contract with Norton and that he had the ability to promote a fight with Ali. We had two principal defenses: 1) the agreement that Norton had signed with King was not a valid contract because it didn't contain enough specific terms to be an enforceable contract — in legal jargon, it was an agreement to agree, not a contract; and 2) King could not have promoted the fight because he had had a falling out with Elijah Muhammad, Ali's manager.

Because this was an action to enjoin the fight that was to take place in a few months, the case was on a fast track. In light of the time pressure, I needed help and I asked Pete Putzel, my opponent in the Buzzie case, to work with me. Pete had left the US Attorney's office and was subletting an office from our firm.

I had the opportunity to cross-examine Don King twice — once during his deposition and again during a hearing before Judge Brieant. It was clear that King was not wedded to the truth.

The highlight of the case for me occurred during the hearing. King had testified that, given his relationship with Muhammad Ali, he could have promoted a Norton-Ali fight. In doing research for the case, I found an article by Dick Young, then the sports editor of the New York Daily News, in which Young quoted King as saying that he realized he could not promote the fight because he had a falling out with Elijah Muhammad, Ali's manager.

Dick Young had been a friend of my father, so I called him and asked if he would testify to that conversation and he agreed. With this testimony in my back pocket, on cross-examination I asked King, "Did you ever tell Dick Young of the Daily News that you could not promote the flight because you had a falling out with Elijah Muhammad?" Given my experience with King at his deposition, where truth did not seem to stand in the way, I was shocked when, after pausing for a moment, King answered my question, "Yes.

At the next break, Norton's manager explained to me the reason that King would not deny what he had said to Dick Young. He said that Dick Young's columns could put more people in seats for a boxing event than any other sportswriter. Don King did not want to get on the bad side of Dick Young.

The fight went forward and one of the benefits of the litigation for me was that Pete Putzel and I ended up in a ringside seat at Yankee Stadium. We thought that Norton had won, but the decision went the other way.

My Best Results

When you do criminal defense work in the federal courts, you have to be prepared to accept a lot of defeats and I had my share of them. One of them involved a doctor charged with Medicaid and Medicare fraud. The proof was overwhelming, including evidence that he was charging patients for visits to his office In Westchester County when he was on national guard duty in upstate New York. I urged him to accept a plea deal which I thought would keep him out of jail. When we went to trial, I urged him not to testify. When he decided to testify, I required him to sign a statement saying I had urged him not to testify and that he was testifying against my advice. He testified, was convicted and Judge Connor sentenced him to jail. Judge Connor was one of the lightest sentencers on the court and I am sure he would not have sentenced my client to jail if he had not testified.

The most successful representations you have as a criminal defense lawyer you cannot talk about. They are the cases where you represent someone who is under investigation and are able to persuade the prosecutor not to indict. The client reasonably wants no one to ever know he was suspected of a crime and the canons of ethics provide that a lawyer cannot unnecessarily disclose information that is detrimental to a client. As a result, I never could talk about the details of the most successful representations I had.

The restriction on discussing information that could be embarrassing to a client did cause a couple of awkward moments. Within two or three years, I represented a fairly well-known New York politician and a lobbyist. The lobbyist gave an annual party — it was quite elaborate — to which Peggy and I were invited several times. At one of these parties I ran into my former client, the politician, who greeted me warmly in the presence of the host. Later on, each of them asked me separately how I knew the other. I responded that I had been introduced by a mutual friend — substantially true since I had been introduced to each client by a lawyer who had referred the client to me.

I always recognized that my client's life was in my hands and did my best to persuade the prosecutor not to file charges. When I failed and charges were filed I felt terrible, but I also learned that the clients for whom I had worked so hard were not always loyal. It was not uncommon for a client who had been indicted to decide they wanted someone else to represent them in the case. It was never an easy decision to accept.

JOHN S. MARTIN JR.

Jobs I Did Not Get

One of the truisms of life is that you often do not know whether a particular event is good or bad for you. The best example is that of Christa McAuliffe who must have been terribly excited on July 19, 1985, when it was announced that she would be the first teacher in space. However, when her mission was launched on January 28, 1986, the spaceship exploded killing all aboard.

While my life has not had any event as dramatic as that, during my time in private practice in the 70s I was severely disappointed when I was turned down for two important government positions. However in retrospect I was lucky that I was not selected because had I accepted either of those positions I probably never would have become United States Attorney for the Southern District of New York or a federal judge.

In the summer of 1977 I was asked if I was interested in being considered for the position of Assistant Secretary of the Treasury for Enforcement & Administration, which involved among other things supervision of the Secret Service. I forget how this opportunity came to me but it looked like an exciting job. After discussing it with Peggy and Bob and Otto, I decided to apply. I traveled to Washington and was interviewed by the then Secretary of the Treasury, W. Michael Blumenthal. He selected Richard Davis, a former SDNY Assistant.

About a year later, I received a call from Benjamin Civiletti, then the Deputy Attorney General asking me if I wanted to be considered to be the Assistant Attorney General for the Criminal Division. I then consulted with Peggy and my partners and decided to apply for the job. A day or two after I met with Civiletti, I talked to my brother Frank, who was then working in the Department of Justice and had previously worked for the Watergate Special Prosecutor. In the course of our conversation Frank said that he thought he knew who the new assistant AG for the Criminal Division would be. He said he had recently been in Civelletti's office when he received a phone call. When he hung up, Civiletti told Frank that he had been speaking to Phil Hyman, who was under consideration to be the Assistant

Attorney General for the Criminal Division and asked Frank if he knew Phil. Frank said "I told Ben we worked together in the Special Prosecutor's office and you couldn't find anyone better for the job." I said to Frank, "You schmuck, I have my name in for that job." Prior to that Frank did not know I had applied. When Ben called to tell me he had selected Phil, he tried to persuade me to come to Washington to serve as his principal deputy but I decided not to.

Phil Heyman was still serving in the Criminal when I became US Attorney and he and I had a good laugh when I told him about Frank's recommendation.

While I am sure I would have enjoyed either of the two jobs for which I applied, both would have involved a move to Washington which might have dramatically changed my career. In any event, had I taken either job I would not have applied to be the United States Attorney for the Southern District of New York. I was lucky to have been turned down.

Baer & McGoldrick

Martin, Obermaier & Morvillo was a reasonably successful law firm, but the nature of the practice was such that we had no recurring business. At the end of the year, we would sit down and say, "We had a good year, but where will the business come from next year?" When I raised this problem with a friend, he replied, "You guys are like undertakers. You do not know who it will be, but every year there will be people out there who need your services."

Otto and I became persuaded that we would be better off practicing in a full-service firm. That way, if we developed a good relationship with a client, that client might be able to send us their non-litigation business and the non-litigating partners could also be a source of new business for us.

From the time I opened up in 1969, cases had been referred to me by the firm of Baer & McGoldrick. That firm had been established about the time I opened my office by a group of young lawyers who had been associates at major firms. They were equal partners and used the names of the two of them that they thought sounded most prestigious.

Tommy Baer had been a colleague in the US Attorney's office and another partner, Charles Goldstein, had been a law clerk for another circuit judge when I was clerking. Tommy was supposed to be the litigator, but early on he began representing a good-sized corporation that was run by a friend of his. Thus, when one of the firm's clients needed a litigator, they would often call on me. On several occasions, the firm raised the question whether I would like to join them.

In 1978, I was again approached about joining Baer & McGoldrick, but this time the proposal was that we merge the two firms. Otto, Bob, Tom and I had a series of discussions about the possible benefits of such a merger. In the end, Bob and Tom decided they would prefer to remain together concentrating on criminal defense work and not be part of the firm, but they encouraged Otto and I to do it if we thought it made sense. Otto and I agreed that we should do it and we began serious negotiations. The proposal was very attractive; we would join as full partners on the same level as their founding partners, all of whom received the same percentage of the partnerships profits, with the exception that at the end of the year a small portion of the profits would be allocated on the basis of the individual's partners contribution to the firm during the year. Otto and I agreed to join the firm, but, as we got to the very end of the road, Otto said to me, "Will you still go ahead if I decide not to"—meaning that he would go along with me if necessary. I said that we were too old to make that type of commitment to each other and he should do what he felt was best for him, but I was prepared to join Baer & McGoldrick. Otto said he wanted to remain with Bob and Tom.

My tenure at Baer & McGoldrick began on January 1, 1979. At my first partnership meeting, my friend Charles Goldstein announced that he would leave the firm unless he was provided with certain benefits, e.g., a car and driver. At the time, Charles was one of the biggest income producers, but what he was proposing was anathema to the concept that had brought me to the firm—the senior partners were equal—and I joined the others voting against him. Welcome to the new firm.

My stay at the firm did not last long. In late October or early November 1969, I attended the annual luncheon of the American Friends of the Hebrew University - - an event that usually honored some litigator who I knew or who I wanted to know. At some point, I ran into Chet Straub, then a member of Senator Moynihan's judicial selection committee. Chet told me that the committee was beginning to consider applications for a new United States Attorney for the Southern District of New York because Bob Fiske would be leaving in February. I told Chet that I would love to do it, but I had just joined Baer & McGoldrick and I did not think I could walk away from the firm in less than a year.

That afternoon, I told some of my partners about my conversation with Chet and they all urged me to submit an application. I did and Chet helped shepherd me through the process. In late January Senator Moynihan announced that he was recommending my appointment to lead the Southern District. The confirmation process took several months but I was eventually sworn in on May 22, 1980.

ELEVEN

United States Attorney

The office of the United States Attorney for the Southern District of New York ("SDNY") has a rich history and for years had been regarded as the finest prosecutor's office in the country. Among my distinguished predecessors were Henry Stimson, whose long career included service as Secretary of War under both William Howard Taft and Franklin Delano Roosevelt and as Secretary of State under Herbert Hoover. Alumni of the office included Supreme Court Justices John Marshall Harlan and Felix Frankfurter and New York Governor and Republican candidate for President Thomas Dewey.

Since the appointment was political, not all of my predecessors were as distinguished and admirable. Each change of administration would bring a new US Attorney. It was not uncommon when a new US Attorney took office anywhere in the United States that all of the people serving as assistants were fired and replaced with individuals of the prevailing political party. Although this was not always the case in SDNY, it was not unusual.

JOHN S. MARTIN JR.

The New US Attorney and his Family

Beginning with the appointment of J. Edward Lumbard as United States Attorney in 1953, however, SDNY's hiring policy changed. Assistants were hired on the basis of merit and continued to serve despite changes in the political leadership of the office

As a result of this policy, when I became United States Attorney, I took over an office that had been well run for years and had an exceptionally talented group of lawyers. My main job was not to screw it up.

I took the oath of office on May 22, 1980, first privately in my office and later as part of a ceremony in courtroom 318, the largest courtroom in the building. The court room ceremony is brief but impressive. The judges of the court assemble in several rows on the bench, the Presidential commission is read, the oath is administered and the court adjourns. The most memorable event of my ceremonial induction was that Ed Koch, then New York City's Mayor, got stuck on a stalled elevator with several people. When one of the Assistant Marshals dealing with the problem shouted to the people stuck on the

A Life Begun on Third Base

elevator, "what's going on in there?" Someone responded, "What do you think, I'm having a drink with the mayor!"

I had been nominated to replace Robert Fiske, an outstanding lawyer and a person whom I would grow to respect and admire. Bob had resigned in February, and William Tendy, his Chief Assistant, had been appointed by the court to serve as United States Attorney on an interim basis.

Early on my first day in office, Bill, the Chief of the Criminal Division, and several other assistants came to see me. They said that there were three cases that involved major policy issues that had been deferred because they thought the issues should be decided by the new US Attorney.

The first case they mentioned involved a narcotics investigation in which the agents were posing as sellers of pharmaceutical cocaine. In a normal narcotics investigation, agents act as purchasers to get evidence on the sellers. In this case, by posing as suppliers, the agents hoped to get mid-level cocaine dealers.

In order to avoid ensnaring simple users, the agents indicated that the minimum amount they would sell was 1 ounce at a price of $10,000. Among the people who agreed to purchase the cocaine were a movie producer, Robert Evans, his brother and his brother-in-law. Their lawyers were arguing that these were simply rich people purchasing cocaine for their own use and that, as a general matter, the office did not prosecute drug users. However, 1 ounce of pure pharmaceutical cocaine was a lot more than three individuals could consume and was a strong indication they were distributing the cocaine to friends.

We ultimately decided we could not ignore the purchase of so substantial an amount of cocaine. We also recognized these were not drug dealers. The decision we reached was somewhat of a compromise — they would not be charged with felonies if they agreed to plead to misdemeanor charges, with the likelihood of no jail time and far less serious collateral consequences. It was not an easy decision and when I have talked about it to student groups in explaining the function of a prosecutor, some of them strongly argued that I was using a double standard.

Next up was a narcotics case in which the question was whether we should get a wiretap warrant. The difficult issue in this case was whether we would include the lawyer for the major drug dealer involved as a potential defendant.

In response to problems of organized crime, Congress had passed the Racketeering Influenced Corrupt Organization Act ("RICO"), which made it a crime to invest the proceeds of certain illegal activities, including narcotics, in a legitimate business. In this case, there was no evidence the lawyer was involved in any way in the narcotics distribution but there was evidence he knew his client was a drug dealer and he was helping him acquire legitimate businesses.

I made the decision to go forward with the case and the lawyer was ultimately indicted. The decision was controversial and one of the newspapers quoted my friend and former colleague from the US Attorney's office, Andy Lawler, as criticizing the decision. It was always my belief that, if all the facts were laid out publicly at a trial, people would see there was a reasonable basis for our decision. The lawyer was in fact acquitted but I never read or heard any criticism of our decision to indict him after the trial.

One humorous incident from that case involved a wiretap conversation between the drug dealer and the lawyer. One of the techniques used in association with a wiretap is referred to as "tickling the wire." During the course of the investigation the agents will do something likely to spark conversations among the subjects of the wiretap. In this case the agents arrested one of the drug dealer's top lieutenants. Thereafter, we overheard a conversation between the lawyer and the drug dealer. At the outset of the conversation, the lawyer made some joke about the arrest to which the drug dealer showed little reaction. However, after we heard the click of the lawyer hanging up, the drug dealer muttered, "asshole."

The final decision with which I was presented on my first day was the one that generated the most substantial adverse publicity. It involved a long-term investigation of bribery used to induce ship captains to bring their ships needing repair to the shipyards of the Bethlehem Steel Corporation. The investigation revealed that the practice had been going on for years, and the people who had instituted it were no longer with the company and could not be prosecuted because their conduct occurred so long ago prosecution was barred by the statute of limitations. The people who we could prosecute had nothing to do with the institution of the scheme and simply inherited it as part of their job when they were promoted. The Corporation was willing to plead guilty if we were willing to forgo prosecuting the individuals.

Again, there was no simple answer. It seemed unfair to prosecute individuals who were simply told this goes with the job when we would not be prosecuting those who set up the scheme. In addition, developing sufficient evidence against these individuals would involve extending an already lengthy investigation, which was a questionable use of resources.

In the end, I decided to take the plea. I do not recall any strong objection to that decision. Several months later, however, the *National Law Journal* did an article entitled "John Martin's Rocky Start." It claimed, among other things, that Jane Parver, an Assistant working on the Bethlehem Steel case, had been outraged by my decision. Jane had never complained to me and denied the assertions made in the article. Over the years Jane has become one of the most loyal of my former assistants, and she now organizes the annual gathering of people who served with me in the office. As someone we know might say, this was "fake news." That is not to say that someone in the office might not have supplied information to the *National Law Journal*—while I believe I had a very good relationship with most of the people with whom I served, I know I did not make everyone happy. That was not my job.

As my first day in the office indicated, this was not necessarily an easy job. My role was not to try cases. I had other important responsibilities. One of them was to serve as a liaison to all of the federal and state agencies that conducted investigations of the cases SDNY would prosecute. We worked with the agencies to determine the most important areas to be investigated. I had little day to day involvement with most of the cases we prosecuted, other than the cases deemed higher profile either because of the defendants involved or the nature of the criminal activity.

My most important job was to hire the new Assistants who would carry on the work of the office and to select the leaders of the various units to which criminal and civil cases were assigned. I often told my staff, "you do all the work and I get all the credit." This was because we didn't want SDNY's lawyers to be influenced by publicity. All press releases went out in my name as United States Attorney. This was true whether I knew about the investigation or not.

Ultimately, while I could not personally make the call for every case, the decision of whether to prosecute or not to prosecute was my responsibility. If there was a difficult decision to be made, I was brought into the loop. In addition, my door was always open to a defense attorney who wished to appeal a decision to prosecute. Since most cases were routine, I did not entertain many such appeals. However, I was always willing to listen. I would often tell defense counsel, "I am willing to consider any argument other than the claim, 'my client couldn't have been so dumb as to do the things with which he is charged.'" Experience had taught me that plenty of people were that dumb.

Some people questioned the fact I would hear appeals from defense lawyers who were my friends. It never bothered me because I knew, and they knew, the decision would have nothing to do with our friendship—the only question was what was the right thing to do for that particular defendant. I rejected do not prosecute pleas for my former partner Bob Morvillo and my good friend Ron Fischetti. For years thereafter Ron delighted in telling the story of how I refused his offer to have his client plead to a single count because of an SDNY policy that any plea involving a conspiracy had to include a plea to the conspiracy and one substantive count. In the case to which Ron was referring, after I refused his offer to plead to a single count, the case was assigned to one of the harsher criminal sentencers on the court and Ron had a horrible experience.

A Life Begun on Third Base

Weberman v. National Security Agency

The *Weberman* case almost resulted in my having the shortest tenure of any presidentially appointed United States Attorney in history. It was not a terribly complex case, legally or factually, but it was one that was vitally important to the National Security Agency ("NSA").

Weberman was an historian researching a book on the Kennedy assassination. He made a request under the Freedom of Information Act asking the NSA to produce a copy of a telegram allegedly sent by the brother of Jack Ruby, the assassin of Lee Harvey Oswald, to Cuba in April 1962. The NSA informed him that the existence or nonexistence of such a telegram was classified information that he was not entitled to receive. Weberman then brought an action in the Southern District seeking to compel the NSA to produce the document.

The government moved to dismiss the complaint arguing that, as a matter of national security, the NSA could not be forced to admit or deny whether it had such a document. Judge Brieant rejected the government's argument and granted summary judgment to the plaintiff in April 1980. The government then moved for re-argument, asking the judge to review in camera an affidavit from the NSA describing why the Freedom of Information Act request was appropriately denied for national security interests. In the decision filed in early June 1980 Judge Brieant denied the application and ordered the NSA to respond to the plaintiff's request.

To this point, this was a routine civil case handled by an SDNY Assistant in the Civil Division. However, as the case was being readied for appeal, I was told the Justice Department had determined the case should be argued by a lawyer from the Department of Justice. The justification was that this lawyer had worked on an NSA matter before and had the confidence of Admiral Inman, then the director of the NSA.

The request set off a firestorm. From Judge Lumbard's time, it had been a tradition that SDNY handled all of its own cases and lawyers from the Department of Justice were not welcome. Indeed, as a young

Assistant, I had heard of a conversation in which a lawyer in the Justice Department's Tax Division was telling a senior SDNY Assistant that the Assistant Attorney General of the Tax Division wanted him to argue a certain case. The Assistant's response was "Tell the Assistant Attorney General to go fuck himself." Bob Morgenthau, then the US Attorney, got involved and, as a result of his personal relationship with Bobby Kennedy, then the Attorney General, the dispute was resolved in SDNY's favor.

A brief bit of background. At the time the issue arose for us, Ben Civiletti was the Attorney General. I had met Ben about 2 1/2 years earlier when he interviewed me for the position of Assistant Attorney General for the Criminal Division. He had decided on someone else, but tried to convince me to serve as one of his deputies.

I had a number of conversations with Ben in which I was unable to convince him that the SDNY's independence was important to my staff. I said if there was concern about the quality of the argument, I would argue the case myself. He insisted the case would have to be handled by the Justice Department lawyer.

This decision launched a series of conversations as to whether or not I should resign as an act of protest. Although it seems trivial in retrospect, there was unanimity at the time that SDNY should not accept interference from Washington in a SDNY case—an issue that would rise again years later during the Trump administration. Before making a decision I consulted with all of the then living former US Attorneys of the Southern District of New York, Bob Fiske, Whitney North Seymour Junior, Paul Curran and Bob Morgenthau. All of them supported my decision to resign.

Fortunately, Bob Fiske took it upon himself to fly to Washington to talk to Civiletti and explain the significance of the issue to him. Bob had a much better relationship with Ben than I did because, for two years, Bob had served as the Chairman of the Attorney General's Advisory Committee, which was composed of a number of United States Attorneys from around the country.

The resignation letter I had prepared was never sent and I argued the case in the Second Circuit. The Circuit Court reversed Judge Brieant and ordered him to accept the ex parte affidavit from the NSA. After reviewing it, he dismissed the case.

The issue may seem trivial on its face, but, for SDNY, it was and is important. One of the benefits of the whole situation was that I got to know Bob Fiske better and I will always remember the thoughtfulness of his trip to Washington.

United States v. Newman

The next case I argued in the Second Circuit was of more substantive importance. During Bob Fiske's tenure, SDNY had indicted a stockbroker, James Newman, for insider trading. The charges were based on general fraud provisions of the Securities & Exchange Act and on the mail fraud statute. The case was assigned to Judge Haight, who would later become a beloved colleague.

The Judge dismissed the indictment, finding the Securities Act did not give the defendant adequate notice that his conduct was criminal and the mail fraud statute did not encompass taking information from brokers working on a merger and acquisition and passing it on to others who would buy the stock.

After the District Court opinion dismissing the indictment, the appellate attorneys and the Chief of the Criminal Division came to me and said they thought I should personally argue the appeal. The question of whether insider trading could be prosecuted criminally was of great importance, and it was their view that my arguing it would reinforce its importance to the Circuit Court.

The problem was, if I argued it, I would be taking the appeal away from the Assistant who had obtained the indictment. One of the things that made being an Assistant an attractive job was you were told you could handle your case from indictment through appeal. While I was reluctant to take the case away from the Assistant involved, the importance of the case carried the day. Fortunately, Lee

Richards took the decision well and was a great help to me in preparing the brief and argument. We won the appeal.

Omega 7

Omega 7 was a terrorist organization of anti-Castro Cubans that was believed to have been responsible for a series of bombings at foreign consulates in New York City in the late 70s and early 80s, as well as the 1980 attempted assassination of the Cuban ambassador to the United Nations

In 1982, I was contacted by members of the FBI terrorist task force and told that an individual named Eduardo Arocena had come to the FBI office and advised agents that he was Omar, the code name used by the alleged leader of Omega 7. He was apparently disgruntled because he had been overthrown as the leader. He provided the FBI substantial detailed information about various Omega 7 terrorist acts and identified the key participants.

The reason the agents had come to see me was Arocena told them, if he were allowed to travel to Florida, he would be able to locate the cache of explosives Omega 7 had stored there. The question for me was whether, despite Aroceno's admission he engaged in a series of terrorist acts, the FBI should allow him to go unaccompanied to Florida. Given the fact he had voluntarily came to the FBI office, there seemed to be little risk he would not return, so I authorized the trip to Florida.

We immediately began preparation of arrest warrants for the individuals. Arocena identified as participants in the terrorist acts. Given his admission of his own participation, the details he provided and other evidence the FBI had developed over the years, we had ample probable cause to justify arrest warrants.

Shortly after we arrested the seven individuals Arocena had identified, Arocena disappeared. We were left with seven individuals who had participated in a series of serious criminal acts but no witness. Our first effort was to question the individuals in the hope that one of them would cooperate. Unfortunately, none of them did.

What were we to do? The issue was discussed with a number of SDNY's senior people, but I believe I was the one that came up with the solution. I told the Assistants handling the case to rank the potential defendants from 1 to 7 on a scale of culpability. We would then grant immunity to number seven and call him before the grand jury and compel him to testify about the others. If he refused to testify we would seek an order sentencing him to jail for contempt.

In reverse order of culpability, each of the seven was granted immunity and called before the grand jury. None of them cooperated and as a result each of them spent approximately 18 months in jail. We did not obtain criminal convictions but we did keep seven very dangerous individuals off the streets.

Sometime in 1984, after I had left the office, Arocena was arrested, tried, convicted and sentenced to life imprisonment.

Leroy Nicky Barnes

Nicky Barnes ran one of the largest and most violent drug operations in the Harlem area during the 70s. Although his role as a major figure in the drug world was well known, law enforcement authorities had not been able to gather enough evidence to prosecute him. He became known as, "Mr. Untouchable." In fact, the *New York Times Magazine* section carried his picture on its cover with that title. He did not remain Mr. Untouchable for long. My predecessor, Bob Fiske, indicted, personally tried and convicted Barnes, who was then sentenced to life in prison without the possibility of parole.

One of the many benefits that Bob Fiske conferred on SDNY during his tenure was that he brought back as Chief Assistant United States Attorney Bill Tendy. Bill was a wonderful man who had served as Chief of the Narcotics Unit when I was an Assistant and had left the office several years later to head the New York State Organized Crime Task Force.

Bill knew the underworld of narcotics better than anyone. Several times after I became US Attorney, Bill said to me, "Barnes will ultimately call us." He was right. In July 1981 Bill received a call from the warden of the prison where Barnes was incarcerated saying Barnes wanted to talk to him. Barnes was ready to cooperate. Apparently, Barnes had become disgruntled because his former associates were not paying his legal bills, were not properly taking care of his family and one of them had the nerve to be sleeping with his former mistress.

Barnes ultimately provided detailed information on the criminal activities of his associates, including a substantial number of murders. We could not go to trial on his word alone, but the DEA, in cooperation with the New York City Police Department, developed enough corroborating evidence to support the indictment of a number of his most senior associates.

The press conference in which we announced an indictment charging Barnes and these individuals with a series of crimes including a number of murders was one of the most unpleasant in my experience. Along with the indictment, we distributed to the press a copy of the plea agreement that had been entered into with Barnes, after consultation with his attorney. In that agreement, Barnes agreed to plead guilty to a major criminal violation and cooperate with the government completely. In turn we agreed that, if Barnes was ever to seek Executive Clemency, we would bring his cooperation to the attention of the Pardon Attorney and, if he was successful in having his sentence reduced, we would support his application to be admitted to the Federal Witness Protection Program.

The first 10 minutes of the press conference were spent with the reporters beating me up about our agreement with Barnes. Questions such as "how could you make an agreement with somebody as vicious as Barnes and agree to him getting out on parole?" I would carefully explain that we had promised Barnes nothing of substance. He had agreed to plead guilty to serious charges and all we said was that we would bring his cooperation to the attention of any appropriate authority in the future. My answers did not satisfy the reporters and a

A Life Begun on Third Base

series of hostile questions continued. Finally, the New York City Police Commissioner, my friend Bob McGuire, asked me to let him respond. He took the microphone and said, "ladies and gentlemen, Mr. Martin and I want to apologize to everybody in this room for the fact that we have indicted these murderers." At that point the questions finally turned to the substance of the allegations against the defendants.

Barnes' cooperation ultimately led to the prosecution 48 individuals. Four of his principal associates were sentenced to life without parole and several others received lengthy prison sentences. The moral of the story is "if you sup with the devil, he may testify against you." More important is the recognition that it is often necessary to make deals with those who have committed serious crimes in order to prosecute others who pose a great threat to the public.

The Brinks Robbery

On October 20, 1981, as I was crossing the Skyway connecting the US Attorney's office to the courthouse, I heard someone say Kathy Boudin has been arrested. Boudin was a well-known fugitive who had last been seen in the 70s running from a house in Greenwich Village where a bomb had exploded. Her fellow members of the Weather Underground, a radical terrorist organization, had apparently blown themselves up while preparing a bomb.

Earlier on the 20th, a group of armed black men emerged from a brightly colored van in Nanuet, NY, to rob an armored Brinks truck after it arrived at a bank. In the process, they killed one of the armored car personnel. After an alert went out to look for a group of black men in a brightly colored van, a woman who lived on a hill overlooking the parking lot of an abandoned store called the police to say that she had seen black men with automatic weapons getting out of a brightly colored van and into the back of a U-Haul truck. Shortly thereafter, police officers at a roadblock in Nyack stopped a U-Haul truck driven by two women. One of the women, later identified as Boudin, told the officers that their shotgun made her nervous and asked him to put it away. As the officer was putting the gun away, the robbers emerged from the back of the truck firing their weapons and killing two police officers. Escape cars swooped in to pick up the others but Boudin was arrested as she tried to flee down the highway.

One of the escape vehicles sped down one of the hilly streets in Nyack and crashed as the driver tried to make a turn. The occupants were arrested. My nephew Tommy Hekker, who went to school nearby, happened to be present and saw the car crash.

From the outset, the case generated substantial publicity. Although the defendants who were arrested were in state custody, the District Attorney's office asked the federal government to take custody of the prisoners because of a concern for the security at the local jail.

A. The Brinks Robbery - Chokwe Lumumba

The first major issue that I confronted occurred when the Assistants and agents working on the case came to see me to express a concern that a lawyer named Chokwe Lumumba, who claimed to represent one of the defendants, wanted to be admitted to the Metropolitan Correctional Center ("MCC"), the federal holding facility, to confer with his client. The FBI had reliable information that Lumumba was an active member of what they considered to be a terrorist organization, The Republic of New Africa. The purpose of the organization was to separate the states of Louisiana, Alabama, South Carolina, Georgia and Mississippi from United States to form a separate "African Republic." The organization stated that, if they were not given the five states, they would have to "go to war with the United States."

Since the Brinks defendants have been taken into federal custody because of a concern about security and the possibility of an attempt to affect their escape, there was a concern that Lumumba could communicate escape plans to the defendants if he was allowed into the MCC. However, SDNY recognized that any attempt to keep Lumumba from visiting someone he claimed was a client would end up being contested in court.

If we wanted to keep Lumumba out of the MCC there were two options. The first would be to dispute Lumumba's right to represent the defendant. As an out-of-state lawyer, Lumumba did not have an automatic right to represent a defendant in New York. He would have to make an application to the court to be admitted to practice pro hac vice — for this case. Such applications are routinely granted.

The second option would be to consent to Lumumba's application for admission so that he could represent the defendant but simply tell the warden not to admit him to the MCC. To me, it seemed less defensible to agree that Lumumba could serve as the defendant's lawyer but refuse him access to his client.

Since every jurisdiction requires any lawyer seeking admission to the bar to establish not only that he has the appropriate training and knowledge, but also that he is of good character, we decided to oppose Lumumba's application to be admitted pro hac vice on the ground of his association with the Republic of New Africa.

One of the things you learn as you practice law is that often the result in a case will depend upon the judge to whom it is assigned. That turned out to be true here.

Lumumba's application for admission would be heard in Part I, the court room where proceedings in a criminal case are heard prior to assignment to a judge for trial. Part I assignments were rotated among the judges of the court on a biweekly basis. Judge Weinfeld, one of the most respected judges in the country, whose decisions were rarely reversed on appeal, had been scheduled to be in Part I the week that Lumumba's application would be heard. However, Judge Weinfeld asked his friend and colleague Judge Irving Ben Cooper to handle Part I for him. Thus our application to deny Lumumba's request for pro hac vice admission would be heard by Judge Cooper not Judge Weinfeld.

After conducting a hearing, Judge Cooper wrote an opinion in our favor and denied Lumumba's application for admission. As anticipated, the matter was quickly appealed by the defendant to the Second

Circuit, which reversed. I took a lot of heat in the press for attempting to deny the defendant his counsel of choice.

Ironically, sometime later I happened to see Judge Weinfeld at a social event and he told me he agreed with our position on the Lumumba application. I remain convinced that, if the decision to deny Lumumba's application had been written by Judge Weinfeld, it would have been sustained on appeal. In any event, our concerns about security proved baseless and there never was any effort to break the defendants out of jail.

Epilogue

Lumumba served as a lawyer representing radical causes for a good part of his career and had more than one run in with judges assigned his cases. However, he ended his career as the respected mayor of Jackson Mississippi.

B. The Brinks Robbery - Who Should Try the Defendants

The robbery of the Brinks armored car and the associated killings violated both state and federal law. Cases in which state and federal prosecutors could prosecute the same crime often resulted in jurisdictional battles. In the Brinks case, it was always my view that because the crime involved three murders in Rockland County, with two victims being local police officers, the local interest was paramount and the case should be tried by the District Attorney of Rockland County. The incumbent District Attorney, Ken Griebtz, desperately wanted the case, but was always suspicious that at the last minute I would come in and prosecute the case federally. There was no reason for his concern and Griebtz prosecuted those arrested at the scene or reasonably quickly thereafter.

The Brinks robbery was one of the series of robberies conducted by a combined group of black nationalist radicals and white members of the Weather Underground. SDNY therefore extended its investigation and ended up indicting several other individuals who were not caught at the scene of the Brinks robbery or shortly thereafter. I offered this case to Ken Griebtz, but he had no interest in taking it on. It was a more difficult case and there was a possibility of acquittal. The case was successfully prosecuted by Assistant United States Attorneys Bob Litt and Stacey Moritz.

Patrick J. Cunningham and John J. Sweeney

It was not many months after I had been sworn in as US Attorney that I ran into John Sweeney on the courthouse elevator. I had known John because we served together on a charitable board, I don't recall whether it was the Catholic Big Brothers or the lawyers' division of the Cardinals Committee of the Laity. When we reached the lobby, John told me he had been there to testify before the grand jury and complained that the Assistant assigned to the case, Dominic Amoroso, was overly aggressive.

Unfortunately for John, the only result of that conversation was that I took a special interest in the case after discussing it with Dom and I ultimately personally handled the criminal trial of John and his brother-in-law Pat Cunningham. Pat Cunningham was, and had been for number of years, the Chairman of the Bronx Democratic Committee and the New York State Democratic Committee. For several years, the IRS had been investigating Cunningham's tax returns. At various times, Cunningham and Sweeney had been law partners. At other times they practiced as individuals, although they continued to share office space.

The tale is too complex and not interesting enough to recount here in detail. What we ultimately uncovered is that during a period in which they were not practicing as partners, Sweeney had been paying some of Cunningham's personal expenses out of an escrow account Sweeney maintained in conjunction with his practice. We would discover that these payments were the means by which Sweeney split with Cunningham the profit that Sweeney made on appointments that he had received from various judges in the Bronx. Apparently Cunningham was reluctant to have it known that he was receiving income as the result of judicial appointments from judges whom he had placed on the bench.

As Judge Walter Mansfield of the Second Circuit noted in his decision affirming the conviction of Cunningham and Sweeney for tax evasion and obstruction of justice: "Experience teaches that the unlawful cover-up offenses are often more heinous than the crimes sought to be concealed."

This was certainly the case with Cunningham and Sweeney. While we ultimately obtained a conviction for tax evasion, the amount of income tax evaded was relatively small and I doubt we would have prosecuted the case if that was all there was. However, from the time in 1976 when Cunningham became aware that he was under investigation, he and Sweeney engaged in a variety of conduct designed to obstruct the investigation, including the creation of false records, destruction of records, inducing others to make false statements to the IRS and the grand jury, perjury by Cunningham and the destruction of evidence.

One of the early efforts to obstruct the tax investigation occurred in 1976 when Cunningham's 1975 tax returns were being prepared. Apparently concerned that the agents would uncover that he had spent cash received from some illegal activity, Cunningham told his lawyer to include on the 1975 returns $8,000 in otherwise unidentified cash income. He would later claim that $2,000 of this amount came from a friend John Spain, another $4,000 from another friend, Joseph Cioccolanti and the final $2,000 from George Steinbrenner, the owner of the New York Yankees. (Cunningham had served as general partner of the Yankees in Steinbrenner's place when Steinbrenner had been suspended by the baseball commissioner for making an illegal campaign contribution.)

As part of the grand jury investigation, John Spain was called to testify. When asked if he had ever given $2,000 in cash to Cunningham, he said no. When asked if he ever told IRS Agent Rippa he had given Cunningham $2,000 in cash, he also said no. Since Spain had

A Life Begun on Third Base

told Rippa and another agent he had given Cunningham $2,000 cash in 1975, he was indicted for perjury.

The Spain perjury trial began my substantial personal participation in the case. As part of his defense, Spain called Marie Falco, Cunningham's secretary. She testified that, while the IRS investigation was going on, she was tasked with talking to people the IRS had interviewed to determine what had been said. In that role, she had spoken to Spain shortly after his IRS interview. She said that Spain told her he had been asked if he had ever given Cunningham $2,000 in cash and said no. To corroborate her testimony she produced a memorandum which she claimed to have typed shortly after this conversation with Spain.

Suspecting that this memorandum was a recent fabrication, Amoroso had a forthwith subpoena for Falco' typewriter served on Cunningham's office that evening . When the agents arrived, Mark Krieg, a younger partner of Cunningham told them to wait. After some interval they were handed the typewriter.

When they got it back to the office and were able to examine it they found evidence of an obstruction of justice. At that time, typewriters had a ribbon that was held up in front of the paper and, as a typed letter was struck, it hit the ribbon, which then imprinted the letter on the paper. Since the ribbon moved continuously as new letters were typed, one could read on the ribbon exactly what had been typed. When the agents examined the seized typewriter they found that the ribbon was new and the only thing that had been typed on it was some gibberish that someone had obviously typed to give the impression that the ribbon had been used.

The next morning we asked the trial judge, Judge Wyatt, to order a hearing to determine whether anyone had tampered with the typewriter after the subpoena had been served. Since Judge Wyatt did not want to delay the trial, he asked Judge Palmieri to conduct the hearing. Since Amoroso would have to be at the trial, I conducted the hearing for the government.

The first witness was a temporary secretary at the Cunningham office who testified that, on the afternoon before the typewriter was seized, she had been typing a series of envelopes to members of the Democratic National Committee because Cunningham was in the process of running for the position of Chairman of the Committee. She was directed by the judge to return to the office and get the envelopes she had typed. However, the envelopes were nowhere to be found.

At some point around this time, Mark Krieg contacted us and said he did not want to get in trouble. He told us that, while the agents were sitting waiting for the typewriter to be produced, he saw Sweeney carrying the typewriter into Cunningham's office.

After Krieg testified to this effect, we called Cunningham to the stand. He ultimately testified that the day after the typewriter was seized, as he was leaving the office, he passed by the desk where the envelopes had been left in the box by the woman who typed them. He said at this point he was so frustrated by the fact our investigation would ruin his chances of becoming the Democratic National Chairman that he reached into the box grabbed the envelopes and stuffed them into his coat pocket. When I asked him what he done with them, he said he'd walked around the area for some time and ultimately took the envelopes out of his pocket and threw them in a trash can. Not surprisingly, he could not remember where.

Another issue that arose at the hearing concerned efforts by Cunningham and his secretary Marie Falco to persuade Krieg not to testify. Krieg told us that on the evening of the day he had come to the office to tell us about the movement of the typewriter, he received a call at home during which he spoke to both Falco and Cunningham, who attempted to persuade him not to testify. Both Falco and Cunningham denied having such a call with Krieg. When I asked Cunningham where he was that night, he said that he and Falco had gone out to dinner but he could not remember where they ate. Unfortunately for him, the telephone company had records which would show where the call Krieg received that evening came from. It was a restaurant near the office where Cunningham and Falco often dined. The owner ultimately testified that he recalled them being there that evening, and Cunningham had asked to have a phone brought to the table.

Cunningham and Falco were both charged with perjury relating to this conversation. The charge was one of many on which Cunningham was tried. Falco was indicted in a separate indictment and I personally tried that case. as I did the case of Cunningham and Sweeney.

There was nothing particularly memorable about the Falco trial but there was one incident in the Cunningham trial that became a legend in the office. Prior to his indictment, Cunningham had testified that he could not recall who had given him the $8,000 in cash he reported on his 1975 tax returns. By the time of the trial, however, he found that it was in his interest to say that he did remember—among other things John Spain, who had been convicted at his perjury trial, was cooperating with the government and testified at the trial that Cunningham asked him to tell the false story that he had given Cunningham $2,000 in 1975.

Cunningham testified in his own defense and during the direct examination by his lawyer Michael Tigar he was asked about the various components of the $8,000 in cash reported on his 1975 return. The following is my vivid memory of what occurred:

> "Q. Mr. Cunningham did there come a time in 1975 when you received $2,000 in cash from George Steinbrenner?
>
> A. Yes, I remember it well. It was a night game at Yankee Stadium—don't ask me the score. I was with George up in one of those owners' boxes that he has at the stadium—I can't remember whether it was box 262 were 264 but it was one of those boxes. At some point George said to me, Pat, you've done a lot for the club that we really haven't paid you for. At that point, George, who always carries a lot of cash, reached into his pocket, took out $2,000 and gave it to me."

While there was much more to his direct testimony and my cross-examination, the highlight of the cross-examination went in substance as follows:

Q. Mr. Cunningham I believe you told us that you have a distinct recollection of receiving $2,000 in cash from George Steinbrenner at Yankee Stadium in 1975, it is that correct?

A. Yes

Q. Now you told us, you don't remember the score, correct?

A. Yes.

Q. And it is also true that you do not recall the box number of Mr. Steinbrenner's box but it was one of those fancy boxes that Mr. Steinberger has at Yankee Stadium, is that correct?

A. Yes.

Q. But you are certain as you sit here today, Mr. Cunningham, that at a night game in Yankee Stadium in 1975 you received $2,000 in cash from George Steinbrenner while sitting in one of his boxes in Yankee Stadium.

A. Yes.

Q. Isn't it a fact Mr. Cunningham that in 1975 the Yankees were playing in Shea Stadium?"

Cunningham said nothing for several seconds and then blurted out "Well, they have boxes in Shea Stadium."

There was nothing else for me to do on that subject.

I wish I could claim that it was my own brilliance that led me to realize that the Yankees were playing at Shea Stadium during 1975 while Yankee Stadium was being rebuilt. However, I had an inside source of information. Steinbrenner was represented by Bill Shea, the senior partner of Shea & Gould. Shea, who had been a good friend of my father. Shea had a young associate in court during Cunningham's testimony because he had been alerted that there would be testimony about Steinbrenner. At a recess after Cunningham had testified on direct examination about the receipt of the money at Yankee Stadium, the associate approached me and said, "I just spoke to Mr. Shea to tell him about the testimony today and he told me to remind you that the Yankees were playing in Shea Stadium in 1975."

Before closing a discussion of the Cunningham case I should note that, as US Attorney I had the ability to pick who I wanted to assist me at the various trials. Proving that my mother did not raise any stupid children, I picked Gerry Lynch, a brilliant young lawyer who had clerked on the Second Circuit and then for Justice Brennan on the Supreme Court. He later served on the faculty of Columbia Law school. He was not only one of the most brilliant people you could meet, he was also one of the nicest. He would later serve as a colleague on the District Court and then be promoted to the Circuit Court.

Many years later, at the dinner for Mary Jo White when she resigned as United States Attorney, the Toastmaster, Paul Schectman, was setting up a joke about the fact that, as US Attorney, Mary Jo had not tried a single case although generally US attorneys tried at least one case during their tenure. His comments went something like this: "When Bob Fiske was US Attorney, he tried Nicky Barnes, known as Mr. Untouchable—proving nobody's untouchable. When Rudy Giuliani was US Attorney he prosecuted the political leader Stanley Friedman—proving no politician is above the law. When John Martin was US Attorney he prosecuted Patrick Cunningham —proving anybody can win a case if he has Gerry Lynch helping him."

Day-to-Day Life as US Attorney

I never knew when I went to work in the morning what I would face during the day. There were personnel matters, administrative matters, liaison with the District Court, meetings on cases, meetings with agencies. There was such a wide variety of cases that there was always a number of important cases requiring my attention.

As with the Brinks case, I could be in the middle of a relatively routine day and a case would come in that would require a substantial amount of my attention and time. Among the more high-profile cases we had were the prosecution of Croatian terrorists involving bombings in

New York City, and organized crime cases, including a case in which an undercover agent Joe Pistone infiltrated the Bonanno Organize crime family. (Joe's story was ultimately made into a movie.) There were also fires that had to be put out arising from disputes among the agencies or with other prosecutors' offices.

One of the jurisdictional disputes involved a bank robbery in the Bronx where the arrests had been made by a joint task force of FBI agents and police officers on a tip from an informant of one of the task force members. The defendants were taken into federal custody and indicted.

Although I had been informed about the case, I had no personal involvement prior to receiving a letter from Paul Gentile, the Chief Assistant to Bronx District Attorney Mario Merola. The letter argued strongly that the case should be prosecuted in the Bronx and Gentile claimed to have been lied to by Tom Fitzpatrick, the Chief of the Criminal division. According to Gentile, he asked Tom why the case had gone federal and Tom told him that the head of the task force said the reason the case went federal was because the information came from an informant of "one of their guys" and that one of their guys" had been shot. Gentile said this was a lie; the informant was an informant of one of the cops and it had been a cop that was shot.

I asked Tom about the incident. After checking with the agents Tom told me it was a New York cop who had been shot and it was a cop's informant. He said he had misunderstood the situation because the head of the task force, who was a federal agent, had referred to each of the cops only as "as one of our guys." I asked Tom to prepare letter from my signature explaining to Gentile how the confusion developed and why we thought it was appropriate for the case to be prosecuted in federal court.

The next day my inbox contained a letter for my signature that Tom drafted containing a detailed explanation of all that had occurred. It ended as follows: "I hope you can appreciate that there was never an intent to deceive you. Please convey to Mr. Merola my hope that our two offices can work cooperatively in the future. As for you Mr. Gentile, go fuck yourself."

Fortunately, I read the letter before signing it. We took out the last line.

My Decision to Resign

As a result of the policy that Senator Moynihan adopted when he was selected as the US Attorney for the Southern District of New York, Bob Fiske had been allowed to serve the full four-year term provided by statute, though always subject to the right of removal by the president. After President Reagan and Senator D'Amato were elected in 1980, D'Amato announced that he would follow Moynihan's example and that I would be allowed to serve my full four-year term. However, the Republican administration was not as welcoming to me as the Carter administration had been to Bob Fiske and I ultimately resigned after three years.

My first major problem involved my first major confrontation with Rudy Giuliani. After the Reagan election, Rudy became Associate Attorney General. In that position, all United States Attorneys were under his jurisdiction. In late '82 or early '83, Rhea Neugarten, the chief of our narcotics unit, came to me and said that she had received information that the Attorney General was going to announce the next day the creation of Narcotics Task Forces to combine the supervision of anti-narcotics prosecutions in multi-district units throughout the country. The head of the task force in our region was to be Raymond Dearie, the United States Attorney in the Eastern District of New York, headquartered in Brooklyn.

Although the Southern District had been a leader in narcotics prosecutions for years, Rhea said that she had been told that the reason I was not selected to head our regional task force was that, "I was not one of their guys." I told Rhea that I would talk to Giuliani.

Several calls to Giuliani that day went unanswered — he was always in a meeting and would always call me back. I waited in the office until about 6:30 when I called his office again. When I was once more told he was unavailable, I told his secretary to have him call me at home and that, if I did not hear from him before they announced the regional narcotics task forces, I would have something to say to the press.

When I arrived home, Peggy told me that Rudy had called and left his number. When I got him on the phone, he asked what the problem was and I recall saying, "I am being fucked and I've been told it is because I am not one of your guys." I then said that, given all the Southern District had done over the years in prosecuting narcotics, it was a slap in the face to the office for the US attorney from some of the district be placed in charge of prosecutions in the Southern District. He said that one of the reasons was that the airports were in the Eastern District and I said that was bullshit. The conversation went nowhere for a couple of minutes and I concluded by saying, "I heard you, you heard me and if this goes as planned I'm going to have something to say to the press in the morning."

Not long after, I got a call from Rudy who said that he'd conferred with the Attorney General, and that they had decided that because prosecutions in the New York region were so important, they should have co-heads for the task force. H asked me to come to Washington in the morning to be present when they announced that Ray Dearie and I would head our regional task force.

The fact that I was not their guy was beginning to become obvious in other ways. Our budget for manpower and supplies was being impacted. One afternoon, after I returned to my office from a lengthy meeting uptown, my secretary informed me that I had received a number of calls from my friend Mike Armstrong, asking that I call him. When I reached Mike, he said the reason he called was that his good friend, John Keenan, a highly respected state prosecutor, had received a call from a reporter who said he had information from a reliable source that John Martin was going to be replaced as US Attorney and that he, Keenan would be nominated for the position. Mike said John had prepared a response that he had wanted me to hear before he put it out, but because of the delay they had to release it.

In one of the classiest statements I have ever seen, Keenan said: "I know nothing about any plan to replace John Martin. The only time I ever discussed the issue of his replacement was shortly after the election, when I told my friend Michael Armstrong, who was on Senator D'Amato's judicial selection committee, that John Martin was doing a good job and should be kept on as US Attorney."

I did not know John well at the time but I admired his willingness to make a statement that might put his chances of becoming US Attorney in jeopardy. Ten years later, I would become John's colleague on the Southern District and he would be one of my most valued friends and mentors.

I asked Mike to find out from D'Amato what was happening and he reported that Al was under a lot of pressure from Republican leaders to replace me. He suggested that I should have dinner with the senator which I did.

I had met Al D'Amato on several occasions but did not know him well. One funny incident occurred when I gave a speech at a large luncheon at which I had received a medal in honor of Emory Buckner, a highly regarded former US Attorney. In the course of that speech I talked about the responsibility of the US Attorney to see that justice is done in each case and said, "sometimes a prosecutor's finest hour comes not when he indicts some prominent public official but when he has the courage to decline such a prosecution." At the time D'Amato was under a criminal investigation in the Eastern District and as I passed by him on my way out of the luncheon he said, "Great speech Johnny, I only wish that the little prick who was investigating me had heard it."

The dinner I had with Mike and the Senator was pleasant and D'Amato said that he would not force me out. He did indicate however that it would be preferable if I finished up any major cases I had and resigned before the four years were up.

This conversation, coupled with the fact that I thought the office was being hurt because the Republicans in the Justice Department considered me "not one of their guys" persuaded me that I should resign. In announcing that I would resign I said I would stay in office until my successor was appointed and took the oath of office.

Rudy Giuliani wanted the job and his nomination and confirmation were expedited. He took the oath of office as United States Attorney on June 3, 1983, and as he did so my tenure ended.

Rudy's service as United States attorney resulted in more aggravating incidents. The first occurred when Peggy and I and the children were on a trip through the national parks out West that summer. Somehow I picked up a copy of the *New York Times* and saw a front-page article reporting that United States Attorney Rudolph Giuliani had announced that his office was abandoning the policy of sealing the indictments and pleas of cooperating defendants — a long standing policy designed to permit the government to get guilty pleas from cooperators without the fact that they were cooperating being known publicly. The article stated that Giuliani said that he had never personally approved of the practice. That was a lie.

The practice of using sealed indictments to protect the identity of informants was long-standing. Near the end of the Carter administration, some in the press had began to question the use of sealed proceedings in a variety of judicial proceedings. As a result, Deputy Attorney General Charles Renfrew had issued a memorandum saying that no US Attorney could consent to a sealed proceeding without the approval of the Deputy Attorney General. His memorandum stated, "this will not apply to matters ancillary to a grand jury proceeding."

When I received the memorandum, I immediately recognized its impact on our practice of sealing indictments and pleas of cooperators. I therefore wrote a letter to Renfrew saying in substance that I had received his memorandum and I was not sure how it would apply in the case of cooperating defendants and their pleas. I said that, since their cooperation was generally "ancillary to a grand jury investigation," I would consider his memorandum as not applying to the

A Life Begun on Third Base

sealing of indictments and pleas of cooperators and asked him to let me know if he disagreed. Renfrew left office without ever responding to my letter.

Shortly after Rudy became Associate Attorney General, I had a meeting with him in his office in Washington. At that time, I said I thought he should know about the Renfrew memorandum and my response to it. He said that he knew how important it was to protect informants by sealing their indictments and pleas and that I should continue the practice.

Not long after this conversation there was additional press comment and criticism of the practice of sealing indictments and pleas. I thought it appropriate to memorialize my conversation with Rudy in writing and I sent him a letter to that effect. He responded in a letter which acknowledged that we had the conversation but said in substance, "given the public controversy about this issue, I think it best that you request my permission before sealing an indictment or plea. Be assured that I will promptly approve any request.

I could document that when Giuliani said he never approved of sealed pleas, he was lying. Fortunately for Rudy, I was out West in a remote national Park and my correspondence relating to the issue was in New York. I, therefore, did not write to the *Times* to contest his statement.

The next time Giuliani made a statement disparaging my tenure as US Attorney, I did respond. Approximately six months to a year after I left office, Rudy announced the indictments of the heads of the five organized crime families in New York on conspiracy charges. In a subsequent article in the *National Law Journal* praising Giuliani as a rackets buster, Giuliani was quoted as saying, "At the time I took over the office, it was not set up to handle this type of case."

I promptly fired off a letter to Giuliani pointing out that the idea of indicting the heads of the five organize crime families in a single indictment had come from the FBI while I was US attorney. I said that, when I left we were working toward that goal and had wiretaps in place on three of the crime families. I noted that those investigations were proceeding under the supervision of the same Assistants who had the cases when he took over. I copied the Assistants involved. I may have also noted that he had retained my Chief of the Criminal Division.

My final confrontation with Rudy was triggered by his appearance on Meet the Press when he was running for President. Rudy was being beaten up by Tim Russert over the fact that he had appointed as police Commissioner Bernard Kerig, who had later been indicted. Russert said this raised questions about Giuliani's judgment, to which he replied, "I may have had poor judgment in that case, but I must have had good judgment because I turned around the US Attorney's office and I turned around the city." I was watching a tape of the show and immediately rewound it to listen again to his attack on the office I left him.

The next day the *New York Times* published an op-ed I prepared which pointed out that Giuliani had taken over an office that had been well-run for decades. I then discussed most of his better known cases and pointed out that those cases had arisen, not as a result of anything Giuliani did, but rather as a result of the hard work of the agencies which had developed the information leading to the prosecutions. A copy of the op-ed is available online.

Serving as United States Attorney was the most difficult job I ever had. It was interesting and exciting but there was no precedent for many of the life altering decisions that had to be made. Every decision to prosecute had a dramatic impact, not only on the defendant but his or her family. A decision not to prosecute could mean the lack of justice for a victim or that a dangerous individual would remain at large and a risk to others. In addition, the difficult decisions that you made often became fodder for critics in the press.

While I enjoyed my service as United States Attorney, I was not sorry to be relieved of the burdens. My departure was made more pleasant by the fact that I was able to take the following summer off and spent six and half weeks traveling with Peggy and the children through the beautiful national parks in the western United States.

TWELVE

Return to Private Practice

When it became known I would be resigning as US Attorney, I received inquiries from several firms about possibly joining them. Although I was relatively confident that I would return to my prior firm, which had changed its name to Schulte Roth & Zabel, I thought I should at least explore other possibilities. I did return to Schulte Roth but, I think, the fact that I had considered other offers caused some resentment at the firm.

Returning to private practice after having a job like being US Attorney is not easy. The work is not as interesting and, rather than supervising a large group of lawyers, you spend your days dealing with clients, reviewing drafts of legal documents, taking depositions, and occasionally getting into court. In addition, there is the matter of generating business and competing with other lawyers in the firm for compensation.

The first few months are the most difficult because you go from being very busy to waiting for new cases to come in. It takes time to develop a backlog of cases.

My work involved cases that came to me directly and also handling important litigation for clients of the firm. One of those was Asher

Edelman, a major client of my partner Burt Lehman. Asher was a player in the takeover game and I worked on some of that litigation. It was always high-pressure and involved a lot of work over short periods of time. My friend Mike Armstrong, who worked on a major takeover with our friend Bernie Nussbaum, said after it was over, "Takeover work is just the opposite of doing legal aid work. The matter is always interesting, you have all the resources you could possibly need, and it pays very well, and, unlike legal aid work, it has no social value." It was financially but not professionally rewarding.

I also worked on some cases for the accounting firm Coopers & Lybrand. Harris Ahmowitz, the General Council of Cooper's, was a close friend of my partner Bill Zabel. I had known Harris from my time as a law clerk when he was clerking for a District Court Judge in the same building. Cooper's was a good client and generally easy to work with. There were a number of in-house lawyers and a group of accountants specifically assigned to work on the firm's litigation.

One of the more interesting cases involved work that had been done for a client that was developing a software program that would enable banks to operate, as they do today, with real-time electronic reporting of all transactions. While this is common today, the development of the software programs was highly complex and took several years. Ultimately, the company developed a software system that could perform all of the necessary functions. Unfortunately, when they tried to implement it in an actual operating environment, it took forever to process the vast amount of data at issue. I forget what the precise accounting issue was but, as was often my advice, I urged an early settlement and Harris agreed.

There was one case I handled about which I remember nothing but the settlement negotiations. My basic approach to settlement was to give my adversary an offer and stick to it. In this case, I told the adversary what my final number was and that it was final and would not change. There were at least 4 or 5 calls thereafter in which he made counteroffers and I repeated that I had given him my final offer. Ultimately, he accepted it.

A Life Begun on Third Base

I recalled this incident often after I left the bench and was conducting mediations on a fairly regular basis. Parties were often reluctant to make the best offer at an early point because they were afraid it would just lead to further negotiation. I used this case to emphasize that no one can force you to make a better offer and that trying too hard to negotiate some lower figure would often result in a failed negotiation.

Hertz

As United States Attorney I was accustomed to seeing my cases reported on the front page of the *New York Times*. As a defense lawyer, it was one of the worst things that could happen to a client. However on August 5, 1988, the *Times* carried a front-page story reporting that my client Hertz had pleaded guilty to engaging in a scheme to overcharge customers who had accidents while driving a Hertz vehicle for the repair of the vehicle. The company agreed to pay a fine of $6.85 million and to establish a restitution fund of over $13 million to compensate the customers who had been overcharged.

As often happens in cases of corporate crime, the illegal activity was unknown to senior management and the people who started the practice probably never thought that what they were doing would be considered fraudulent. In essence, the scheme was simple: after a customer returned a vehicle that had been damaged in an accident, the company would have the vehicle repaired. Because of the volume of the business it provided to repair shops, Hertz was able to obtain substantial discounts from the normal cost of repair. However, it billed its customers what the retail cost of such repairs would have been. The employees we interviewed saw nothing wrong in keeping for Hertz the savings that the company was able to generate because of the volume of its repair business. They failed to recognize that, in billing the customers for repairs costs in excess of what the company actually paid, they were making a false statement that could be prosecuted under the mail fraud statute.

We conducted a lengthy investigation and were able to work out a plea agreement. Although the fine was substantial, the US Attorney, Andy

Maloney, acknowledged at his press conference that this scheme had been carried out by low or mid-level employees and that senior management was not involved.

One of the major benefits of this matter was that, over the course of our investigation and negotiation with the US Attorney's office, I got to know Frank Olson, the company's chief executive. At the time, Hertz was sponsoring the Bay Hill classic at Arnold Palmer's resort. After the case ended, Frank invited me to be one of the guests at what was known as the Hertz Bay Hill Pro-Exec. Forty of the most important Hertz customers were invited to Bay Hill to attend the final round of the tournament and to spend the next two days staying at the resort, eating, drinking, and playing golf with ten of the best known professional golfers. The group included Greg Norman, Curtis Strange, and Andy Beame, among others. There were two days of golf, one at Bay Hill and the other at Islesworth, which would later become famous as the scene of Tiger Woods' car crash during the breakup of his marriage. I was impressed at what nice people the pros were. Unfortunately, my golf game did not merit the company.

The Martin Commission

On Sunday, January 19, 1986, I was at home when I received a call from Ed Koch, the New York City Mayor. I first met Ed in 1966 when I hosted a going away party for my friend Bob McGuire who was leaving the US Attorney's office to take a position in Somalia as the chief aide to the head of the police. The party was held at my dad's magnificent house in Nyack on the Hudson. One of my colleagues who had been invited said he was traveling upstate that day with a friend who was a member of the City Council named Ed Koch and asked if they could both stop by. I next saw Ed a few years later when he was in Congress at a party for Bob Morgenthau. Ed asked how was that magnificent house on the Hudson and when I told him we sold it because we could not afford the upkeep, he said, "Oh, couldn't you just open it to the public on weekends?" When he was elected Mayor, Ed made Bob McGuire his first Police Commissioner and appointed my friend Alan Schwartz as Corporation Counsel.

Shortly before Ed called me on the 19th, there had been several newspaper stories about the fact that the head of the New York City Parking Violations Bureau had been arrested for taking bribes and rumors that some of the city's major political leaders were part of a bribery scheme. Donald Manes, the borough president of Queens and Stanley Friedman, the Bronx Democratic leader had both been mentioned in the press as possibly being involved. Ed said that he wanted to appoint me to lead a commission to investigate possible corruption in city contracts.

After talking to some of my partners, I called Ed back and told him that I would be willing to serve. It was understood it would be a part-time job for me for which I would not take any compensation. Ed asked me to meet him the next day at his office in City Hall.

We spent a good part of the next morning drafting the press release that would announce my appointment. That press release turned out to be my charter and set forth the parameters of the inquiry to be conducted. There was a large press conference that Peggy and the children attended and the next day there was a picture of me on the front page of the *New York Times* with the story of my appointment.

When I accepted the appointment, I could not have anticipated how quickly things would change. Shortly before my appointment, Donald Manes, who would be one of the principal targets of the investigation, had been found bleeding in his car. He told the police he had been kidnapped and attacked. On January 20, the day after my appointment, I called my friend Michael Armstrong, who had served as the Chief Counsel of the Knapp Commission, which had investigated police corruption in the early 70s. I told Mike I was interested in getting together with him to discuss how I should go about setting up a commission. Mike said he would be happy to talk to me about it but he could not do it then because he represented Donald Manes and he was about to hold a press conference to announce that Manes had not been kidnapped, he had attempted suicide.

That was Tuesday. Wednesday morning as I arrived at the train station heading for work, I saw a front page article in the Daily News by

Jimmy Breslin saying that a lawyer named Michael Dowd had told him that Manes made him pay bribes to get a contract with the Parking Violations bureau. In the two days since I had been appointed, vague allegations had been turned into substantiated charges and now the District Attorney's Office and the US Attorney's office were about to get into the fray.

I went about setting up an office and hiring a staff. One of the first people I called was Mary Jo White, who had served with me when I was US Attorney and would later become the US attorney and head of the SEC. I told Mary Jo I would like her on my staff. She gave me one of the most flimsy excuses for not doing it — she said she was going into the hospital the next day to have a cesarean to deliver her first child. I could not understand why she could not defer that for a few months.

I ultimately selected my good friend Marty Perschetz to be my Chief Assistant. Marty has never had a legal job that I did not give him. I hired him at Martin & Obermaier, then as an Assistant United States Attorney, and, after serving with me on the Martin Commission, I brought him to Schulte Roth.

Since there had been a great deal of press coverage of my appointment and of my first efforts to set up the office, Marty was expecting prominent media reports concerning his appointment. Indeed, the press conference I called to announce his appointment was attended by representatives of the major newspapers and television stations. But timing is everything and Marty's appointment was not mentioned in any paper or on TV. Shortly after my press conference, we got word that the Challenger spacecraft had exploded on takeoff and that story dominated the news the next day.

I thought the best way for us to proceed was to quickly hold public hearings at which we could call the senior political officials who had been implicated in the press. I recognized that ultimately this would turn into a criminal case, but I thought that getting these public officials on record would ultimately help in any criminal prosecution. The political leaders involved would have a hard time taking the Fifth

A Life Begun on Third Base

Amendment at a public hearing, although they would no doubt do that if called before the grand jury. Thus, getting them on record publicly would aid in the future prosecution by either locking in their story or providing the basis for a perjury prosecution.

I could not, however, hold public hearings without first clearing it with the principal prosecutors, Bob Morgenthau, then the District Attorney in Manhattan, and US Attorney Rudy Giuliani. I met first with Rudy and, to his credit, he said at the outset of our meeting, "You and I have had our issues in the past, but we've got to put that behind us and not let it interfere with what we should be doing now." I explained my thoughts about a public hearing and he agreed with the plan and said it would be helpful to any investigation they would be conducting.

Bob Morgenthau was another story. Although I had worked with him and we had a good relationship, Bob was very protective of his jurisdiction and did not want me involved in a matter that he might ultimately prosecute. I could not go forward with the public hearing and have Bob Morgenthau telling the press I was interfering with an ongoing criminal investigation. So we held no public hearings.

We never got deep into any investigation because I decided to resign on March 14, 1986, less than two months after it all began. As noted above, the environment in which I was operating changed dramatically within the first two days after my appointment. The admission by Manes that he had attempted suicide was viewed as an admission of guilt and, together with Michael Dowd's confession to Jimmy Breslin, stirred up the interest of Giuliani and Morgenthau.

If we were not going to hold hearings there was little we could do to expose corruption that was not already being done by either the district attorney or the US attorney. I thought we might continue and focus on ways to improve the procedures governing the awarding of city contracts and we started down that road. However, the political firestorm that was growing from the disclosures of the corruption in city contracting also attracted the attention of the governor. Under pressure from the governor, Koch agreed to the appointment of a joint state and city commission to look into the problems of corruption in the city's contracts. The committee was headed by John Feerick, an outstanding lawyer who was the Dean of the Fordham Law school. John was also a good friend since we served together on the board of Holy Child, where my daughters were in high school. In the small world category, John's daughter Rosemary shared the general excellence medal at graduation with Kate.

There was one incident worth noting that occurred during our consideration of ways to improve the procedures for city contracts. The computer was just coming into its own and IBM was the world leader in computer science. As a result, I thought it would be worthwhile to speak to the General Counsel of IBM to learn what procedures they found particularly helpful in uncovering contract fraud.

I traveled to IBM's headquarters in Armonk for a meeting. I asked the IBM representatives what was the major source of their information about kickback schemes relating to their contracts. They said the information generally came from a disgruntled coworker or perhaps an unhappy wife or girlfriend— the same way so many cases of wrongdoing were exposed. Life at IBM was no different than anywhere else.

Claus von Bülow

One of the most notorious figures of the 1980s was Claus von Bülow, who had been convicted of causing his wife to be in a vegetative state by injecting her with excessive amounts of insulin. The conviction was reversed, however, and at a retrial he was acquitted. After his acquittal, his wife's children by a prior marriage brought a civil case against him for assault on their mother.

My recollection is that Peggy and I were on a trip to Europe when I received a call asking me if I would meet von Bülow in London to discuss representing him in the civil action. We met for lunch and I was retained.

Our first major move was to move to dismiss the complaint — I do not recall the grounds for the motion. Judge John Walker of the

A Life Begun on Third Base

Southern District set the case down for oral argument and I appeared in his courtroom where my opponent, the lawyer for the children, was my good friend Mike Armstrong. There was nothing memorable about the argument. However, what occurred immediately thereafter did make the NBC local evening news.

The argument occurred shortly after I began my service at the Martin Commission, where one of the subjects of the investigation was Donald Manes, who was represented by Michael Armstrong. As I left the courthouse after the argument in the von Bülow case, I was approached by Ellen Fleischer, a TV reporter for NBC. I knew Ellen because she had served as press spokesman for my friend Bob McGuire when he was police commissioner. After I agreed to go on camera, we had the following dialogue:

Q: Mr. Martin, you have just come from arguing a case in which you represent Claus von Bülow, who is being sued by his wife's children, who are represented by Michael Armstrong. At the same time, you are conducting an investigation for the city and one of the subjects of that investigation is Donald Manes, who is represented by Michael Armstrong. Isn't that odd?

A: Ellen, Michael Armstrong and I were sworn in as Assistant United States Attorneys on the same day in 1962. Since that time, we've been on the same side and we have been on opposite sides. There is nothing strange about it."

I left and thought nothing more about it until I turned on NBC news that night. After the clip of my interview, they showed an interview that occurred shortly after I left, when Mike Armstrong was leaving the courthouse. The dialogue was as follows:

Q: Mr. Armstrong you have just come from arguing a motion to dismiss against John Martin. This is happening at the same time that you are representing Donald Manes in an investigation that Mr. Martin is conducting for the city. Isn't that odd?

A: Ellen, John Martin I were sworn in as Assistant United States Attorneys on the same day. Since that time we been on the same side we been on opposite sides. There is nothing strange about this.

Q: Did you rehearse this?

A: Rehearse?

The segment on NBC ended with Chuck Scarborough, the news anchor saying, "Isn't it odd how lawyers think alike?" Of course, Mike and I had not rehearsed it. We were just speaking the truth as we knew it, but it did seem odd.

We lost the motion to dismiss and shortly thereafter von Bülow decided to get another lawyer. I was not particularly upset because he was not the easiest client and Peggy was very happy that she did not have to defend me to her friends.

Ending Private Practice

I do not recall when I began to seriously consider trying to become a federal judge but, in early 1988, I decided the time had come. Being a federal judge would bring me rewarding work and considerable prestige but, for my family, it meant only financial sacrifice, since I would be making hundreds of thousands less than I could earn in private practice. But, once again, Peggy urged me to do it because of the great value she placed on public service.

Under a long-standing arrangement between Senator Moynihan and his Republican colleagues, the Senator whose party was out of power would be granted the right to select every fourth candidate for a District Court judgeship. I, therefore, had lunch with Chet Straub and asked him if Senator Moynihan had a judgeship available. There was a vacancy and I put in my application. Although Senator Moynihan's position was that his judicial selection committee should send him three names for each vacancy, I later learned that the Senator told the committee that, if they were going to recommend me, they would not have to send two other names.

I was recommended and in due course an announcement was made that I was being recommended for a position in the Southern District

A Life Begun on Third Base

of New York. Because of the political nature of the arrangement between the Senators, the recommendation was made by Senator D'Amato and, in connection with the confirmation hearings, I was shepherded through the process by the office of the ranking Republican Senator on the Judiciary Committee, Strom Thurmond.

I believe that the recommendation was made in early March of 1989, but I was not confirmed until late April or early May 1990. The delay had little to do with me but arose from the fact that one of the other nominees from New York was controversial and, indeed, was never confirmed. Since there were several nominees from New York, we were treated as a group and thus all of us were delayed because of the concern about one nominee.

Although I was frustrated by the delay in the processing of my nomination, a wise friend correctly observed, "John, your nomination will ultimately go through, and, after you are on the bench, you will be happy to have the extra money." I was happy with the extra money and also with the fact that, during the waiting period I was able to conclude two significant matters.

American Express

Not long after it was announced that I was being recommended for the District Court, I received a call from the General Counsel of American Express, for whom I had done some work in the past. He asked me how long the confirmation process would take and, when I told him several months, he said, "Good. We need to have an internal investigation conducted and I would like you to do it."

Shortly before I had been called, American Express had been contacted by Stanley Arkin, a well-respected criminal defense lawyer and friend, who said he represented Edmond Safra, the former head of the American Express International Bank and the then head of the Republic National Bank. Arkin said he had evidence American Express had orchestrated a campaign to defame Safra by giving members of the press false information that Safra's bank had been engaged in money laundering for international narcotics dealers. He said unless a settlement could be reached, Safra would bring suit. My job was to find out if the allegations that Arkin made were true or false.

I met with Stanley and pointed out that this was a delicate situation for both of our clients. I asked him if he knew the story of the dentist who was treating a patient and, when he put the drill into the patient's mouth, the patient grabbed him by the testicles. When the dentist appeared shocked the patient said, "Neither one of us is going to hurt the other, are we?" Obviously, a public lawsuit would be damaging to both parties and I was hopeful that we could ultimately resolve this matter amicably.

The investigation was interesting and it took me to Europe, where most of the adverse publicity had occurred. In the end, we concluded that what Stanley said was true. People at American Express had leaked what turned out to be false information to the press. Apparently when, after leaving American Express, Safra became a competitor, and this caused substantial resentment. As a result, an attempt was made to dig up dirt on Safra. The information that was eventually leaked to the press came from an overseas investigator American Express hired. It was hard to determine whether any American Express personnel knew that the information they were distributing was in fact false.

Stanley and I were able to work out an amicable resolution. James Robinson, the president of American Express, issued a public letter to Safra apologizing for the fact that the company had been responsible for the dissemination of false information and American Express agreed to make payments totaling $8 million to charities of Safra's choosing. Without admitting that he knew what was going on, the Executive Vice President of American Express resigned because the defamation campaign had been carried out by his subordinates.

Young & Rubicam

On October 12, 1989, the cameras clicked as I walked with my client, Art Klein, the Executive Vice President of Young & Rubicam, into the United States Courthouse in Hartford, Connecticut, for his arraignment. As we passed the photographers, Art said to me, "The last time I generated this much publicity was when I sank a half-court shot at the end of the Princeton Harvard game to win the Ivy League basketball title for Princeton."

Art was another client I believed to be totally innocent of any criminal wrongdoing. Fortunately, in this case, the facts proved me right.

Through friends at Cravath Swain & Moore, I was asked to represent Young & Rubicam after it was informed that it was the subject of criminal investigation involving allegations that the firm had paid bribes to Anthony Abrahams, the Minister of Tourism in Jamaica, to obtain the advertising contract for Jamaican tourism.

Robin Moore, a successful author whose books included the bestselling *Green Berets*, and who had a residence in Jamaica, had been under investigation for tax evasion by the US attorney in Connecticut. In attempting to negotiate a disposition, he told the prosecutors that, through contacts in Jamaica, he became involved in the process that resulted in the advertising contract for the Jamaican tourism account being awarded to Young & Rubicam.

Moore had contacted Y&R in March 1981 about the possibility of taking over the tourism account. In the course of his initial meeting with Y&R executives, he was accompanied by Arnold Foote, who operated an advertising agency in Jamaica. Moore said that, from the outset, the Y&R executives were told that to get the contract they would have to agree to hire Foote as their local advertising agent because he would be paying the Minister.

Moore later arranged a social gathering at his residence in which he introduced the Minister of Tourism to Klein and Walter Spangenberg, another Y&R official who had been present at the initial meeting.

A few days later, on April 3, 1981, Y&R was one of three advertising agencies that made pitches to the Board of Tourism. On April 6, 1981, Y&R signed a contract with Jamaica for the tourism account. Three days later, on April 9, Klein, on behalf of Y&R, executed a contract retaining Foote as its local agent. Once all the contracts were signed,

Klein dropped out of the picture and had no day-to-day involvement with the Jamaica account.

Over the years that followed, comments made by Foote and other things led people working on the Jamaica account to speculate that the local agent was paying off the minister. One of the things that we had to determine as part of our investigation was whether anyone knew at the outset that bribes were being paid and, if not, whether subsequent events had led any of the Y&R people working on the account to know that bribes were being paid.

Moore had originally approached a neighbor of his in Connecticut who was a Y&R executive about the possibility of representing Jamaica. This executive brought this opportunity to the leadership of Y&R and it was agreed that a team headed by Art Klein would meet with Moore. What occurred at the initial meeting would become a focal point of our investigation. Moore's assertion that it was clear from the outset that Foote would be passing money on to Abrahams was vigorously denied by Art and the other Y&R people present at the meeting.

In our interviews with people who attended the initial meeting with Moore and Foote, several of the participants recalled that a now retired executive who was present at the meeting had recorded the meeting. Despite our best efforts and a grand jury subpoena, this crucial piece of evidence was nowhere to be found.

As the possibility of an indictment became more evident, it was decided that I would represent Art Klein and Cravath would represent Y&R. Despite my best efforts, the US Attorney believed Moore's assertion that from the outset everyone knew that Foote would be paying off Abrahams. As a result, an indictment was filed charging Y&R, Klein, and Walter Spangenberg with conspiracy and RICO violations, and Steven McKenna, the Y&R account executive on the Jamaica account, with perjury.

From the time the indictment was filed in October, 1989, until we were to start trial the following February, we continued our unsuccessful efforts to find the missing tape recording of the initial meeting between the Y&R executives and Moore and Foote.

In early February 1990, I set off for Hartford for a long trial at which I would be representing another individual whom I believed to be innocent. Everything changed, however, when I arrived in Hartford and met with Tom Barr and the other Cravath lawyers working on the case. They told me in one of their last interviews with a retired executive, he had told them that he had a copy of the missing tape. The tape contained very explicit statements by Moore that hiring Foote as an agent was not necessary for them to obtain the Jamaica account—it would simply be very helpful to them to have an agent in Jamaica to coordinate local activities. Nothing on the tape suggested that money was going to be paid to anyone with the Board of Tourism.

We quickly arranged a meeting with the United States Attorney's office at which they were given a copy of the tape. After hearing the tape, the US Attorney agreed to dismiss the charges against Klein and Spangenberg and to accept a guilty plea by the firm to a single count of violating the Foreign Corrupt Practices Act and to dismiss all of the other charges against the company. Although the US Attorney would not agree to dismiss the perjury charges against McKenna, a few days later, at the end of jury selection, it was agreed that the prosecution of the McKenna would be deferred and would be dismissed after some agreed upon period of good behavior.

On February 10, 1990, Art Klein would once again find his photograph prominently displayed in the press, but this time it appeared with an article in the *New York Times* which quoted the United States Attorney for Connecticut as saying that the transcript which we had given him, "... made quite clear that Arthur Klein was not aware of what was going on." I admire Stan Twardy, the US Attorney, for his willingness to candidly admit they had been wrong.

Thus ended the case that would have been the last criminal trial of my career. It was also a great ending for my career in private practice.

THIRTEEN

District Judge

I took the oath of office on May 22, 1990, 10 years to the day from my swearing in as US Attorney. I left the law firm at the end of April and Peggy and I traveled to Ireland to play golf. Since the 22nd was within the window of reasonable times to begin my judicial career, nostalgia made the 22nd a logical choice.

No one comes to the federal bench totally prepared to for the job. Every new judge will ultimately be called upon to decide cases in fields of the law with which he or she has had no prior experience. Since I had handled both civil and criminal cases both in private practice and government service, I was probably better prepared than most. However there were vast areas of the law with which I had no prior experience, e.g., patents, copyright, employment discrimination and admiralty law.

Fortunately, our judicial system makes it possible for a judge to gain a sufficient understanding of each of the legal issues presented so that a reasonable decision can be reached. There are basically two sources of law that will provide guidance for the outcome of any particular dispute. The first are statutes—laws passed by legislatures, either Congress or the states, that set forth rules that must be followed in a variety of contexts. However, no statute can be detailed enough to provide clear guidance for every case and, therefore, judges must decide whether a particular statute governs the conduct in a pending case. For example, did this employer discriminate against this employee on the basis of race or was the employee discharged for legitimate reasons.

US District Judge John S. Martin, Jr.

While statutes have become the major source of governing law, that has not always been the case. In the English tradition, which we adopted at the time of the founding of this nation, rules of law had been derived from principles set forth by individual judges in the course of deciding cases that came before them. For example, two adjoining landowners have a dispute because one of them has constructed a dam on a stream that had traversed both of their properties for years. With no written law specifically addressing that issue, the judge would have to decide whether it was fair to allow one landowner to appropriate for himself the benefit of a common natural resource. The judge would have to rely on common sense, enlightened by the arguments of counsel, to render a decision. Once that decision was made, it would be cited as precedent the next time two abutting landowners had a similar dispute. This is how, over the course of centuries, what we now call the Common Law developed rules of conduct governing vast areas of human behavior.

For a new judge called upon to decide an issue in the field of law with which he has had no experience, there are thousands of volumes of reported cases which can provide guidance for the decision. There are some prior cases that a judge must follow, e.g., if an appellate court that has supervision over his or her court has decided a case involving the exact same legal question. Other cases simply provide the reasoning that other judges have used in similar cases, which the deciding judge is free to either accept or reject. These would be cases from other states, or other federal trial courts or from federal appellate courts in other parts of the country.

Due to the vast quantity of relevant case law that is accessible through various legal research tools, judges are rarely faced with making a decision for which there is not substantial precedent. Sometimes that precedent will provide a definitive answer, but in other cases the peculiar facts of the pending case will not quite fit within the framework of existing case law and the judge is left with the responsibility of determining how the law should be applied to the case at issue.

Although I was called upon to decide many cases involving fields of law with which I had no prior experience, I was never intimidated by the decision-making process. In part, that was the result of the accumulated experience of my years in private practice and in government service. Indeed, my service as Chief of the Criminal Division in the US Attorney's office prepared me well for my role as a judge. In that position I spent my days meeting with agents or talking to them on the phone and deciding whether to make an arrest, get a search warrant, issue a grand jury subpoena or do nothing with respect to a potential criminal matter. I learned that you have to make decisions that will have consequences because deferring the decision will also have consequences. I learned to make decisions and not look back.

One of the interesting things I learned through experience was that there are judges who hate to make decisions and judges who agonize over the decision-making process. Fortunately, that was not my problem. I recognized that I might not always be right, but attorneys needed a result in their cases and it was by job to provide that result. If I was wrong, the Circuit Court of Appeals could reverse me. Over the course of 13 years on the bench, my decisions were reversed many times. Sometimes I agreed with the appellate court and other times I felt they had the right to be wrong.

Doing the Job

As a new federal judge you have to learn not only how to go about deciding cases but also how to manage your caseload. A judge may have 50 to 100 pending criminal cases and 400 to 500 civil cases. You have to determine how to ensure that each case gets the attention it deserves and that the many issues that must be decided get resolved promptly.

Each judge has a personal staff with four positions allotted: a secretary, a courtroom deputy and two law clerks. I was fortunate to have an extraordinary staff. My secretary, Karen Harris, came with me from the law firm. I interviewed a number of candidates from the courthouse staff to be my courtroom deputy and fortunately selected Linda Thomas, a delightful woman who maintained a wonderful relationship with the court reporters, the US marshals and the lawyers who appeared before me. One of my daughter's friends who was particularly taken with Linda called her "the woman who stares," because in the courtroom she just sat in front of the bench looking out into the audience.

In the federal courts, the common practice is to hire as clerks young lawyers recently graduated from law school. Some judges required a two-year commitment with one of the two starting each year so there would be a continuity with at least one experienced clerk. I decided a two-year commitment was not fair to the young lawyer because the pay was lower than that of private practice and two years of experience was of no more value to the clerk than a single year. I did, however, stagger the arrival of the new law clerks by a month so that one of them would have time to learn our procedures from an outgoing clerk.

During my 13 years on the court, I never had a law clerk who was a problem or could not do the job. I was fortunate to have an extremely able and affable group of assistants. I was particularly lucky in my first year because Janet Neustaetter, a senior associate with whom I worked at the firm and who had previously clerked for a Southern District Judge, volunteered to serve as my first clerk. She was outstanding and, near the end of my tenure as a judge, I was able to arrange for Janet and another of my former clerks, Marnie Stetson, both of whom had young children, to share a clerkship with each of them working two days in the office and part time at home.

In addition to my own staff, I could also call upon the wisdom and experience of my colleagues. When I was first appointed, I went to see Ken Conboy, who I knew previously, and asked him what I should know. Fortunately for me, Ken was highly organized and he spent a morning taking me through a looseleaf book of forms that he used for routine administrative matters. In the course of reviewing these forms, he explained the nature of the issues that arose and how to expedite the decision-making process. His help was invaluable, and after I gained experience, I made a point to reach out to new judges to offer them similar advice. One of the new judges who took me up on my offer was Sonia Sotomayor.

New judges also spent a week in Washington in new judges' school. The federal court system is operated under the Administrative Office for the Courts under the supervision of the Chief Justice. Periodically, they bring a group of new judges from around the country to DC for a week of classes in which experienced judges cover some of the most important areas of the law that a new judge will have to decide, and also provide guidance in how to administer your caseload. One of the highlights of new judges' school was a dinner at the Supreme Court with several of the Justices, which I described earlier.

The procedures of the Court were designed to ease a new judge into the job. You are reassigned your percentage of the court's civil caseload from each of the courts' active judges, but you are not reassigned any criminal cases. Your name is immediately placed in the wheels maintained in the clerk's office for the distribution of cases among the judges. During the time I was on the bench, the clerk's office actually maintained 13 separate wheels into which the name of each judge was placed so that when a new case was filed, a name would be drawn and the case assigned to that judge. There were three criminal wheels and 10 civil wheels, each with different categories of cases, so there would not be an unfair distribution of one type of case to a particular judge.

As I began to receive my share of the civil cases from other judges, I came to realize that not all judges followed the rules. Prior to the time I became a judge, a judge was allowed to pick any case on the docket to assign to the new judge. This resulted in the new judge receiving cases that consisted primarily of matters which the reassigning judge considered "a dog." Shortly before I arrived, the Court changed its rules and cases were supposed to be assigned based on the docket number. For example, if I were to receive 5% of the docket of a judge who had 200 cases, every 10th case by docket number should have been transferred to me. However, the reassigning judge could withhold the case if it was related to another case or if the judge had already invested substantial time in the case. It became clear that, in some cases, a judge with a dog on the docket a number or two removed from the one scheduled to be reassigned would find some reason to keep the two cases so that the dog would be reassigned.

While I started to work my way through my cases, I came to realize that not every case would be interesting and exciting. One of my colleagues, I think it was Milton Pollock, said, "There is no case too trivial for the federal courts." My first trial proved that to be true. It was a nonjury case under the admiralty jurisdiction of the court. Matters arising from commerce on the navigable waters have been part of federal court jurisdiction from the outset and there was no monetary limit that had to be satisfied to bring an action in Admiralty. Although I do not remember the precise amount, my first trial

A Life Begun on Third Base

involved a claim for damage to cargo that was less than $1000. Being a federal judge did not necessarily mean I would always be deciding significant cases, but I recognized the wisdom of Judge Weinfeld when he said that "every case is important to the litigants."

I cannot mention Judge Pollock without recalling the conversation I had with his daughter Stephanie shortly after I joined the court. Stephanie had been a housemate of Peggy's at Smith and we had dinner with Stephanie and her husband from time to time. Her father Milton Pollock was one of the most feared judges on the court. He was brilliant and in control and quick to correct or silence a lawyer. At the dinner in question, Stephanie asked me, "John, since you practiced often in the federal courts before you became a judge, what was the most difficult change for you when you became a judge?" My answer was straightforward: "Learning to call your father Milton." Milton became a friend and loved the story.

The story illustrates another issue in starting a judicial career. All of a sudden you are a colleague of people you have looked up to for years—treating them as equals and calling them by their first names take some time. Another major issue is the nature of your relations both on and off the bench with the lawyers who appear before you. When I first became a judge, I thought I should think of myself as just another lawyer in the courtroom guiding the proceedings. I soon recognized, however, that I had a responsibility to maintain decorum and to see that the time of jurors and the court personnel was not wasted. This required a certain toughness and the willingness to impose discipline on lawyers. I always tried to treat lawyers with respect, but I had to run a tight ship.

Another issue that had to be confronted was my relationship with my former colleagues at the bar. At new judges' school, one of the instructors said that after he left his law firm he never returned and tried to avoid close social contact with his former partners and colleagues. This was one piece of advice I did not take. When you become a judge and people call you "Your Honor," it is quite easy to become impressed with yourself and develop what some people call "Judgeitis." For me, it was my friends and former colleagues who would keep me from getting too big a head. This is perhaps best illustrated by what my very good friend and former and future partner, Otto Obermaier said to me shortly after I became a judge: "Remember John, there are only two professions in which you can make a living in a black nightgown." It was people like Otto and Peggy who I hope saved me from Judgeitis.

Managing a caseload and at the same time doing justice in individual cases requires a recognition that you have to use time and resources wisely. One of the things I told new colleagues was "remember, you are going to die with a caseload." This was simply a recognition that, if you tried to dispose of every case on your docket, you could not lead a reasonable life or provide prompt justice in all of the cases before you. There had to be a balancing of the need to resolve the individual case appropriately while maintaining sufficient time for other cases and for life outside the court, particularly with your family.

Although I never reduced my caseload to the lowest of any member of the court, I believe I developed a system that let me do a reasonable job in disposing of cases while still maintaining a balance between my court and personal lives. One of the most important things in managing a caseload is learning how to use the resources available to you. In addition to having law clerks who can help with research and drafting opinions, the court had a number of magistrate judges who could be assigned some of the routine tasks involved in managing a caseload.

It took time for me to learn how to most efficiently use my law clerks. A general rule followed by most judges was to divide the cases assigned to the law clerks by docket number—one would work on all cases ending in an even number and the other on the odd numbers. That was easy but what were they to do? The principal job of the law clerk is to help with the writing of opinions, which are generally generated by motions to dismiss cases or for summary judgment. When I started on the court, the clerks were told that when a new motion came in, they were to review it and give me their views as to how the motion should be resolved. But I quickly learned that this resulted in a substantial waste of law clerk time. A law clerk might spend hours drafting a memorandum summarizing legal principles with which I was totally familiar. I therefore changed the system and took responsibility for being the first one to review a motion file. I could then explain to the law clerk the legal issues that needed research and ask for a memorandum addressing those issues.

Another issue was how much of an opinion should reflect my own writing. I soon realized that the vast majority of cases I would decide did not involve some new and important issue. The questions presented could be answered from existing case law and whether I wrote the analysis of those cases or my law clerk did made no difference. As a result, there are many opinions that I signed in which I did very little of the writing. However, each of those decisions reflected my decision, and my decision alone, as to how the case should be decided.

There were other cases where the answer to the question posed was not as easily derived from existing authority or where the importance of the matter required my attention. Therefore, there were a number of cases where I wrote the first draft of the opinion and simply asked my clerk for editorial assistance. In other cases, I might make substantial revisions to a draft provided by a clerk. Ultimately, the system enabled me to work a reasonable schedule and still dispose of the matters before me promptly.

This was a result that a number of judges were not able to obtain. Some judges felt that they had to write the majority of the opinions themselves with only research assistance from the law clerks. Others agonized over difficult and unprecedented decisions. The result was that there were very able judges who fell behind in their disposition of pending motions. I attempted, without success, to get the court to adopt some procedure that would provide some form of relief to judges with a backlog of pending motions. The response to my suggestions was that reassigning some of the backlog to another judge would simply be rewarding lazy judges. I doubted that much of the backlog was because of laziness but was rather a delay caused by a desire to see that every opinion was the best possible. But even if they were lazy judges, I still cannot see how a court can tell a litigant whose motion has been pending for over a year, "unfortunately your case was assigned to a lazy judge."

As noted above, the court also had magistrate judges, judicial officers authorized to handle most pretrial procedures in civil cases and preliminary matters in criminal cases. The court had approximately 15 magistrate judges and a total of approximately 45 District Judges, some of whom were semiretired. Cases were randomly assigned to the magistrate judges and each of them would end up with a docket of cases from every district judge. This was highly inefficient. Most other federal district courts had systems in which each magistrate judge was assigned to a single group of district judges. This enabled the district judges to work much more closely and efficiently with the magistrate judges. Our court resisted this practice because some judges feared they would be paired with one of the less able magistrates.

Given the limits of our system, I decided not to use a magistrate judge in most of my cases. However, I recognized that there were categories of cases, such as admiralty cases and negligence cases, which generally settle after discovery was complete and without substantial motion practice. I, therefore, assigned all of those cases to the magistrates and would rarely have anything to do with them again.

Looking back at my judicial service, I recognize that I was not a great judge but I think I think I would be rated above-average. I say this recognizing one of my favorite statistics — 75% of the people in the United States think they are of above average intelligence.

What separates the great judges from journeyman like me is that they have the ability to articulate in their decisions all of the visceral factors that go into determining the right result in an individual case. The classic example is the opinion of Judge Henry Friendly in a case in which the Polaroid Corporation sought to prohibit another party from using the term Polaroid in its trademark. After noting some confusion in the prior case law, Judge Friendly articulated eight separate factors that should be considered in determining when a trade name should be protected. In a few words, he was able to articulate a standard still being applied 60 years later. I can reasonably believe I would have come to the same result, but I doubt I could have so clearly articulated all of the considerations that lead to the conclusion that it was fair to allow Polaroid to prohibit another from using the same name.

If I did my job well, it was because I recognized some basic principles. First, and most important, as Judge Moore taught me, I tried to treat everyone who came before me with respect. Treating people with respect is more than addressing them politely. Treating others with respect requires a recognition that their time and convenience is no less important than yours. I believe I was popular with the court reporters, not because of some sparkling personality, but because I ran the train on time and did not waste their time — I started court when I said I would, the recesses ended on time and I did not work unreasonable hours.

I made it a practice to go into the jury room, after a verdict, to thank the jurors for their service. It was not unusual to have someone who had prior jury service thank me for how efficiently I ran the courtroom. I tried to remember that the courthouse personnel, the litigants the lawyers and the jurors all had lives outside the courthouse.

Being a good judge involved recognizing the job was not about me. It was about doing the right thing for the litigants who came before me. Among other things this involved not allowing concerns for public reactions to an opinion to play any role in the decision-making process, a healthy skepticism of attempts to measure a judge's performance by statistical analysis and a willingness to risk appellate reversible in cases where a just result was not necessarily consistent with existing law.

It is vitally important for judges not to be overly concerned about their record on appeal. After I was on the court for about three or four years an article appeared in the New York Law Journal entitled "The 10 Most Often Reversed Judges in the Second Circuit." While I was not far behind those judges in my reversal rate, the fact that I was not in the top 10 gave me the opportunity to write a letter to the editor pointing out this was a terrible article because it assumed that a judge who was reversed often was not a good judge. I noted that for a

District Judge to avoid being reversed there were only two things that had to be done: 1) never grant a motion to dismiss or for summary judgment in a civil case, and 2) never depart from a guideline sentence in a criminal case. However, these are two things district judges should do to ensure that the judicial system does justice.

Since a decision denying a motion to dismiss or for summary judgment is not appealable, some judges avoid granting such motions to avoid appellate review and possible reversal. However, a refusal to grant a meritorious motion to dismiss or for summary judgments forces the parties to expend considerable time and money to take a meritless case to trial. Often such costs compel parties to make payments in settlement even though the claim has no merit.

Departures from guideline sentence are absolutely necessary to prevent grave injustices to individual defendants. I have given several examples earlier in this chapter. Unfortunately during the time I was on the court, judges did not use the power to depart often enough.

Near the end of my judicial career, I was at a reception honoring Jack Weinstein of the Eastern District, one of the most highly regarded judges in the country. When I saw him, I said, "Jack, someone recently paid me a great compliment; they said that I must be doing something right because I'm being reversed almost as often as Jack Weinstein." Jack was not someone worried that he might get reversed for doing something he knew was right. More judges should have that attitude.

The Civil Cases

The docket of a federal judge consists of both civil and criminal cases. Civil cases are lawsuits between two parties involving claims for money damages, injunctions, or a declaration with respect to the law that might apply to a future dispute between the parties. Criminal cases are brought by the government to punish some form of conduct prohibited by statute.

By far the largest number of cases a federal judge has on the docket are civil cases. Criminal cases, however, tend to take a substantial portion of the judge's time because a greater number of them go to trial and, in every criminal case, the judge must take time to manage the case, take guilty pleas and impose sentence.

The civil cases include a wide range or disputes including complex patent infringement, securities class action, employment discrimination, prisoner civil rights claims, etc. Before discussing some of the more interesting civil cases that came before me, I want to note briefly some of the more routine matters. Proof of Judge Weinfeld's maximum that "every case is important to the litigants involved," is found in what I consider to be the most important thing I did as a federal judge.

The case was never reported in any newspaper nor did it involve a published decision. It was simply a settlement discussion in which I contributed to a resolution of the dispute between an insurance company and the husband of an insured. The man's wife was in the last stages of a losing battle with multiple sclerosis. Her husband, who had retired so that he could provide full-time care for his wife, thought that she was entitled to the aid of a full-time practical nurse paid for by the insurance company, but the insurer took the position that her policy would reimburse only necessary skilled nursing care and that she only needed skilled nursing care for a couple of hours twice a week.

As a matter of law, the insurance company was probably right. However, unlike the stereotype of an insurance company often depicted in the press or by politicians, the insurance company was not unsympathetic to the burden this husband was carrying. As a result, I was able to promote a settlement in which the insurer agreed to provide for a practical nurse for two full days a week and also for a week or two during the year. This would enable the husband to have some time off from the day-to-day care of his wife, which he obviously needed during this stressful period. Getting this resolution for someone in desperate need was more significant in the long run than any decision I would make in other cases some might consider more important, some of which are set forth below.

Groden v. Random House

This case could have made me the most famous trial judge in the country. More famous even than Lance Ito, the judge in the O.J. Simpson case. The plaintiff was an author who had written a book saying that Lee Harvey Oswald had not acted alone when he assassinated John F. Kennedy and he hoped to have a trial in federal court to prove it.

The case started with an ad Random House placed in the *New York Times* to promote a book written by Gerald Posner in which the author set out to prove that there was no basis for any of the conspiracy theories with respect to the Kennedy assassination and that Lee Harvey Oswald had acted alone. The ad started by stating in bold type "Guilty of Misleading the Public," under which were pictures of six of the leading conspiracy theorists, including Groden, with a brief quote from each author. Under those quotes, the ad said, "One Man, One Gun, One Inescapable Conclusion." The ad ended by saying "Read Case Closed by Gerald Posner."

Groden's principal claim was that the ad violated the Lanham Act, which gives people injured by false advertising a right to sue. Groden said he would prove the ad was false by proving that there was, in fact, more than one assassin involved in the Kennedy shooting. A trial of the Kennedy assassination would have filled the courtroom with reporters and television cameras.

Unfortunately for Mr. Groden, and for my career as a celebrity, I threw the case out. My decision was based on prior cases that said the Lanham Act covered only the making of false statements of fact and not statements of opinion. I found that by 1994 the question of whether the Kennedy assassination involved more than one assassin could only reasonably be considered a matter of opinion because it could not be reliably proved either way.

My decision granting summary judgment to Random House and dismissing the case began one of the most bizarre series of events in my judicial career. It started when Groden's lawyer, Roger Bruce Feinman, made a motion seeking to disqualify me as the judge in the case. While I had no quarrel with a lawyer who sought to disqualify me because he or she thought, for some reason, that he or she could not get a fair trial before me, I had no patience for applications to disqualify made after I had rendered an adverse decision.

In this case, Feinman alleged three reasons that I should never have acted in the case: 1) I had served in the Justice Department at the time the Warren Commission report was prepared with the help of Justice Department people and that would have prejudiced me against Mr. Groden's claim; 2) One of the in-house lawyers for Random House, Leslie Oelsner, had served as an Assistant US Attorney under me in the 1980s; and 3) I was the brother of Kevin Martin a lawyer who had worked with Mr. Feinman in the past and who would have prejudiced the against Feinman. I denied the motion on two grounds: 1) All of the facts on which Feinman relied were matters of public record that would have been known to him when the case was first assigned to me and any motion to disqualify should have been made then and 2) In any event none of the items he alleged required disqualification.

The fact that I served in the Justice Department at the time it was working with the Warren Commission was not disqualifying because I had no involvement in the work related to the Warren Commission. Although it was true that Leslie Oelsner had served in the US Attorney's office under me, we had no ongoing social or professional relationship so there was no basis for disqualification. As to the fact that my brother Kevin may have prejudiced me against Mr. Feinman, I wrote:

"The factual assertion, unqualified by any allegation that it is based on information and belief, or any similar caution, is an outright falsehood. I do not even know an individual named Kevin L Martin, and I doubt that my deceased parents would have failed to disclose a fact of such significance to their six children."

When I summoned Mr. Feinman to court to require him to explain why he should not be sanctioned for making such a blatantly false allegation, he said, "Well, you look like Kevin Martin."

In addition to the bizarre allegations about Kevin Martin, Feinman had sent a letter to me in which he referred to the fact the lawyer for Random House, Victor Kovner, who was active in Democratic Party politics, had accompanied President Clinton to the Mideast as "his token New York Jewboy." In another letter to me he referred to Kovner and me saying, "you two fellas can play with each other all you want. I'm going upstairs to talk to The Man"—referring to the Second Circuit.

Feinman had also sent a letter to a federal judge in Washington D.C. who was handling a related case in which he said he understood that the judge had received "a copy of Judge Martin's crooked and corrupt decision in our case."

The combination of these bizarre actions by Mr. Feinman convinced me that he should not be practicing law in our courts. I referred the matter to our disciplinary committee and he was disbarred. I have never before or since encountered such bizarre behavior by a lawyer.

Copyright Cases

Ringgold v. Black Entertainment TV

Although I had no experience with copyright law prior to becoming a judge, copyright cases were an important part of the docket that often presented interesting questions. For example, in one case a television show centered in the black community had a scene that was to take place inside a church. To add an air of authenticity, one of the rooms was decorated with a poster of a painting entitled "Church Picnic" by Faith Ringgold, a respected African-American artist. The painting was owned by the High Museum of Art which sold the poster under a license from the artist. The posters sold for $20.

The poster appeared in the background of the scene that lasted for about five minutes and was visible on the screen approximately nine times. I dismissed the claim on the grounds that the incidental use of the poster simply as background was protected by the "fair use" doctrine in the copyright law. In my view, the use of the poster is a background did no economic harm to the artist, since it would not have an adverse impact on the sale of the poster or of her other paintings. My decision was ultimately reversed by a learned opinion of Jon Newman, one of the finest judges on the Second Circuit and someone for whom I had great respect. Despite my admiration for Jon, I think as a practical matter I was right and that the appellate court decision over-intellectualized the issue.

Willis v. HBO

Arli$$ was a popular HBO series about a sports agent named Arliss. In 2000, Patricia Willis sued HBO, claiming that Arli$$ was based on an outline for a TV series—known in the trade as a Treatment—which she had submitted to HBO before it produced Arli$$. HBO moved to dismiss her claims on the ground that it violated no copyrightable interest of the plaintiff because Arli$$ did not contain any material that was unique to Ms. Willis's Treatment. I wrote a fairly detailed opinion dismissing the copyright claims on the recognized ground that the copyright law does not give anyone the rights to stock characters or typical situations—it only protects original ideas or modes of expression. However, to make this ruling I had to do a detailed analysis of the characters and themes from Arli$$ and the show that Ms. Willis had pitched to HBO. The following brief excerpts from my opinion give some idea of the analysis involved:

> Many people would consider the phrase "sleazy talent agent" to be redundant. While this is no doubt as unfair a stereotype as is the "sleazy lawyer," no one could reasonably claim a copyright in the concept of a sleazy talent agent. The question presented here is what degree of detail must an author add to such a well-recognized stock character in order to obtain copyright protection."
>
> 'A stock character or basic character type ... is not entitled to copyright protection.' *Robinson v. Viacom International, Inc.*, 93 Civ. 2539, 1995 WL 417076, at *9 (S.D.N.Y. Jan. 4, 1995); *Sinicola v. Warner Bros.*, 948 F. Supp. 1176, 1185 (E.D.N.Y. 1996). 'No character infringement claim

can succeed unless plaintiff's original conception sufficiently developed the character, and defendants have copied this development and not merely the broader outlines.' *Smith v. Weinstein*, 578 F. Supp. 1297, 1303, *aff'd mem.*, 738 F.2d 419 (2d Cir. 1984); *see also Nichols v. Universal Pictures Corp.*, 45 F.2d 119, 121 (2d Cir. 1930) ('the less developed the characters, the less they can be copyrighted; that is the penalty for marking them too indistinctly').

Almost as unsuccessful is Plaintiff's expert's attempt to prove that Arliss's secretary Rita Wu is substantially similar to Maricait Barker. Aside from the fact that they are both female, there is little that Rita and Maricait have in common. While Maricait is described as 'a persistently horn-rimmed dishwater blonde who evokes the warmth and flaky brilliance of a young Diane Keaton,' Treatment at 10, Rita is a with-it Asian American who would remind no one of Diane Keaton. Rita does wear dark rimmed glasses but they are stylish and would not ordinarily be described as horn-rimmed. While Maricait is described as 'good-hearted, yet cerebral' and 'happiest with her face in a book,' Treatment at 10, no one but Plaintiff's expert would describe Rita as 'cerebral' or think of her as happiest with her face in a book. In asserting that Rita, like Maricait, serves 'as the 'moral voice' of the series,' Expert's Report at 31, Plaintiff's expert apparently overlooks those episodes in which Rita is shown attempting to overhear the conversations in Arliss's office by kneeling outside his office with a glass to the door, and other instances where she lies without compunction and sleeps with a variety of his clients."

My decision dismissing the case was affirmed in a brief Summary Order by the Second Circuit.

West Publishing

Perhaps the most significant copyright case in terms of economic impact involved the West Publishing Company, which for over 100 years had been printing the opinions issued by state and federal courts throughout the country. West's volumes of cases were the principal source of cases used by lawyers in advising their clients and in the drafting of their legal briefs. In some states, West was the official reporter for the courts of the state and it had very little, if any, competition throughout the country.

The computer age brought a challenge to West's control over the market for judicial opinions. To compete with West, companies no longer had to print thousands of volumes of reported cases. Rather, cases could be scanned onto computer discs and the product sold to law firms. Since West was in many cases the sole source of printed cases, anyone who wanted to compete by scanning decisions onto computer discs had to begin the process by scanning material from one of West's volumes of cases. When that happened, West threatened to sue, claiming that it had a copyright interest in the cases it published.

Faced with such a threat, one of the incipient competitors brought an action seeking a declaratory judgment that its scanning of an opinion from a West volume did not violate the copyright law. The case was assigned to me. West recognized that it could not claim to have a copyright interest in one of my opinions, or that of any other judge, simply because it was the first to publish it. It claimed, however, that it made certain editorial changes to the opinions it published and, therefore, no one could copy one of its published opinions without violating its rights under the copyright law.

When it published an opinion, West did not simply reprint verbatim the opinion of the court. It added certain features that would enhance the ability of lawyers to find relevant cases, such as brief synopsis of the legal issues decided, to which key numbers were assigned so lawyers looking for similar cases in digests published by West could find under that key number all of the cases that had considered the issue. To facilitate the ability of the attorney to find the relevant portion of an opinion considering an issue raised in the headnote, West added numbers to the opinion at points where it began a discussion of a new issue. In addition, since many cases were reported in official volumes issued by the states involved, as well as regional volumes, West might add what is known as a parallel cite, i.e., a citation to the same opinion in a different published series.

West claimed that the additions it made were significant and therefore it had a copyright interest in the materials it published that was violated when its competitors used its published opinions by scanning them onto computer discs. West's competitors said that they blacked out all of West's head notes and key numbers before they scanned the opinions and that any remaining original work by West was so insignificant that it was not entitled to copyright protection. I agreed and ruled that the scanning of the West opinions did not give West a claim under the copyright law. The Second Circuit affirmed.

I did not realize at the time how significant the ruling in the West case would be. The effort to put cases onto computer discs was the start of a sea change in legal research. As the Internet developed, computerized research almost completely replaced reliance on printed books as the source of case authority. Now a lawyer researching a case simply goes to the computer and enters the research terms and can gain immediate access to all cases around the country dealing with a similar issue. If the case seems particularly important, with the click of a mouse the lawyer can download the case and store it in a file on his computer.

Prior to the decision in West, every law firm had a huge library filled with volumes of reported cases. Not long after I left the bench, I was on an arbitration panel in Chicago. Our hearings were held in a space that someone had developed with the sole purpose of hosting arbitrations, mediations, conferences, etc. The facility covered several floors of a major office building and had previously served as the headquarters for one of Chicago's largest law firms. At the end of an arbitration day, we stopped for a drink at a cocktail lounge that was part of the facility. It was lined with law books—it was where the library of the law firm had been. The computer age had ended the law firm's need for its printed books, so they were left behind.

Insurance Coverage Cases

If, before I became a judge, I had met a lawyer at a cocktail party who told me that his or her specialty was insurance coverage, I would have

A Life Begun on Third Base

quickly walked away thinking how boring that must be. I would have been wrong. By luck of the draw, I ended up with a higher percentage of insurance coverage cases than most of my colleagues and found that they involved a variety of interesting factual and legal issues.

National Gypsum

The first major insurance coverage case I was assigned involved claims for coverage for both personal injury and property damage being asserted against National Gypsum, one of the leading producers of asbestos products, including wallboard. In the late 70s early 80s, it was discovered that asbestos was a major carcinogen, and National Gypsum was sued by various building owners who had installed its asbestos-containing wallboard and were now required to remove it, and by thousands of individuals who claimed various medical conditions from which they suffered were the result of exposure to asbestos-containing products.

A common question in many disputes over property damage and personal injury claims involves the meaning of the term "occurrence." Insurance policies often provide a set amount of insurance "per occurrence." Each separate occurrence entitled the insured to the coverage to the full amount of the policy limits. For example, if a building owner has a property damage policy that provides $100,000 of insurance per occurrence and a group of vandals set three fires in the building at about the same time, doing total damages of $300,000, if each fire is considered a separate occurrence, the building owner would be entitled total insurance of $300,000. If, however, the events were considered a single occurrence because they were carried out by a group of individuals acting at about the same time, the insured would only be entitled to $100,000 of insurance. The definition of occurrence would also be important in determining what part of the loss was included in the deductible the insured would have to pay before the insurer had to pay anything. In the above example, if each of the three fires was a separate occurrence and there was a $20,000 deductible, the insurer would only be liable for $240,00, the amount of damages in excess of the three $20,00 deductibles.

In the *National Gypsum* case, one of the major questions was whether each individual sale of an asbestos related product or each individual installation of an asbestos-containing product in a building was the occurrence that gave rise to insurance liability—in the jargon of the insurance world was that what "triggered" the obligation of the insurer to pay. In the property damage cases, the occurrence issue was important because if each installation of asbestos was an occurrence triggering a deductible that was the responsibility of the insured, National Gypsum would have received millions less in insurance proceeds. I ultimately determined that, under the applicable New York law, the decision to manufacture and sell asbestos was the occurrence which gave rise to liability and therefore National Gypsum was only responsible for a single deductible.

The issues with respect to insurance coverage for personal injury claims turned out to be fascinating. Most product liability insurance for personal injury claims provides that the insurer will provide insurance coverage for injuries that occur during the policy period. Most of the personal injury claims involved conditions such as cancer or mesothelioma, which developed over a long period of time. That raised the question of which of the insurers that provided insurance to National Gypsum over a 25-year period was liable to National Gypsum on any individual claim.

To understand the issue, the following example may help. Assume an individual who worked in a shipyard and was exposed to asbestos during the years 1959 to 1965 was diagnosed with lung cancer in 1983. He files a lawsuit against National Gypsum claiming it is liable for the damages caused by the cancer. Since the plaintiff was exposed to asbestos in the years from 1959 to 1965, National Gypsum would go to the insurers it used during those years and ask them to defend the case and pay any liability. The insurers might say, "we insured you only for any injury that occurred during the policy period and this individual was not injured until he was diagnosed with cancer." If National Gypsum then went to the insurer who provided coverage in 1983, that insurer might say, "We agreed to insure you for any claims made by an individual who was injured during the policy period and

A Life Begun on Third Base

this plaintiff wasn't injured when his condition was diagnosed, he was injured when he was exposed to the asbestos that caused his cancer." The question of when an individual, who was exposed to asbestos years ago and then, 20 or 30 years later, is diagnosed with cancer, was actually injured became central to the personal injury claims and resulted in some of the most interesting testimony I would hear in my judicial career.

In the ordinary personal injury case in the federal court, the expert witnesses who testified were rarely the top practitioners in that field. In the National Gypsum case, however, there was so much money at issue that each of the parties retained some of the leading medical experts in the country to testify about how the various conditions caused by exposure to asbestos developed over a number of years.

By the time I was assigned these cases, the law had developed a rule that any injury, even if microscopic, could give rise to liability if the injury could be established with reasonable medical certainty. Thus, I got an education in how cancer develops when a single strand of asbestos becomes implanted in a single cell in the lung. During the course of a person's lifetime, that injured cell is regularly replacing itself by generating new cells, each of which bears the scar from the original damage. In addition, over time mutations occur in the cells that ultimately may cause them to be cancerous. It usually takes four of five separate mutations to change a perfectly healthy cell into a cancer cell. The cancerous cell then generates rapidly into a major malignancy.

There were a number of insurance companies that were defendants in these cases and some of them wanted the issue resolved by a jury and others thought they would be better off having me decide the issue after a bench trial. Therefore, the issues of the trigger of coverage for personal injury cases ended up being decided both by a jury and later by me after a separate nonjury trial.

Originally, I planned to hold a single trial and simply submit some of the claims to the jury and decide others myself. On the day set for trial, the parties told me that the combined trial would take at least a week longer than had been originally estimated. My problem was I had an important criminal trial scheduled for that week. I therefore told the parties we would hold the jury trial first. Because the jury trial would involve many fewer lawyers questioning the witnesses, it could be accomplished in the original time allotted. I said that after my criminal trial, I would conduct a bench trial and the evidence from the jury trial would be part of the record of the bench trial, with the insurers having the right to call back the jury trial witnesses for cross-examination. The result was two trials that in total were much shorter than the original estimate.

With respect to the cancers, both the jury and I found that all of the insurers who provided insurance to national Gypsum from the time of the initial exposure to asbestos until the time of the diagnosis were required to provide insurance coverage to National Gypsum with respect to any claim. The net result was that National Gypsum was covered by insurance for the personal injury claims arising from its sales up to the full amount of insurance that it had for all of the years from the time of the initial injuries through the last personal injury claim.

The case was different with respect to mesothelioma, another major disease caused by asbestos, in that the cells injured by the asbestos do not continue to generate new injured cells. Rather, they simply die and are not replaced. As more and more cells are exposed to and damaged by asbestos, the individual's condition becomes worse and worse. However, once exposure to asbestos ends, there is no further injury from asbestos. Unfortunately, even though no further damage is done from the asbestos, that damage coupled with damage from some other source, such as smoking, may ultimately contribute to a person's death. Both the jury and I found that on the mesothelioma claims, only the insurers who provided coverage to the company during the period when the individual was exposed to asbestos had an obligation to provide insurance to National Gypsum for those claims.

Even though National Gypsum was entitled to recover from its insurers the total amount of insurance it had purchased over more than twenty years, that amount was substantially less than the total of the property damage and personal injury claims and National Gypsum had to declare bankruptcy. In the bankruptcy proceeding, the amount of the insurance coverage was set aside and administered separately to compensate those who had been injured.

Squibb

This was another case involving the question of which of a number of insurance companies who had provided personal injury insurance to Squibb, a large pharmaceutical company, would be responsible for defending and paying the claims of people injured by DES, a drug that for years had been given to pregnant women who were having difficulty carrying to term. Years later many of these women developed cancers, as did some of their children and grandchildren. In addition many of their daughters and granddaughters developed anatomical conditions such as endometriosis.

While the details of some of the numerous legal and factual issues posed by this case would be of little interest to almost anyone, it is worth noting how complex cases like this could be. The easiest way to demonstrate the complexity of this case is to set forth the following short excerpt from the 29-page Circuit Court opinion that affirmed all but one minor ruling:

In addition to the question of subject matter jurisdiction, we address the following issues going to the merits of this case: (a) whether, given another court's ruling that one of Squibb's primary insurance policies was triggered by the manifestation of DES injury, Squibb is estopped from benefitting in this case from an injury-in-fact trigger of insurance coverage; (b) whether the district court erred in excluding evidence proffered by the Excess Insurers on the question of whether DES caused certain injuries in children of women who ingested DES during pregnancy; (c) whether certain claims by the grandchildren of these women are covered under the insurance policies at issue; (d) whether the district court properly allocated responsibility for Squibb's losses among its various insurers; (e) whether the district court erred in the procedures it established for addressing new postjudgment information and claims; (f) whether the district court erred in its interpretation of when a deductible in certain policies applies; (g) whether certain statements in the final judgment's preamble should be stricken; (h) whether there is a case or controversy concerning the policies of certain Excess Insurers which provide coverage to Squibb only if its liability reaches very high levels; and (i) whether CNA's policies cover Squibb's defense-related costs between January 1, 1971 and January 1, 1976.

In this case, which I took over after the case had been pending for many years before a judge who became sick, over 10 years of the time and effort of lawyers and clients came close to being wasted because of a basic question of the jurisdiction of the federal courts. In addition to having jurisdiction over cases involving federal laws, the Constitution provides that the federal courts have jurisdiction over cases "between Citizens of different States." Most of the insurance coverage cases in the federal courts are based on diversity of citizenship because the insurers are incorporated in one state and the insured in another.

The jurisdictional problem in the Squibb case arose because some of the insurance was provided by Lloyds of London. Lloyd's is not a single company that provides insurance; rather it is a marketplace in which a group of individuals—referred to as "names"—agree to participate in the insurance of a certain risk that Lloyd's is asked to insure.

After I had spent well over a year getting the case ready for trial and conducting the trial and post-trial proceedings, the insurers appealed from the judgment holding them liable to Squibb. Unfortunately for them, one of the Circuit Judges to whom the case was assigned was Guido Calabrese, a delightful and learned man who for years had been the Dean of the Yale Law School.

Even though the question of jurisdiction had never been raised by the parties, the jurisdiction of the federal courts is an issue of its power and can be challenged at any time even though not raised earlier in the proceedings. Apparently, Guido was familiar with other federal courts cases in which the issue of diversity jurisdiction in cases involving

Lloyd's had been raised. Lloyd's involves a vast number of "names," some of them are US citizens and some of the names who were US citizens had agreed to be liable on the Squibb policies. Therefore, the Circuit Court sent the case back to me to decide the factual and legal issues necessary to determine whether the federal court ever had jurisdiction over the case.

In its opinion sending the case back to me, the Circuit Court noted several theories that might sustain jurisdiction but recognized potential problems with each of them. It concluded by saying that these questions should be resolved by the District Judge in the first instance. Sometime later, I saw Guido in the judges' dining room and started kidding him about what he had done to me. He is a delightful individual and enjoyed the banter.

Although I had decided each of the possible bases of jurisdiction mentioned in the Circuit Court opinion, when the case went back to the Circuit Court it simply affirmed on the easiest option and said it did not have to address all of the other issues they had forced me to decide.

In the *Squibb* case, the insurers had demanded a jury trial and the complex medical and legal issues had to be decided by a jury. Once again I was impressed with how well the jury did its job.

The testimony of the experts covered a wide range of conditions that DES caused. The testimony concerning some of the conditions that developed in the daughters and granddaughters of women who took DES was that the fetus was injured at the time the mother took the DES but, after birth, the injured cells remained in the quiescent state until puberty. As in the *National Gypsum* case, the jury found that the cancers caused injury from the time of exposure to diagnosis. However, for the cases in which the testimony indicated that the injured cells remained dormant until puberty, the jury found that the injury occurred to the daughters and granddaughters when the daughter was in utero but did not begin again until puberty. The jury reached a very sophisticated judgment which both I and the Court of Appeals found to be correct.

At the trial, Squibb called the most impressive expert witness I have ever seen. In giving his background he testified that he was an obstetrician-gynecologist, microbiologist and a geneticist and had studied under some of the leading experts in the field. He was also a teacher. During his direct examination the following occurred:

Q. Doctor, aside from teaching, do you treat patients?

A. Yes.

Q. Please give us an example of the type of patient you treat.

A. For example, there was a woman who had had a child born without an immune system—a bubble baby. The child was kept in a bubble for several months but ultimately developed an infection and died. At the time she came to see me, she was pregnant and I tested the fetus and found it did not have an immune system. So, I took some bone marrow from her husband, aspirated it, cleaned it up and inserted it into the fetus. That child is over a year-old today."

Later, my law clerk who had been in court said to me "God testified in your courtroom today." He wasn't God but he made what I was doing on a day-to-day basis seem rather insignificant.

The World Trade Center

The terrorist attack on the World Trade Center did incredible human and property damage. Like similar disasters, the attack resulted in a wide variety of litigation, including a suit between, Silverstein Properties, the leaseholder and operator of the Center, and a group of insurers who provided approximately $3.1 billion of property insurance. I was assigned the case.

One could teach a course on insurance law based solely on the issues raised by the terrorist attack on the World Trade Center. I set forth the basic issue in one of my early opinions in the case:

A Life Begun on Third Base

The extent of the liability of the insurance carriers may ultimately depend upon resolution of the question: Which of the two following statements best describes what caused the destruction of the World Trade Center on September 11, 2001?

1. In a single coordinated attack, terrorists flew hijacked planes into the twin towers of the World Trade Center.
2. At 8:46 A. M. on the morning of September 11th, a hijacked airliner crashed into the North Tower of the World Trade Center, and 16 minutes later a second hijacked plane struck the South Tower."

Since most property damage insurance is written on a "per occurrence" basis—the maximum insured amount will be paid for each covered occurrence—the Court would normally expect to find the answer to the question of whether the events of September 11th constituted one or two "occurrences" by looking at how the parties to the insurance contract defined that term in the policy they negotiated. In the case of the World Trade Center, however, with minor exceptions, there were no insurance policies in place on September 11th, although each of the insurers had signed binders setting forth in summary form their agreement to provide property damage coverage. Some of these binders expressly stated that the precise language was "to be agreed upon."

Since Silverstein Properties had policies that would pay up to $3.1 billion per occurrence, a finding of two occurrences would provide up to $6.2 billion of insurance. With no written policies defining occurrence, the principal questions to be resolved were:

1) At the end of the negotiation process, would the term "occurrence" have been defined; and

2) if so, how?

At the time Silverstein was taking over the World Trade Center, its broker sent out a package of documents to a variety of insurance companies asking them if they were interested in becoming part of the insurance consortium and what level of liability the insurer would assume. With major commercial insurance, various insurers provide insurance at different levels, e.g. some insurers may agree to provide the first hundred million dollars of insurance less the deductible and other insurance would agree to ensure different amounts above the first $100,000,000 at different levels up to the total amount of insurance.

The package of documents sent out by Silverstein's broker, Willis, contained a description of the properties and the insurance being sought, along with a form of property insurance contract that Willis indicated would serve as a basis of negotiation. Unlike your typical home insurance, insurance for large commercial operations like the World Trade Center is not written on a standard form; rather, the provisions of the contract are negotiated over a period of time between the building owner and the insurers. At the time of the terrorist attack the vast majority of the insurers were still in the process of negotiating the final contract terms with Silverstein Properties

Under the general principles of contract law, a draft agreement that does not set forth the essential terms of the contract will not be enforced. In the case of property insurance, however, the property owner has relied upon the fact that there is insurance in place and it would be unfair to find that there was no insurance because the final contract had not been signed. As a result, the law requires the court to attempt to look back and divine the terms that would have been in the contract had the final document been produced.

One of the ironies of the case was that the Willis form included in the original package sent to the insurer's provided that the insurer would provide an amount of insurance "per occurrence," defined as follows:

> "'Occurrence' shall mean all losses or damages that are attributable, directly or indirectly, to one cause or series of similar causes."

This was viewed as a pro-owner definition because it would limit the number of deductibles for which the owner would be responsible.

With limited exception, the insurers had not signed the specimen policy that Willis had distributed, and negotiations were ongoing. On September 14, three days after the attack, Travelers Insurance signed and sent to Silverstein Properties its insurance policy, which provided $220 million of insurance "per occurrence," but did not define the term the occurrence.

The language of the Willis form that defined an occurrence as including all losses from "one cause or series of similar causes," clearly supported a finding that the concerted terrorist attack was a single occurrence because two planes hitting two towers only minutes apart were "a series of similar causes." Thus, I granted summary judgment to two insurers who had originally marked up the Willis form and returned it with their binder.

Given the fact that the Willis form made the terrorist attack one occurrence, which would limit the total of the insurer's liability to $3.1 billion, whereas the undefined term "occurrence" could be construed as justifying a finding that the terrorist attack constituted two separate occurrences, increasing the insurer's total liability to $6.2 billion, it was not surprising that a vast majority of the insurers claimed that they were on the Willis form and their insurance contract would have included its occurrence definition. Silverstein Properties argued to the contrary that most of the insurers were going to follow the Travelers form and leave occurrence undefined.

As a result of these conflicting contentions, I determined there would have to be two trials: 1) a trial to determine which of the insurers would have adopted the Willis form and which of them would ultimately have used the Travelers form; and 2) a second trial to have a jury answer the question of whether, if the term "occurrence" is undefined, the terrorist attack constituted one or two occurrences.

I ended up acting something like the man who voted to make a town dry and then moved. After deciding that two trials would be necessary, I retired from the bench and left the case to my colleague and friend

Michael Mukasey, who sometime after those trials resigned to become Attorney General.

The first trial resulted in a finding that a majority of the insurers would have ultimately adopted the Travelers form. At the end of the second trial, the jury found that with occurrence undefined, the attack of the two planes constituted two occurrences, so that Silverstein properties was ultimately entitled to total of $4.2 billion of insurance.

Although he had not been involved in the case when it was before me, my good friend Bernie Nussbaum tried the two cases for Silverstein before Judge Mukasey. When I heard that the jury had found there were two occurrences I called Bernie and said, "Bernie you are a great lawyer. A good lawyer wins the cases he should win; a great lawyer wins the cases he should lose. You should have lost that case." Bernie said, "No John, I won that case because I should have won the case. At the trial we were able to introduce documents found in some of the insurers' files in which the insurers said they liked to leave the term occurrence undefined so that they could argue either way depending upon the facts of the particular case." When I heard about those memoranda, I realized no jury would have found for the insurers on that record.

My resignation from the bench did not end my association with the World Trade Center insurance issues. I ultimately got involved in settling a related case for $1.2 billion.

Other Significant Civil Cases

The Queen Elizabeth II *Runs Aground*

For those who know the meaning of the term snafu, a perfect example can be found in the grounding of the *Queen Elizabeth II* off Martha's Vineyard, which was the subject of a nonjury trial that I conducted.

After the *QE2* ran aground sailing from Martha's Vineyard, its owners sued the United States, claiming that charts produced by the National Oceanic and Atmospheric Administration of the water surrounding

A Life Begun on Third Base

Martha's Vineyard misrepresented the depth of the water at the place where the ship grounded. It was claimed that the chart showed that there was thirty-nine feet of water at the spot where the grounding occurred when, in fact, the water was only thirty-six feet deep.

The evidence at trial established that it was not an error in the chart but a mistake by crew that caused the grounding. When a ship such as the *QE2* is entering or leaving Martha's Vineyard, it is required to have a local pilot who is responsible for setting the course. A ship leaving Martha's Vineyard must carefully follow a set course to avoid shallow water. Even though the ships' crew was not responsible for setting the course, its navigator had plotted a course that called for the ship to make a sharp turn at a buoy, marked on the chart as the N buoy.

Before leaving the harbor, the ship's crew had not coordinated with the pilot to see if he would be using the same course. In fact, the course the pilot set had the ship continue straight past the N buoy and making its turn at another point further on. As the ship was passing the N buoy, the navigator told the captain that he had plotted a turn at that point and there was low water ahead. The captain then told this to the pilot and asked if he had any objection to making the turn immediately. The pilot did not object and the turn was made. Unfortunately for the *QE2*, a large ocean liner cannot make the type of sharp turn you would make in a car. As a result, by the time the ship actually made its turn, it was well past the N buoy and it ran aground in an area properly marked on the charts as having low water. A perfect snafu.

You will sometimes hear a person insult another by saying, "You don't know squat." As a result of the *QE2* trial, I do know squat. Squat is a nautical term used to describe the phenomenon that occurs when a vessel travels through water. As the bow of the vessel parts the water, it actually lowers the depth of the water through which it is passing. In the case of the *QE2* for example, although its bottom was only thirty-six feet below the waterline, as the bow pushed aside the water ahead, the ship dropped another four feet below the water surface so that it would need a total depth of forty feet to clear bottom. The ship squats four feet below the surface. One of the great things about being a lawyer is you're always learning new things from the facts of cases you are handling.

The First Amendment Rights of a Pedophile Clown

Although I made a number of controversial decisions during my 13 years as a federal judge, none engendered more negative publicity than my opinions in the case of William Hobbs. On May 22, 1980, Hobbs sent a letter to Joseph Montalto, the then director of Playland Park in Rye New York, seeking a permit to perform in Playland as a clown, making balloon animals and seeking contributions—activity that is known in the trade as "busking."

Playland, which is owned and operated by Westchester County, consists of an amusement park, an ice-skating rink and a beach and boardwalk on Long Island sound. Hobbs's application was not precise as to the area of the park in which he was seeking to perform. In any event, his request was denied on the ground that soliciting contributions was prohibited in any Park in Westchester County.

Hobbs repeated his request for a permit to perform at Playland in 2001, by which time the Westchester officials had learned that Hobbs had two misdemeanor convictions involving sexual abuse of minors. In denying Hobbs' 2001 application for a permit, Mr. Montalto noted that the prior convictions indicated that granting Hobbs a permit would pose an unreasonable risk to the safety of children.

Based on this record, both sides moved for summary judgment, i.e., they claimed that the facts developed during discovery that were not disputed entitled them to a judgment. While I was not unsympathetic to the County's legitimate concerns about allowing a convicted pedophile to perform for children as a clown, the existing regulations on which the County relied were clearly unconstitutional because they infringed First Amendment rights.

In my opinion, I first recognized that there were separate areas within the park that required different analyses. To the extent that the County was operating an amusement park, it had the same rights, as would any commercial operator, to prohibit certain conduct within the amusement park, including performing and soliciting money. However, the areas of the park outside the amusement areas were like all other public park areas where individuals had the right to exercise their freedom of speech. Those rights could not be limited at the sole discretion of the County and, under existing case law, the County could not bar performers like Mr. Hobbs. On this basis I concluded that the County could prohibit Hobbs from performing in the amusement park area but could not prevent him from doing his act on the boardwalk and the adjoining property.

Although I ruled that the County could not prevent Hobbs from performing under its existing regulations, I was careful to note:

> This is not to say, however, that a narrowly drawn regulation specifically designed to protect children from pedophiles could not pass constitutional muster if it included sufficient procedural safeguards. The Courts have recognized that there are situations in which the First Amendment rights of convicted felons may be limited if there is a reasonable relationship between the restriction and the need to protect the public from the type of behavior for which the felon was convicted.
>
> Similarly, the courts have recognized that the activities of convicted pedophiles may be subject to regulation in the interest of protecting children.

The newspaper reports focused on the fact that I had ruled that a pedophile clown had the right to perform at Playland and totally ignored the fact that I said he could be barred under a properly drafted regulation. I was portrayed as the bad guy, not the county officials.

This did lead to one amusing incident. Shortly after my decision, Peggy had lunch with her friend and colleague Jane Mickitavage. At some point during the lunch, Jane said, "Peggy, did you see that some judge said that a pedophile could perform at Playland?" Peggy said, "Yes, it was John." Apparently shocked, Jane replied, "Then it must be all right."

Saying that a pedophile clown could perform at Playland was bad enough but the situation was compounded in my final ruling in the case. After my original opinion saying that Hobbs could perform at Playland, the County took my implied advice and adopted a regulation that focused on preventing pedophiles performing acts that would be attractive to children.

My final opinion the case was issued approximately one month before I retired. I ruled that the new regulation that the County had enacted was constitutional and that Mr. Hobbs could be totally barred from performing at Playland. However, in the same opinion, I had to deal with Hobbs' claim that he was entitled to damages because the County had improperly denied him the right to perform at Playland in the years prior to its adoption of the regulation targeting pedophiles. He was right and I reluctantly awarded him $2500 in damages. Although the award was small, the negative public reaction was not.

I would have preferred to end my judicial career on a higher note.

Criminal Cases

Civil cases tend to be the more interesting and complex legally, but criminal cases are the most important in human terms. Every criminal case involves an individual whose life can be affected dramatically, as can as can his or her family's. I recall that when my daughter Meg was in college, she told me about a classmate who had talked about the fact that her family had been dramatically impacted by the fact that her grandfather had gone to jail almost 40 years ago. It is hard to understand what a terrible impact a jail sentence has on the family of the defendant.

Criminal cases take up a good part of a judge's time. There are motions before trial, scheduling conferences, applications for bail, sentencing, and the supervision of defendants on probation or who have been recently released from prison.

Perhaps the most significant responsibility a District Judge has is imposing a sentence on another human being. Before I became a judge, if I asked a judge what the toughest part of the job was, the answer was almost always sentencing. In those days, a judge had wide discretion to impose a sentence anywhere in range that could be as broad as from 0 to 20 years. All of that changed at about the time I became a judge. Congress established a system pursuant to which judges were required to impose a sentence within guidelines established by a Sentencing Commission.

This system was adopted because the discretion given to sentencing judges prior to the guidelines often resulted in substantial disparities, with two offenders with similar records getting substantially different sentences simply because they were sentenced by two different judges. The problem was real, but the remedy was worse. To boil it down to its essence, the guideline system that was adopted ensured that there would be no disparity by imposing equally unjust sentences on large groups of offenders.

The basic problem with guideline sentencing is that there is such a wide variety of factors that have to be considered in imposing a just sentence that is impossible to develop a system that appropriately accounts for each of the variables.

Among its major problems were that the sentencing guidelines, in accounting for the seriousness of the offense, tended to put too much weight on things like the quantity of narcotics involved in the crime or the dollar value of a fraud.

Pedro Lara

The problem with putting too much stress on the quantity of narcotics that was attributable to a defendant's conduct is demonstrated by the case of Pedro Lara, a narcotics dealer who went to trial before me. Lara was part of the crew of a major drug dealer named Maximo Genao. Because Lara's case is such a good example of the problems with the sentencing guideline system, I am setting forth at some length the beginning of my opinion on the sentencing issues raised:

In this case, the Government is seeking to have the Court impose lengthy guideline and mandatory minimum sentences on relatively low-level drug dealers. The factual record before the Court clearly demonstrates the injustice that results from a system that has the sentence of a defendant predetermined by people who have never seen the defendant, know nothing of the defendant's background and are unaware of the particular factual circumstances of his crime.

The draconian sentences mandated for drug dealers are adopted to punish a stereotypical drug dealer, such as those described in the following excerpt from the Congressional record: 'They live in the fast lane. They drive big cars — usually several — like BMWs and Mercedeses ... They like gold. Big gold chains and big gold diamond rings ... They spend most of their money on themselves and their women. 134 Cong. Rec. S3127 (1988) (Sen. Graham).

While harsh mandatory minimum and guideline sentences are totally appropriate for such high-level drug dealers, they all too often are applied to people such as the defendants in this case, whose lives are far from those described above.

For approximately six and one-half months, Lara worked twelve hours a day, six days a week and was paid $500 per week (or $6.95 per hour) for his efforts. While there is a semantic dispute as to whether Lara should be considered a "manager" of the spot or a "look out," there is no substantial dispute as to what his role was. Lara took bundles of crack prepared by other members of Genao's organization, delivered them to "pitchers" who sold them on the street, looked out for the cops while the sales were taking place, and then collected the proceeds from the pitchers and delivered them to another member of Genao's organization.

On the basis of this conduct, the pre-sentence report presently before the Court calculates Pedro Lara's offense level under the Sentencing Guidelines as 38, which would require the Court to sentence Pedro Lara to jail for 19 years and 7 months, with no possibility of parole.

In the opinion that followed, I pointed out a serious flaw in the narcotics guidelines was that it placed too much weight on the quan-

A Life Begun on Third Base

tity of drugs involved without considering the time it took to distribute that quantity. I doubt that anyone would dispute that the people who deal in large quantities of narcotics deserve greater punishment than street-level dealers. Indeed, law enforcement places a priority on investigating those who deal in kilogram level quantities of drugs. However, because he was part of a conspiracy with the drug leader, Maximo Genao, Lara, who never distributed more than 25 grams of crack in any one day, had his guideline sentence based on the 7.3 kilograms of crack distributed by the Genao organization over a six-month period.

Under the Guidelines, a judge can impose a sentence lower than that mandated by the guideline if the judge finds that there is some factor present in the case before him that was not "adequately considered" by the Sentencing Commission in setting the guideline. In the Lara case, I said that the Sentencing Commission had not adequately considered the relationship between the quantity of drugs sold and the time period over which that quantity was sold. It thus made major violators and street-level dealers equal, which was irrational.

Under the guideline calculation urged by the government, which would have made Lara responsible for all of the drugs distributed by the Genao organization, the sentence would have been 235 months, or more than 19 1/2 years. Because I was willing to depart from the guideline, I sentenced Lara to only 10 years in jail. While even this sentence seemed harsh, 10 years was the mandatory minimum sentence provided by Congress and I was compelled to impose it.

Since the question of whether I could depart from the guidelines was one I knew would be controversial, I did so only after raising the possibility with the parties, hearing oral argument and writing an opinion setting forth my conclusions and the sentence I would impose. Thus, when it came to the actual sentencing, Pedro Lara knew exactly what sentence I would impose. When asked whether he wanted to address the court before sentence was imposed, Lara said, in substance, that he had discussed my opinion with other prisoners in the MCC and he knew he was very lucky to be sentenced by such a wonderful judge. I am sure that other defendants who I sentenced more harshly did not think I was wonderful. However, it was satisfying to know that I had done something that made life a little better for someone else. I often wonder whatever happened to Pedro Lara?

Other Sentencing Cases

Another good example of the unfairness in our sentencing system also involved a low-level crack dealer. I do not recall his name but he was an addict who had been arrested making a street-level sale. He had been released on bail and the case lingered for a period of time. By the time it came to sentencing, the defendant had cleaned up his act, was off drugs, had a wife and child he was supporting and had not been involved in any narcotics activity for well over a year. Given total discretion, I probably would not have sentenced him to jail but rather placed him on probation for a substantial period, with a warning that, if he went back to drugs, he would go to jail. Unfortunately, I had no discretion, and was therefore forced to impose a mandatory minimum five-year jail sentence. I thought it was totally unjust and I told the defendant so when I imposed the sentence. I also said that I hoped that he would not let the unfairness of the sentence cause him to become bitter and to revert to the drug life after he was released from prison. I am willing to bet that he did not.

The problem created by the drug guidelines' reliance on drug quantity as a major factor in calculating sentencing was similar to the problem in fraud cases where the guidelines relied too heavily on the dollar value of the fraud. A good example of this is provided by a number of cases I had involving food stamp fraud.

People who receive food stamps can only use them to purchase food in grocery stores. As might be expected, some food stamp recipients desire to use the food stamps for other purposes. The cases to which I refer all originated in Chinese restaurants in poor neighborhoods and involved purchases of food stamps for cash by the owners or managers of the restaurants. The food stamps could not be used in restaurants, the restaurant owners could not cash them or deposit them and so a system developed where they would pass up the food stamps through their supply chain. Ultimately someone, usually a Chinese immigrant, who was induced to do so by others, would open up a sham grocery store with only a few and often outdated products on the shelves. These store owners would end up depositing over $1 million in food stamps to their bank accounts, which was often more than what the neighborhood supermarket would deposit.

The way the chain worked, the food stamp recipient might receive only $0.50 on the dollar for the food stamps, and as they were passed up the line, the various intermediaries would pay increased percentages of the dollar value. The owner of the sham grocery store at the end of the chain would usually pay approximately 97% of the value of the food stamps that were ultimately deposited.

Most of the cases that came before me involved sham grocery store owners who had deposited over $1 million of food stamps into their bank accounts. Since the fraud guideline gave great weight to the dollar value of the fraud, the sham grocery store owners I sentenced generally received between 2 1/2 and 3 1/2 years in jail.

Finally, I had a case involving a Chinese restaurant owner. The owner had purchased food stamps from an undercover agent. On the second occasion, when the agent went back to make another undercover sale, he was told that the man he was looking for was not there. On the third occasion, he went back and made another sale of food stamps and the defendant gave him his cell phone number so he could be contacted in the future. Because there were only undercover sales involved, the total dollar value of the food stamps purchased by the restaurant owner was less than $1000 and therefore his guideline range was only zero to six months.

Having had to sentence several sham grocery store owners to 2 1/2 to 3 1/2 years, I was outraged that the restaurant owner could receive probation. It seemed to me that the restaurant owner, who engaged in his conduct knowing it was illegal and solely out of greed, was more culpable than the immigrants who had been persuaded to open the sham grocery stores so that the food stamps could be deposited. I therefore gave the parties notice that I was considering departing upward in this case because, in my view, the guidelines did not adequately consider the culpability of those who ultimately bore the primary responsibility for the food stamp fraud.

Since the government had entered into a plea agreement with the defendant in which they agreed that the appropriate guideline sentence range was zero to six months, and that they would not urge any greatest sentence, the government took the position that I should impose sentence within that range as did the defendant. I ended up saying that the guideline range in this case did not adequately consider the fact that this defendant was a regular dealer in food stamps, as evidenced by the two purchasers, his giving a cell phone number to the undercover agent so he could be reached in the future and by the fact that, on the one occasion he was not present, the agent was told the person you need for this is not here. I said, since he was in the business of buying food stamps, there should be some enhancement of his sentence similar to that provided in the guidelines for people who are regular dealers in stolen goods. As I recall, adding that four point enhancement to the guideline calculation for the defendant increased the possible sentence range to over a year. I do not recall the specific sentence I imposed but it was imposed on the basis of my calculation, not the range stipulated in the plea agreement.

The defendant appealed my sentence. At the time the US Attorney was my friend and former colleague in the office Mary Jo White. Since the office had entered into the plea agreement that said that the government would not urge any higher sentence, Mary Jo concluded that the government would not support my position in the Court of Appeals. Thus the case went to the Court of Appeals with only the defendant's argument challenging my decision.

In what I still consider an intellectually dishonest decision, the Circuit Court issued a memorandum order, which could not be considered as precedent for other cases under the rules of the court, in which it found that my factual determination that the defendant was a regular dealer in food stamps was "clearly erroneous" — a standard that basically says there was no reasonable basis for my finding. I continue to strongly disagree.

Probably my most dramatic moment in court was a result of another unjustified guideline. One of the criminal cases which I was assigned involved a narcotics and gun conspiracy in which approximately 15 people were charged. The defendants were arrested and bail was set before the case was assigned to me and none of the defendants, most of whom were being held in custody, asked me to modify the bail status.

After I had the case for a number of months, a female defendant was brought before me with an application to change her plea from guilty to not guilty. In the process of accepting her guilty plea, I was required to ask what she did that made her guilty of the crime to which she was pleading guilty. She said she was home with her husband one night when they were visited by a friend, whom they did not know was cooperating with the government. The friend asked her husband if he knew where he could get a gun and the husband said he did. The defendant then drove her husband and the friend to a location where someone else sold the gun to the informant.

At that point I said to the Assistant United States Attorney, "is that all this woman did as part of this conspiracy." He responded it was and I asked what was the sentence range she was facing. I recall he said it was approximately three years. I then asked how long she had already been in jail and was told seven months. I said that we should begin talking about bail because when I eventually got the pre-sentence report several months later, I would in all likelihood determine that this was a case where a departure from the guidelines was justified and I would not impose a sentence of anything more than the time already served. As we began to discuss the amount of bail, it took some time for the woman to realize that we were talking about her going home to her three children. When she realized this, she began to cry. She went home that night and when the time of sentencing came, I imposed time served. It was another case that made me feel good about what I was doing.

There was a similar situation in a food stamp case. In that case, the woman was married to a store owner who was buying food stamps for cash at a discounted price and depositing them at full value. According to the government, the wife had occasionally made the bank deposits. She was facing 3 1/2 years in jail. Once again, I departed on the ground that the guidelines did not adequately consider the minimal role that this defendant played in her husband's operation and gave her a six month sentence.

This highlights a problem which, I believe, has been exacerbated by the laudable goal of treating women equally with men. I had no problem sentencing a woman who knowingly engaged in insider trading to the same sentence a man would receive for the crime. However, when we are sentencing women from lower economic circumstances who, with her children, depend for support on a drug dealer with whom she lives, treating the man and the woman equally does not do justice. Under our mandatory minimum sentences, a woman who moves in with a drug dealer who becomes the major support of herself and her children will have to be sentenced to the same mandatory minimum sentence he would receive if the drug dealer asks her to take messages from his associates. This is true even though it is evident that, on her own, she would never have instituted a drug transaction or become involved in a drug conspiracy. I know of a woman who was sentenced to life plus thirty-five years because she helped her boyfriend in his drug operation. Treating her "equally" was not treating her fairly.

Because of my experience as a prosecutor and defense lawyer for over thirty years, I have a stronger sense of the injustice in our sentencing system then many of my colleagues. Judges who had only handled civil cases in private practice often do not have the experience to recognize how unjust many of the guideline sentences are, or to appreciate the fact that there is some flexibility to depart from the guideline sentence. I recall discussing a particular sentence with a colleague who was surprised when he heard that I had departed from the guideline sentence. He was not aware that anyone was doing that. To remedy that situation, I asked all of my colleagues to send me a copy of the judgment of conviction in any case in which there was a departure from the guidelines. I then circulated those documents to the other members of the court so they would have some sense of what other judges were doing.

One of the most egregious sentencing cases I had involved a crack distribution conspiracy in which a defense lawyer asked that the trial of his client be deferred until after the other defendants were sentenced. When asked what reason would justify such a deferral, he said, if the other defendants had been tried and convicted, they would be willing to testify that his client was not part of any conspiracy. I asked the Assistant United States Attorney what this defendant's role in the conspiracy was. He said this defendant, who was an addict, would sit on a stoop outside an apartment building and, if anyone asked him where they might buy crack, he would tell them of the defendants' operation in one of the apartments. As a reward for this activity, the defendants would occasionally give him some crack for his personal use. I asked what the guideline was and was told it was in the range of sixteen years but that was not relevant since the defendant faced a twenty-year mandatory minimum sentence. I granted the application. For reasons I do not recall, this defendant's case went to another judge, who when he learned of the sentence the defendant was facing, found some reason to suppress the evidence against him and the case was dismissed. Twenty years in jail for sitting on a stoop and answering a question; the system is irrational.

Sentencing involves more that the imposition of a term of imprisonment. Often the Judge speaks for the community in expressing outrage at the crime committed. Over the years, I learned to temper that moral outrage. There is one case where I particularly regretted a statement I made at sentencing.

The defendant was a narcotics dealer who had been convicted of murdering two other rival dealers. At his sentencing I made some statement about what an evil person he was for doing this. He replied in substance, it is easy for you to say but if I hadn't killed them, they would have killed me.

It made me realize, in words Pope Francis would later use with respect to homosexuals, "who am I to judge?" While it may be important to enforce certain laws, like the laws against narcotic distribution, we should not become overly self-righteous. I ultimately recognized that no drug dealer that I sentenced had turned down an offer to be an investment banker in order to take up a career as a drug dealer. The sad fact was that almost every narcotics violator whose plea I accepted responded to my question "how far do you go in school?" with the answer "10th grade." They never had a chance.

King Blood

The most vicious individual ever to come before me was Luis Felipe, also known as King Blood. Felipe, who was born in Cuba, came to the United States in 1980 as part of the Mariel Boatlift, an exodus sanctioned by Fidel Castro that included many people recently released from prison.

Within a year of arriving in the United States, Felipe was convicted of attempted murder and sentenced to nine years in prison. While in prison, he started the New York chapter of the Latin Kings, an organization that had been founded in 1940. The organization said its purpose was to foster Hispanic pride but under Felipe's leadership, it became a violent criminal gang.

During a subsequent period of incarceration, Felipe began ordering the series of murders that ultimately led to his conviction before me. Even though his correspondence was being monitored, those monitoring the mail did not realize that when Felipe said "José Rodriguez TOS," he was saying, terminate José Rodriguez on sight. As a result, using his correspondence and contacts with visitors and other inmates, Felipe orchestrated the murder of at least three individuals, one of whom was beheaded, and the attempted murder of six others.

When it became time for me to impose sentence, I was determined Felipe should not again have the ability to order murders from his jail cell. I decided to impose several special conditions on his incarceration that would later become highly controversial.

A Life Begun on Third Base

At the outset of the sentencing I said that, even though I did not believe in the death penalty, I would have imposed it if it had been available because that would be the only way to ensure that Felipe did not order more murders in the future. To prevent that from happening, I imposed the following conditions: 1) Felipe was to be held in solitary confinement and have no contact with other prisoners; 2) he could only have visits from his attorney and close family members; 3) he could only correspond with his attorney and close family members; and 4) none of these conditions of confinement could be changed without my prior approval.

I did not know at the time that Felipe did not have close family members and, therefore, there was no one but his lawyer who could visit him or correspond with him. When his lawyer made a motion for me to reconsider the sentence, I did give permission for him to receive correspondence from three additional individuals, but required that all correspondence had to be monitored.

As noted, the sentence was unique and controversial. Although some critics thought I imposed it as a punitive measure, my only concern was the safety of individuals who might become the victim of Felipe's wrath. All of the conditions that I imposed were sustained on appeal.

Looking back fifteen years, I have no regrets about the sentence imposed. I recognize it was as severe a sentence as I could have been imposed in the absence of the death penalty. Although the decision was criticized in an article in the *New York Times*, the article was a thoughtful discussion of a difficult decision and I recommend it. A link to that article is set forth below.

https://www.nytimes.com/1997/10/26/nyregion/testing-limits-punishment-unusually-severe-life-sentence-vs-society-s-need-for.htm

I learned of one unforeseen consequence of my decision to impose a sentence of life in solitary confinement from my son John. Sometime after my decision, when John was clerking for a federal judge in Chicago who had a death penalty case, the defense lawyer asked the judge to include in her instructions a description of the sentence that I had imposed so that the jury would see that, if they did not impose the death penalty, there would be no risk that the defendant could kill in the future.

There was one unusual request that was later made by Larry Feitell, the talented and charming lawyer who served as Felipe's assigned counsel. Several years after the sentence was imposed, I received a letter from Larry saying that he had recently learned that there were three other prisoners in the same prison with Felipe who had similar restrictions that prohibited them from having contact with other prisoners. These three prisoners were, however, permitted to exercise at the same time in an open space in the prison. Although they were separated by wire fences, they were allowed to talk to each other and Larry asked that Felipe be allowed to exercise at the same time as they did.

The three prisoners were Timothy McVeigh, who was responsible for the Oklahoma City bombing that killed 168 people, Ted Kaczynski, the "Unabomber," and Ramzi Yousef, the mastermind of the first attack on the World Trade Center. I said that Felipe could exercise with McVeigh and Kaczynski but denied the request to exercise with Ramsey Youssef, because I feared that Youssef might still have contact with members of his organization.

When my ruling was reported in the press, one of the Assistant US Attorneys working on the case was quoted as saying, "I would love to be a fly on the wall at that coffee clatch."

About two weeks after this ruling I received another letter from Larry Feitell. He said he had made his application after he read in the papers about the three prisoners exercising together but without consulting his client. He said that after he wrote to his client to tell him of my decision, he received a return letter in which his client said, "I don't want to exercise with those bombers."

My last involvement with the Felipe case came several years later when I received a call from the US Marshal for the District who said he wanted to come to my chambers to see me. When he arrived, he informed me that an inmate currently incarcerated in the MCC had told the FBI that the Latin Kings had put out a contract on my life. He said that the Marshall Service had investigated it and thought there was nothing to the claim. To this day, I do not understand why the Marshal Service would tell me about an unfounded rumor when they did not intend to provide any special protection. Prior to writing this, I never told my wife or children.

The Decision to Retire

Once a Federal Judge reaches sixty-five and completes a sufficient number of years of service so that the combination of age and years of service total eighty, she or he has several options: 1) He or she can continue to serve as an active judge and make no change in his or her status; 2) He or she can totally retire from the court, return to practice and still receive a pension for life equal to his salary at the time of retirement; 3) He or she can continue to serve as a judge, but assume what is known as "senior status," which requires that the judge do only 25% of the work normally done by an active judge. In this case, the judge will retain chambers, as well as the staff and full salary paid to an active judge; or 4) The judge can fully retire but maintain his status as a judge and can in the future resume a more active judicial career.

When I became a judge, I intended to spend the rest of my life as a judge. Indeed, my former colleague and friend Marty Perschetz often reminds me that as my desk was being removed from Schulte Roth for transportation to my new chambers at the courthouse, I said to him, "The next time that desk gets moved, I will be dead." As it turned out, the desk was moved again and I am still here.

On May 31, 2003 I would turn sixty-seven and have completed thirteen years of service as a judge. As that day approached, I began to contemplate which of the options available to me I would take. Although I had enjoyed my years on the bench, after 13 years the cases were not as exciting and the frustrations presented by our often inflexible sentencing system made me contemplate retirement.

Becoming a judge involved a substantial cut in pay, and the difference between the salary of a District Judge and the compensation of a lawyer in private practice with my experience had grown dramatically. The job had been great fun for me and often exciting, but for my family it involved a degree of financial sacrifice, which although not overwhelming, was real. In the end, I decided that the satisfaction I derived from being a judge was not worth the financial sacrifice of my family. Peggy had always supported me when I opted for public service and she did not in any way attempt to influence me to leave the bench.

I may not have left the bench were it not for actions of Congress that showed utter contempt for the role of judges in the sentencing process. In April 2003, Congress enacted, as an add-on to an otherwise salutary piece of legislation, a provision that became known as the "Feeney Amendments." This legislation placed limits on a judge's ability to depart from a guideline sentence, reduced the number of judges on the Sentencing Commission that set the guidelines and increased the scope of appellate review of sentences. That did it for me.

When I finally decided to retire, I also determined not to go quietly. I prepared an op-ed submission for the *New York Times*. I think each of my children made some contribution to the final draft, which was published in the *New York Times* on June 24, 2003. A copy of that op-ed is available at the following link:

> https://www.nytimes.com/2003/06/24/opinion/let-judges-do-their-jobs.html

After the article appeared, I received a substantial number of letters from those who agreed with me about the injustice in the federal sentencing system. One was from a federal judge in Georgia who wrote in substance: when I was appointed to the bench by President Reagan I thought my job would be to see that criminals would receive strict sentences. So I can't believe that I spent so much of my time trying to find a way not to impose sentences that are overly severe and unfair.

The *Times* subsequently published a very complementary letter from a criminal lawyer who had appeared before me. It left me with the happy feeling that I had earned the respect of those who appeared before me. Here is a link to that letter:

https://www.nytimes.com/2003/07/02/opinion/l-tying-judges-hands-344435.html?referringSource=articleShare

My decision to retire was clearly the right one for me and my family. It enabled me, among other things, to purchase a house in Florida that would become a major venue for family reunions. Every Christmas since the house was purchased, we have had all of our children and grandchildren with us in Florida. To see 18 people who love each other and enjoy being together gathered in one place is richly rewarding for any parent. When I was contemplating selling the house after Peggy died and I was living alone, it was gratifying that my children asked it not be sold and said they would share the burden of maintaining the house after my death because it was so important to the combined family lines.

The only time that I felt any regret that I was no longer a federal judge was after Peggy died. The loneliness resulting from her passing would have been greatly ameliorated if I had the court to go to every day, where I would share my day with my secretary, my law clerks, my courtroom deputy and my colleagues. Nevertheless, on balance, I am very content with the decision.

FOURTEEN

Retirement

Two days after I retired, we purchased a house in Fort Myers Florida. Although I would go back to private practice, I did not intend to work the hours of a full time lawyer. I was primarily interested in developing a practice as an arbitrator and mediator and occasionally serving as an expert witness or a consultant on a major litigation or doing a major internal corporate investigation.

Debevoice & Plimpton

After meeting with several firms, I decided Debevoise & Plimpton would be the best fit. Mary Jo White, who had served as my Chief Appellate Attorney in the US Attorney's office, was a senior partner there and urged me to join her. Since I was not willing to make the commitment to full-time practice, I did not join as a partner but rather I served in a position known as "Of Counsel." The arrangement was that the firm would supply me with an office and secretary as well as access to all of their support staff without any charge to me and would pay me $1000 an hour for time spent working on any of the firm's matters. I would charge the same rate for matters that came directly to me.

One of the things that attracted me to Debevoise was that it had a lockstep compensation system. This meant that throughout their careers all of the lawyers who became partner in the same year would receive equal compensation. In my view is made for a happier working environment because there was no competition among the partners for credit for bringing in a particular piece of business and no reluctance to work on matters generated by other departments.

Although only a few of the matters on which I worked were as high-profile as many of the cases I had as a Judge, I also did not have the heavy docket of routine cases that could be found in the District Court. All of the matters on which I worked were interesting and, given the amount in controversy, the lawyers were always very good.

As I mentioned previously, when you start with a new firm it takes time to build up an inventory of your own matters. At Debevoise, however, Mary Jo had developed a substantial practice involving, among other things, internal investigations. As soon as I began at the firm, I became involved in an internal investigation for a major securities firm.

When I left the Court, I knew I did not want to try another case. The pressure and time commitment of any major trial was something I wanted to avoid. I did, however, end up conducting a one-week trial. A former colleague from the US Attorney's office asked me if I would represent a judge who was the subject of disciplinary proceedings. When he told me the facts, I became convinced that the charges were not warranted and agreed to represent the judge pro bono. Given the confidentiality of such proceedings, I will not set forth the details but I can recount one humorous incident.

The disciplinary hearing was conducted by retired judge of the New York Court of Appeals. In the midst of the hearing the lawyer prosecuting the case asked an improper question. As I often did when an improper question was asked without objection when I was on the bench, I said "objection sustained." Realizing what I had done I looked at the judge and said, "old habits die hard." Fortunately the judge had a sense of humor.

A Life Begun on Third Base

One incident that impressed me involved one of the senior associates who was working with me on a matter, the substance of which I cannot recall. There was a tight time schedule which called for work over the weekend. Despite the fact that he was leaving the firm and starting a new position with the Justice Department the following Monday, Joe Bianco came in to work over the weekend. I was impressed with how responsible he was and delighted, several years later when he was appointed as a District Judge in the Eastern District of New York.

Sony v. Bolton

I was only at Debevoise a month or two when Bruce Cutler, one of the partners who handled copyright matters came to see me. He explained he had been working with an English law firm providing advice on US copyright law on a matter being litigated in England but where the contract said the case should be governed by US law.

The English lawyers had called to say they had now reached the point where they had to pick an expert witness to testify on US law—if a case is being litigated in a foreign country and the contract indicates that the parties have agreed to apply US law to that transaction, US law must be proved like any other fact and therefore the need for an expert.

Bruce told them the timing was good because the judge who had written one of the US copyright cases on which they previously relied in their submissions to the court had just joined Debevoise. The case involved a copyright license known as a Harry Fox license which is explained below. The English firm agreed to retain me to serve as their expert.

The case was fascinating. In 1991, Michael Bolton, a very popular singer, had recorded a song he had co-authored, "Love Is a Wonderful Thing," on an album he did for Sony music. After the song became popular Sony and Bolton were sued by the Isley Brothers, who claimed that Bolton copied a significant portion of that song from a song they had written in 1964 with the same title. A jury had found in favor of the Isley Brothers and awarded $5.4 million in damages. In affirming that decision, the Circuit Court ruled that, even though Bolton might not have consciously copied the much earlier work, the fact that the earlier work had been widely distributed and Bolton admitted that, as a child, he listened to the type of music the Isley Brothers played, this was enough to establish copyright infringement.

Subsequently, Sony brought an action in England against Bolton. They alleged that, in order to record this song on the Sony label, they had to obtain a copyright license from Bolton and his co-author. They argued that, in granting that license, Bolton had impliedly warranted he had the right to license the song and, since this was not true, Sony was entitled to be reimbursed for the money it had to pay to the Isley Brothers.

The question whether Bolton was liable to Sony turned on an arcane area of copyright law. There was no dispute that ordinarily someone who grants a copyright license is representing that he owns the rights that he is licensing and, if that is not true, he will be liable to anyone who was damaged as a result of their use of the particular work. The dispute in the Bolton case was whether Bolton had actually granted a license to Sony and that issue turned on an aspect of copyright law known as a "compulsory license."

The copyright law provides that, if the owner of a copyrighted work allows someone to perform the work, they are compelled to grant a license to anyone else who wants to perform the work. The statute then sets up a rather complex mechanism for determining the license fee that the user will have to pay to the copyright holder.

Because the compulsory license statute is so complex, the music industry has developed its own procedure for dealing with compulsory licenses. The copyright holders have in essence agreed that anyone desiring a compulsory license to perform the work should submit an application to the Harry Fox Agency, which will issue a license granting all the rights that would be available under the compulsory license and collect the licensing fee.

A Life Begun on Third Base

In the Bolton case, Sony had obtained a Harry Fox license in order to make and distribute the album containing the song at issue. The crucial issue then was whether the party whose work is subject to a Harry Fox license is warranting that he owns the work in question.

The law in England makes it very clear that anyone who gives expert testimony is serving as an expert for the court and not for a party and, therefore, has an obligation of total candor. In addition, the experts from each side are required to meet and confer and to narrow as much as possible the areas of dispute.

The expert for Bolton was Paul Goldstein a professor of law at Stanford and the author of one of two leading treatises on copyright law. His position was that all Sony received from Bolton was a compulsory license and since the license was compulsory there was no basis for finding that the composer had made any warranty as to his right to grant the license.

My opinion agreed with Prof. Goldstein that, if the license was a compulsory license there would be no warranty of title because the composer was not granting a license, it was simply being taken from him. However, this was not a compulsory license because Bolton had authorized Harry Fox to issue a license and that license carried with it all of the warranties that were inherent in any other voluntary license.

We will never know who was right because shortly before I was to leave for London to testify, we received an email saying stop everything the parties have settled.

The English Extradition Case

I did get to do an expert opinion that got me a trip to England. I now cannot recall the name of the individual. He was a British businessman, who was the subject of an extradition request from the United States to England. His lawyers asked me to serve as an expert witness in the extradition proceeding in England.

The client had been indicted for participating in a price-fixing conspiracy in United States and for perjury. Price-fixing was not a crime in England and the extradition treaty said a country would not be required to extradite a person if the crime charged was not a crime in England. The United States Justice Department, represented by British counsel, said that price-fixing involved a fraud on customers and, since fraud was a crime in England, extradition should be granted.

I was asked to provide an affidavit that said, while price-fixing may in certain circumstances involve fraud, this indictment did not charge fraud, it charged only price-fixing. If the Prosecutor's believed this price-fixing involved a fraud, they could have brought fraud charges under the federal mail and wire fraud statutes. I also provided an opinion that under the sentencing guidelines, even if the Justice Department agreed not to prosecute the price-fixing, that conduct could be considered as a relevant factor under the sentencing guidelines and thus result in the defendant being punished for the price-fixing.

Peggy and I traveled to England for my testimony in the case which took place in the Bow Street Magistrate's Court. This was particularly interesting for Peggy and me because we had been reading a series of mysteries by Bruce Alexander in which the primary character was Sir John Fielding, a blind judge of the Bow Street Magistrate's Court. Although the books were fiction, they were based on the real life Sir John Fielding, who was a blind judge of the Bow Street Court in the late 1700s.

My testimony was very brief. In England, they have what I considered to be an odd procedure in which the lawyers read the witnesses' affidavit to the judge. My cross-examination was then very brief. But Peggy and I had a very first class vacation in England with all of my expenses paid by the client.

The case went all the way to the highest court in England, which ultimately agreed that the client could not be extradited for price-fixing. Unfortunately for him, the courts found that he could be extradited to answer the perjury charge. I believe that he ultimately pleaded guilty and received a short jail sentence.

A Life Begun on Third Base

Fidelity Investments

Fidelity is one of the largest investment fund managers in the world. As a result of the size of its portfolio, in 2004 its daily trading in the securities markets generated over $800 million in brokerage commissions. A routine audit of a major brokerage firm by the National Association of Securities Dealers uncovered evidence that brokerage firms were spending huge amounts to lavishly entertain traders at investment management firms like Fidelity. This led to an investigation by the SEC and an internal investigation by Fidelity, which ultimately disciplined 16 of its traders.

The Fidelity investigation revealed that a number of its traders had received lavish entertainment, including all expense paid trips to the Super Bowl and Wimbledon on private jets. The gifts and entertainment received by one broker were valued at approximately $500,000. This included payment for his bachelor party, which involved chartered flights to Florida, chartered yachts, expensive hotels and parties that included a dwarf throwing contest in which Velcro vests were placed on dwarfs who were then thrown against padded walls.

Even though it paid an $8 billion fine to the SEC, Fidelity took the position that no harm had been done to the mutual fund shareholders because it had fixed commission rates with its brokers. Whether or not damage had occurred was a question that Debevoise was asked to answer.

Under the regulatory scheme for mutual funds, the funds are required to have an independent Board of Trustees to oversee the conduct of the money manager. Sometime in 2004, one of the partners. who represented the Fidelity Trustees, told me that the firm had been retained to conduct an investigation to determine whether the entertainment of the traders caused financial loss to the funds. I agreed to be part of the Debevoise team.

One of the interesting things about the investigation was that the Chairman of the Trustees was Robert Gates, formerly the head of the CIA and later the Secretary of Defense under Presidents Bush and

Obama. At our first meeting with the trustees, I was not particularly impressed with Gates until the end of the meeting, when he carefully and accurately summarized all of the key points we had made. It was a pleasure to work with him. At the time, he was the President of Texas A&M and every time I had to call him, I would spend some time on hold listening to the Texas A&M fight song.

The investigation was challenging because there was some merit to Fidelity's argument that the funds had not been injured because the commissions paid to the brokers would be the same no matter what brokerage firm was used. After some deliberation, we decided that even though the brokerage commission that the funds paid was ultimately the same as that which would have been paid to a broker who was not providing entertainment, the funds were deprived of the opportunity to have the trades placed with other brokers and might have gotten better execution-the broker might have been able to obtain a higher price for the securities Fidelity was selling or lower price for those it was buying. While the theory was sound, the issue was how do you prove after the fact that better prices could have been obtained..

We retained the services of a consulting firm specializing in economic analysis. They conducted an exhaustive study comparing the prices Fidelity paid on shares purchased and sold by the brokers who were providing entertainment and those obtained when the firm used other brokers. The study provided statistical evidence indicating that Fidelity did pay higher prices when the traders were using the firms which provided entertainment and gifts. As a result of our investigation Fidelity agreed to pay the funds $42 million as compensation for the damages suffered in the trades of the brokers who had been entertained.

Schering Plough

On June 9, 2004 the SEC announced that it had settled an enforcement action against Schering-Plough, a major pharmaceutical company, which it accused of making improper payments to the head of a Polish government health organization to induce him to cause the government to purchase Schering-Plough products. The injunction to which the company consented required it "to retain an independent consultant to review the company's policies and procedures with respect to compliance with the Foreign Corrupt Practices Act and to implement any changes recommended by the consultant." Shortly thereafter, I was retained as that consultant.

The Foreign Corrupt Practices Act (FCPA) prohibits US companies from paying foreign officials to obtain business from the government. While in most circumstances it is clear that any benefit conferred on a foreign government official is prohibited, the pharmaceutical industry raises much more subtle questions.

All over the world, pharmaceutical companies engage product promotion that requires them to provide information to doctors. This requires them to gain access to speak to the doctor and the doctor's staff and also involves providing the doctor's office with promotional material such as pens with the company logo and other minor items of similar nature. It is also not uncommon for the representative to take a doctor to lunch or perhaps bring in food for lunch with the doctor and his or her staff in the office.

Since in many countries around the world, almost all the doctors are government employees, the question that has to be asked is when does normal product promotion rise to the level of an improper payment. In addition to answering that question, a pharmaceutical company must maintain appropriate records and procedures so it can determine whether any employee is violating the company policy against making improper payments to a foreign government official. My job was to help the company establish guidelines and procedures to ensure its employees would not engage in improper activity.

In order to understand how Schering-Plough interacted with doctors throughout the world, we literally had to travel around the world. Our first trip was a two-week trip that started from New York with a direct flight to Tokyo, where we conducted interviews of Schering-Plough employees from not only Japan but other nearby countries. We then flew to Singapore for interviews of people operating in that part of the world, and then flew directly to Milan. After spending a day or two in Milan, we flew to Budapest and ultimately back to New York.

When I later told people I had taken a two week trip around the world, I was often asked whether my wife went with me. My standard answer was, "No. I love her." While traveling first class made the trip less burdensome, flying into a major city and spending several days in an office conducting interviews and then flying on to do the same in another major city was not a vacation.

One of the more memorable incidents occurred when we were in Tokyo interviewing people about the practices in that country. We were told that the only entertaining they did of doctors was that they would bring box lunches for the doctor and his or her staff when they called on the doctor. They insisted that these were not elaborate lunches and they proved it by providing us with similar box lunches for our lunch that day—some of the worst food I've ever had. Two pieces of bread with a lot of mayonnaise and little else between the bread. No one could conceivably find that subjecting the doctor to such a lunch would constitute a bribe.

We later took a one week trip to South America with stops in Chile, Argentina and Mexico City. Once again far from a great vacation. I think that in all of these countries we were accompanied by armed guards. I remember being told in Mexico about one of their employees who visited from the United States. When he stopped at a light, he thought he was being asked the time until he saw the gun and realized that his watch was being stolen. Fortunately we were well protected. It did make me realize how lucky we are to be living in this country.

Vioxx

One of the most interesting investigations I conducted involved the question of whether a scientist at Merck had acted improperly in any way in connection with the company's development and sales of Vioxx, a popular prescription medication for pain.

A Life Begun on Third Base

In September 2004, Merck withdrew Vioxx from the market, despite the fact that it accounted for over 2 1/2 billion dollars in sales. The withdrawal occurred as a result of a clinical trial that Merck was conducting in which the results achieved by people who used Vioxx were being measured against those of a similar group taking a placebo. After the trial had been in process for some time, Merck scientists became concerned because the data indicated a higher incidence of cardiovascular problems in the group taking Vioxx. Although Merck quickly took Vioxx off the market, there were a number of class action lawsuits brought against the company by individuals who claimed they were injured as a result of their use of Vioxx.

As discovery in those actions proceeded, documents were leaked to the press that suggested individuals at Merck were aware of the cardiovascular risk well before the company withdrew Vioxx from the market. In light of these allegations, Merck announced that a committee of its Independent Directors would conduct an investigation to determine whether any of Merck's people had acted improperly in connection with the distribution and sale of Vioxx.

The head of the Independent Directors Committee was William Bowen, a former President of Princeton, whom I met when he was on the Board of American Express when I did work for American Express before I went on the bench. After the Committee was formed, Bill called me and asked if I would conduct the investigation.

The investigation that we conducted lasted for 20 months and involved a team of between 15 and 20 lawyers and ultimately cost Merck $20 million. Our report was 180 pages long and included 20 additional volumes of documents consisting of a total of 1500 pages.

Although pharmaceutical companies are often pictured in the press as greedy and unconcerned about patient safety, the people at Merck with whom we dealt were nothing like the stereotype. The Board of Directors included three highly respected physicians and others who were truly independent. The scientists we interviewed were impressive both for their professional competence and their concern for the public. The then head of research was a highly respected academic who left that world, as he told us, because with a company like Merck he had the ability to accomplish much more good than he could as a research scientist. The man whom he had replaced as the head of research Dr. Scolnick, was one of the most impressive people I ever met.

The question that we had to answer was, did this group of respected scientists turn a blind eye to the danger that Vioxx posed. Our conclusion was that they did not and they acted responsibly as soon as evidence developed that Vioxx might be causing heart problems for those who took it.

One of the clearest indications that the senior officials at Merck were not concerned about the safety of Vioxx was found in the fact that at the time Merck withdrew Vioxx from the market, the General Counsel, the wife of the Chief Executive and the mother of the Director of Research were all taking Vioxx. I recall Bill Bowen saying at the press conference in which we announced the results of our investigation that he was by training and economist and economist work on the basic principle –don't look at what people say, look at what they do.

Yet the news articles questioning Merck's conduct with respect to Vioxx was not idle speculation. There were documents in Merck's files that, taken in isolation, raised questions about the knowledge of the risks posed by Vioxx. Principal among them were a series of internal documents circulated several years before Vioxx was withdrawn when a trial testing the efficacy in alleviating pain of Vioxx and naproxen, the generic of Aleve, indicated that those taking Vioxx were having a greater number of cardiovascular incidents.

When results from that study indicated higher cardiovascular incidents on the Vioxx arm, alarm bells sounded and people wrote emails and memos expressing their concerns. When we interviewed a doctor who was the author of one of the documents that received a substantial amount of publicity, she told us that she was concerned and she went to see Ed Scolnick, the Head of Research, and her boss. When she reiterated her concerns Ed told her he recognized the issue and was looking into it, and she should be assured that, whatever the

A Life Begun on Third Base

results of that inquiry, Merck would do the right thing. At this point in the interview she began to cry and explained that is had been an emotional experience for because she was so concerned at the time and she so relieved when she was assured the company was committed to doing the right thing.

The problem for scientists attempting to assess the effects of two different drugs being used in a test is that you cannot be certain whether a particular effect is a result of a defect in one of the drugs or a beneficial effect of the other drug. After reviewing all of the data from the trial comparing Vioxx and naproxen, Dr. Scolnick concluded that Vioxx was not causing any higher than normal incidents of cardiovascular events but that naproxen, like aspirin, had cardioprotective characteristics.

I am one of many taking baby aspirin every day at the direction of a doctor because aspirin acts as a blood thinner and thereby reduces the risk of blood clots that can cause heart attacks and strokes. If you were to do a study of people taking aspirin and people taking only water, the results would show a higher incidence of cardiovascular problems among the people taking only water. However, that would not mean water causes heart attacks and strokes.

There were many documents in Merck's internal files that evidenced the fact that its scientists honestly believed that Vioxx was not causing an increased risk of cardiovascular events. One of the things that as a layman I could understand was the data that showed that people taking naproxen had a higher incidence of nosebleeds than those taking Vioxx. As someone who had nosebleeds when I was younger, I recognized that a higher number of nosebleeds supported the conclusion that naproxen was acting as a blood thinner and was, therefore, cardioprotective.

Another thing that supported our view that the scientists at Merck would not intentionally expose the users of its products to an unwarranted risk was the fact that when they became aware that there was a risk in a placebo study, they took Vioxx off the market. That occurred when a trial was being conducted that compared Vioxx to a placebo.

When results came in from that trial indicating that people on Vioxx were having more cardiovascular events, Merck quickly assembled a consulting group of leading cardiologists and rheumatologists. The rheumatologist, who regularly prescribed Vioxx to treat the pain caused by arthritis, recommended that Vioxx be kept on the market but with a clear label warning of its risk. The cardiologists, however, urged that it be taken off the market and that is what Merck did.

Years later, I happened to mention this difference between the cardiologist and rheumatologist to a rheumatologist treating me for arthritis. His reaction was quite strong: "That's just like those damn cardiologists, they don't care how much pain you're in as long as you don't die of a heart attack."

Despite the length of our investigation and report and the volumes of supporting documentation, our conclusions were not totally accepted by the press or by juries in class-action lawsuits against Merck. I observed one positive reaction, however, when I watched a news account of our report on the Jim Cramer CNBC television show the night of our press conference. After showing a brief clip of Bill Bowen and I describing our findings, the report switched to a critic saying we were just saying this because were being paid by Merck. At this, Kramer, a Princeton graduate said, "Bill Bowen, a man of his integrity, don't be ridiculous."

The work we did on the Vioxx investigation was truly extraordinary. It was not a tribute to me but rather to the talented and hard-working team of Debevoise partners and associates, headed by Marc Kaplan and Debbie Todres, who did the hard work of digging into the documents and learning the science. It was amazing to see how this group of lawyers who originally knew nothing of the science of Cox-1 and Cox-2 inhibitors, scientific classification of products like aspirin and ibuprofen (Cox-1) and Vioxx and Celebrex (Cox-2) were ultimately able to discuss the issues with top scientists in the field.

There is, again, an epilogue. The panel of consultants who recommended that Merck take Vioxx off the market, rather than leave it in use but with a strong label warning, did so because there were other products like Vioxx on the market, such as Celebrex and there was no evidence that they caused a similar cardiovascular risk. As it turned out later, evidence indicated that these products carry the same cardiovascular risk as Vioxx but they continue on the market with a strong warning because there is no other comparable product.

Arbitrations and Mediations

When I left the Court, I hoped to develop an arbitration and mediation practice. I correctly anticipated that lawyers who had appeared before me and were happy with the results would come to me when I entered private practice.

I had settled hundreds of cases during conferences as a judge and was confident that experience would serve me well as a private mediator. It did not take me long to realize that there was a substantial difference between being the judge settling the case and a private mediator. The main difference was that a lawyer will not lie to a federal judge but few lawyers have compunction about telling the mediator, "we will never pay more than $1 million in this case," and five hours later writing a check for $10 million. You have to learn early to develop techniques that will help you get a better sense of what the parties are willing to do in settlement.

To some extent, I think the ability of parties to settle cases is frustrated by a desire to try to get the most favorable settlement possible. Mediations often fall apart early in the day because one side or the other proposes a number that is so unreasonable that the other party gets mad and walks out. I spent a lot of my time trying to urge parties to make more reasonable offers early in the mediation and was generally met with the response, "then we will have no room to negotiate." My typical response was that no one can put a gun to your head and force you to make a better offer, but, until there is blood in the water, there is not going to be much interest from your adversary.

One of the most interesting mediations I conducted occurred after an unsuccessful mediation in the same case. I received a call from the lawyers saying that after the mediation they continued discussions and now wanted me to become involved again. I forget the precise numbers but what they proposed was something as follows: "we will each give you in confidence a number at which we are willing to settle. If our numbers are within $500,000 of each other, then you can tell us and we will split the difference. If the numbers are a million dollars apart, you will tell us and we will try to negotiate within that range. If we are more than $1 million apart you should tell us no more than that there is no settlement. As it turned out the numbers were within the $500,000 limit and the case settled.

I strongly believe that more mediations would be successful if parties used a similar approach and made a reasonable estimate of what they willing to settle for and went into the mediation willing to put reasonable parameters around the negotiations.

Almost all of the arbitrations were interesting but due to the confidentiality they cannot be discussed in detail. However, a large number of them were insurance coverage cases in which a property owner had a major fire, flood or hurricane damage. Although the businesses differed, the issues were basically the same. An insurer agreed to provide replacement cost for the equipment that was lost and to pay the property owner the profit that was lost during the period that it was out of operation. The problem arose from the fact that a manufacturer whose 30-year-old plant was destroyed by a hurricane is not going to simply replace what was in the 30-year-old plant. New and more modern equipment will be purchased and configured differently because of improvements in the processes. When the insurer gets the bill for the construction of the new plant, the response is, "we are only responsible for replacing what you had and not for improving your plant and it would have cost considerably less if you simply replaced what you had." Similarly, when the manufacturer asked to be compensated for the profits that it lost during the year that it was out of business while it rebuilt the plant, the insurer might say, "if you only replaced what you had, you could have done that in eight months and so we are only liable for eight months of profit."

The thing that made most of these arbitrations interesting is that, in order for you to determine what was a replacement and what was an

A Life Begun on Third Base

improvement in a business you had to learn about the business. As a result, I learned a good deal about the power business, the chemicals business the auto dealership business and many others.

One interesting thing occurred during an arbitration I was conducting in Los Angeles involving contracts for the delivery of electricity. The arbitration lasted two weeks. The last witness called was someone whom I had observed sitting in the conference rooms every day and whom I may have spoken to from time to time at a break, although I had no idea who he was. He was called as an expert witness for one of the parties and the first question that he was asked was, "what is your current job?" His response was something of a shock, "I am president of the Gulf Oil Corporation." Apparently he had been hired by Gulf only several months before and prior to that he had a business as a consultant which is why he was retained as the expert. I was impressed by the fact that, despite the demands of his new job, he was willing to live up to his responsibility as an expert to be present every day during the arbitration so he could comment on all of the evidence presented. At the break I saw him in the hall and said, "I bet you're not very happy to be here." He agreed.

One of the nice things about serving as an arbitrator is that you meet and become friends with some very terrific people who serve with you on an arbitration panel. One of them was Layn Phillips.

Most arbitrations involve three arbitrators— each of the parties select one and those two select the third. Fairly early on in my arbitration practice I was selected by a party to the arbitration and told that the other party had selected Layn Phillips. I looked Layn up on the Internet and found that he had been the US Attorney and a District Judge in Oklahoma, and in each of those positions he had been one of the youngest ever appointed.

I called Layn and asked him who he might suggest as our third arbitrator and the two of us quickly agreed on Charlie Renfrew, another retired federal judge who also served as Deputy Attorney General. After we agreed on Charlie, Layn, who lives in California, said he would be in New York the following week and asked if my wife and I would like to have dinner with him and his wife the Wednesday of that week. I agreed.

On Monday of the following week I had to call another party appointed arbitrator in a different case, Tim Lewis, a former federal judge from Philadelphia. When I asked Tim who we would suggest as our chair, he said, "My go to guy in something like this is Layn Phillips. Do you know him?" I replied, "No, but I'm having dinner with him and his wife in New York on Wednesday."

The case with Tim settled without any major involvement of the arbitration panel but Layn and I served on three arbitration panels in which the case went through hearings of a week or two. Peggy and I had dinner with them many times over the course of the years and it was always a delight.

Martin & Obermaier II

In the early fall of 2006 I met with John Kiernan and Mary Jo White, the co-head's of the litigation department and told them that, as much as I like working with the firm, I was planning to leave to set up as a sole practitioner. The reason for my decision was that Debevoise had such an extensive practice that I often had to decline arbitrations and mediations because one of the parties was or had been a client of Debevoise. No party to an arbitration or mediation wants to place the fate of its case in the hands of someone who has had a close relationship with the adversary. John and Mary Jo said they were sorry to see me leave but they did understand.

The first thing I had to do was get office space, so I called my former partner Bob Morvillo and asked him if the firm had a spare office I could rent. He said that they did and also that an old lawyer named Otto Obermaier who was facing mandatory retirement at Weil Gotshal also wanted to rent an office.

Otto had left Obermaier Morvillo & Abramowitz to replace my successor Rudy Giuliani as United States Attorney for the Southern

District of New York. When he resigned from that position in 1993 he had joined Weil Gotshal, one of the larger law firms in New York.

One amusing incident resulted from Otto's selection as US Attorney. Selecting the US Attorney is generally the prerogative of the Senator of the President's party in the state. When Rudy heard that Senator D'Amato was recommending Otto, he tried to sabotage Otto's appointment, which caused a falling out between Rudy and the Senator. Although D'Amato did not force me out when I left the Us Attorney's office, he certainly indicated that he would be happy if I would leave early.

Sometime after Otto was appointed and Rudy and D'Amato had their falling out, I ran into D'Amato at some social event. He greeted me and said, "You know John, if you had only served out your full four-year term as US Attorney—as you will recall I wanted you to do—I would not have had all of these problems with that little prick, Giuliani." He laughed.

The launching of Martin & Obermaier II in November 2006, sparked an article in the New York Law Journal about the reunion of two former US Attorneys. The article contained a quote from Bob Morvillo, which I think captures his personality pretty well. When asked what he thought of our reunion, Bob said, "This is great. Now when I get pissed off at my partners, I can go downstairs and we will be Martin Obermaier & Morvillo again and when I get pissed off at them I can go back upstairs to my firm." Unfortunately, Bob would die a few years later.

When we formed Martin & Obermaier in 1972, it was a truly equal partnership—we each took 50% of the profits no matter who had generated the business. When we reunited in 2006, neither Otto nor I wanted a profit-sharing partnership because neither of us intended to work full time and did not want to be under any pressure to try to hold up our end of the firm. Therefore, our partnership was simply an agreement to share the cost of a secretary and the other expenses necessary to support our activities.

JOHN S. MARTIN JR.

United States v. Stein

Although Otto and I worked independently most of the time, there was one major matter on which we worked together. In 2007, we were contacted by several friends from the defense bar, each of whom represented an individual who had been employed by the accounting firm KPMG—a successor to Peat Marwick & Mitchell, where Tony Natelli had been a partner. Their clients had recently had an indictment against them dismissed and they wanted Otto and I to jointly write the brief in opposition to the government's appeal from that order and for me to argue the appeal. We agreed.

The case was extremely interesting and we ultimately prevailed but it placed a strain on my relationship with at least one Assistant United States Attorney who had worked with me when I headed the office. The case also illustrates a problem that exists in many cases, which is that different people in a meeting can emerge from that meeting with different impressions of what was said.

The case centered on the question of whether the government had the right to tell an organization under investigation that it would not look favorably upon that organization if it paid the legal fees of its employees who were the subjects of the investigation. This can be a very difficult choice for an organization, which may believe the protestations of innocence by the individuals the government is investigating but does not want to jeopardize its ability to persuade the government that, whatever the individuals may have done, the organization should not be charged criminally. This pressure is exacerbated by the fact that the conviction of an organization can have collateral consequences that could force it out of business—this happened to Arthur Anderson, a major accounting firm that went out of business after it was criminally prosecuted.

The factual dispute in Stein centered on a series of meetings between the lawyers for KPMG and the Assistant United States Attorneys working on the case, including Shira Neiman, a career prosecutor who had served under me as Chief of the Major Crimes Unit and was a person for whom I had great respect and affection. During these meetings there were discussions focused around a memorandum prepared by Larry Thompson in 2003 when he was Deputy Attorney General which outlined the factors that prosecutors should consider in determining whether to indict an organization. The memorandum directed the prosecutors to inquire, "whether the corporation appears to be protecting its culpable employees ... either through the advancement of attorney's fees, through retaining the employees without sanction ..."

Precisely what was said at the meetings between the KPMG lawyers and the prosecutors will never be known but, after one of those meetings, one of the lawyers for KPMG wrote a memo stating, "[paying] legal fees" and "severance" ... Not a sign of cooperation."

The testimony and documents produced at a hearing conducted by the trial judge, Lou Kaplan, a friend and highly respected District Court Judge, persuaded him that the government had told the KPMG lawyers that if they continued to pay the legal fees of its employees, that fact would be considered against them in determining whether the firm itself would be indicted. He ruled that by persuading KPMG not to pay the attorneys fees of its partners and employees, the government deprived the defendants of the right to counsel and dismissed the indictment against them.

Otto and I had great fun working together on the brief and, along with able counsel for some of the other indicted KPMG employees, were able to persuade the Second Circuit to affirm Lou Kaplan's ruling. I learned through the grapevine that Shira was mad at me because she perceived me as arguing that her testimony that she had not tried to coerce KPMG to not pay the attorneys' fees was false. Knowing Shira I never believed, nor did I argue, that she gave false testimony. I am convinced that she and the other prosecutors never appreciated how defense lawyers might construe statements that the prosecutors believed were relatively benign. I was reminded of a line of Thurgood Marshall when as a law clerk a group of us were discussing a coerced confession and Thurgood said, "if you want to know whether a confession was coerced, just tell me, how big was the cop." It is a good reminder that we have to remember that what we say may often be construed in a manner that we did not intend.

Dennis Kozlowski

Dennis was the perfect whipping boy for journalists and others critical of the pay and benefits many major corporations bestow on the chief executives. How much to compensate a CEO who generates billions of profits for a company is an extremely difficult issue. In the hedge fund industry, fund managers usually charge investors what is commonly referred to as "2 and 20." Investors must pay the manager annually an amount equal to 2% of the amount of the investment and, in addition, the manager is entitled to retain 20% of the profits generated for the funds. That is why many hedge fund managers become billionaires.

Compared to hedge fund managers, many executives who generate billions of dollars of profits for the company may feel under compensated. In the case of Dennis Kozlowski, he generated billions in profit for his company, Tyco and he and his chief financial officer took bonuses of over $200 million in a two year period. Dennis also caused the company to buy and furnish a lavish apartment in Manhattan—one of the more famous items purchased for that apartment by the company was a $6,000 shower curtain. The company also purchased a yacht and bore one half of the $2 million expense of an elaborate birthday party for his wife on the island of Sardinia, which featured an ice sculpture of Michelangelo's David urinating Stolichnaya vodka and a concert by Jimmy Buffett.

Kozlowski was indicted and convicted of defrauding the company of hundreds of millions of dollars that he had received as compensation, either as bonuses or the payment of personal expenses such as fine art. Dennis testified in his own behalf and admitted that his compensation might be considered excessive but he denied doing anything improper. In his view, the huge bonuses he received were appropriate under the company's policies and to the extent any personal item might have been paid by the company it was merely a book-keeping error. His version of events was contradicted by members of the company's Board of Directors, who denied having any knowledge of many of the bonuses paid to Kozlowski or of his maintenance of an elaborate corporate apartment for his use. The jury accepted the testimony of the prosecution witnesses and Dennis was convicted in September 2005.

Dennis had been represented at trial by Steve Kaufman, my old boss in the US Attorney's office, and Austin Campriello, who had worked with me on the short-lived Martin Commission. They asked me if I would work with them on the appeal and present the oral argument. I agreed.

By the time I was retained Dennis was already imprisoned in Marcy, New York, about a four hour drive from the city. Steve, Austin I drove up there so I could meet Dennis and discuss the appeal. He was very pleasant and an easy client to deal with. Imprisonment was particularly difficult for him because he was being held is a very small group of prisoners who could not be let into the general population for fear that they would be extorted or attacked. This former multimillionaire was working in the laundry.

Although we had some reasonable arguments as to why his conviction should be reversed, we were unable to persuade either the Appellate Division or New York's highest court, the Court of Appeals. Dennis was released from prison in 2014 and currently has residences in New York, Nantucket and Florida. He's been active in the Fortune Society and serves on the board of the Women's Prison Association.

The appeal in the Kozlowski case had one particular benefit for me. In 2006 I had hip replacement surgery, which required me to be home for six weeks. It was during that period that I wrote a large part of the appellate brief. I was working at home well before the coronavirus.

The World Trade Center Property Damage Cases

The World Trade Center case that I handled as a judge involved claims by the leaseholder, Silverstein Properties, against its insurers for the damage done to the buildings. This was just one of a number of World Trade Center cases arising from the terrorist attack. Another major case involved claims made by insurers who had paid claims for property damage of businesses that had been operating in the World Trade Center. The law permits what is known as a subrogation claim, which allows an insurer that has paid its insured for an injury it sustained as a result of wrongful conduct by a third party to sue that third party in the name of its insured.

A group of the insurers who paid claims to businesses in the Center brought negligence claims against American and United Airlines and their security companies, claiming that their negligence allowed the terrorists on the plane and as a result they should be liable for the property damage those terrorists caused. In addition, a few of the businesses in the Trade Center who were uninsured brought similar claims. In total, the plaintiffs were seeking $4.4 billion in damages.

Since the insurers who had brought this lawsuit had actually paid the damages suffered by the businesses they insured, Al Hellerstein, the judge to whom the case was assigned, suggested to the lawyers that they try to agree on the amount of damages the insurers might recover if they prevailed, so that any trial could be limited to the issue of liability. When the parties agreed with his proposal, he suggested that they agree upon an individual to serve as a Special Master for the settlement discussions. I was selected for that role.

Although on the surface it seemed reasonable that the parties should be able to agree upon the issue of damages, since the insurers had paid the damages they were claiming, the issue was complicated due to a major difference between tort law and the terms of the insurance policies. The term tort simply refers to any wrongful act that gives rise to a claim for damages. An easy example is a negligent driver who causes an accident. His negligent operation of his car is a tort and anyone injured can recover the damages that were caused.

The problem in the Trade Center case was that someone injured by a tort is only entitled to recover "the fair market value" of the property damaged. However, the insurers' contracts with the businesses they insured obligated them to pay "the cost to replace" the damage property. The difficulty in reconciling these two standards is demonstrated by the following example.

There were brokerage firms located in the World Trade Center whose offices were totally destroyed, including highly sophisticated computer systems. The insurers had paid the cost of acquiring a totally new computer system but, under tort law, they were only entitled to recover the fair market value of a computer system that was five years old. What is a five-year-old computer system worth?

The above is simply one example of a vast number of items of used equipment and furnishings that had to be replaced. Over the course of several months, I had meetings with the large group of lawyers involved and their valuation experts trying to come to some agreement on the myriad of valuation issues involved. There was virtually no success in getting the parties to agree upon any of the valuation issues. However, the parties ultimately agreed that they should abandon the valuation exercise and attempt to reach an overall settlement with me as the mediator.

What was particularly unusual about the World Trade Center property damage case was that it was basically a dispute in which insurance companies were suing insurance companies and, in some instances, suing themselves. After the World Trade Center attack, Congress had limited the airlines' liability for any damage claims arising from the terrorist attack to the total amount of insurance that was available to pay such claims. Thus, the insurers who were suing because they paid claims to business owners were suing other insurers who had provided insurance to the airlines and their security companies. In many cases, the insurers were suing themselves because they had insured both the airlines and some of the businesses operating in the World Trade Center. In light of this fact, all of the insurance companies agreed that they should make a real effort to settle the case, among other things to put an end to the extensive legal fees they were incurring in the litigation.

The mediation sessions took place over a two-week period. One of the interesting things was that normally it would have been one room for all the plaintiffs and their lawyers and a second room for the defendants and their lawyers. In this case there was a third room for one of the insurers who had such a large percentage of both the plaintiffs' claims and potential liability, that neither the plaintiffs nor the defendants wanted this insurer to be part of their settlement discussions.

There were approximately 40 to 50 people present for each side and the issues were very difficult. As noted, the parties were far apart on the total amount of damages that would be recovered if the plaintiffs were successful and there were difficult legal questions concerning the airlines' liability for the acts of the terrorists.

As with most mediations, there were times when I thought we were getting close to a settlement and then there would be a development that made a potential settlement difficult. Near the end of the second week I thought we were close to a settlement but it blew up when not everyone was willing to go along. I finally decided to make a "mediator's proposal."

It is not unusual at the end of a mediation that has not been successful for the mediator to propose a settlement to the parties. I had done this often, not only in mediations, but it hundreds of settlement conferences as a judge. The goal of the mediator's proposal is to provide a settlement amount that each side is willing to accept. This is not simply a "why don't we split the baby?" proposal. The art of settlement involves finding a number that is as little as the plaintiff will accept and the most that the defendant will pay. To make a viable recommendation the mediator has to carefully assess all that is been said in the mediation in light of his own assessment of the likely outcome and then make a recommendation.

My recommendation that the matter settled for $1.2 billion was accepted. However, that did not end the matter. There was still an issue as to how that money would be allocated among the plaintiffs and how much of the $1.2 billion would be paid by each of the defendants.

A Life Begun on Third Base

The allocation among the defendants was not difficult. However, the allocation among the plaintiffs was complicated by the fact that the insurers' plaintiffs had controlled the mediation process but the settlement amount also had to be shared by the uninsured businesses who were also part of the plaintiff group. These were typically small businesses, such as a newsstand or small restaurant, whose claims were important to the business owner but only a minor part of the total overall claims.

Since the $1.2 billion settlement amount was a 72% discount from the total claims of $4.4 billion, it was decided that each of the uninsured businesses would be offered 72% of the amount that it was claiming. I therefore participated in discussions with each of those business owners urging them to accept 72% of their claim. These were difficult discussions because to these uninsured businesses, their recovery was much more important than it was to the major insurers who asserted claims. Although I was sympathetic to these small claimants, they would have had virtually no chance of recovery if they did not participate in the settlement. If the defendants had settled solely with the insurer plaintiffs and agreed to continue the litigation with the uninsured plaintiffs, those plaintiffs could not afford the costs of going forward. They simply had to take whatever they could get. Thus, although the settlement for much less than their claim was not adequate compensation for their loss, it was more than they would have recovered after deducting the cost of going forward with the litigation. For the small business owner the settlement was not ideal but it was practical.

BP

On April 20, 2010 a drilling platform in the Gulf of Mexico exploded killing 11 workers and injuring 94 others and starting an oil leak that would become one of the greatest environmental disasters in history. In the three months that followed, 220 million gallons of oil spread across the Gulf and contaminated beaches, rivers and wildlife. By early June, the oil spread reached 125 miles of the coastline from Florida to Texas

On June 16, 2010, President Obama met with BP executives who agreed to set up a $20 billion trust fund to compensate those who had been injured as a result of the oil spill. Within a few weeks of that meeting, I received a call from lawyers representing BP who explained that they were in the process of recommending individuals to serve as trustees of the $20 billion trust and asking if they could submit my name to the Justice Department. I agreed, and not long thereafter, Kent Syverud and I were selected as the trustees. At the time Kent was the Dean of the law school at Washington University in St. Louis. He later would become the Chancellor of Syracuse University.

Kent was a delightful individual to work with and well organized. He quickly arranged for several of his colleagues on the law school faculty to serve as advisors and recommended Mark Templeton to serve as our Executive Director. I doubt that, on my own, I would have had the wisdom to recognize the need for someone like Mark. He was a it was tremendous help to us in coordinating our work with BP.

The job of the Trustees was not to play any role in determining who was to be compensated or the amount of their compensation. That function would be carried out by Ken Feinberg, a former AUSA who had administered a fund that had been used earlier to successfully compensate veterans who had been injured by exposure to agent orange.

Our major job as trustees was to negotiate with BP the terms of the trust. BP had agreed with the President to establish the trust but how it would be structured and how its commitment of $20 million was to be guaranteed were to be the subject of negotiations with the trustees.

By the time we became involved, BP had agreed to put up $3 billion immediately and to pay another $2 billion into the trust in early 2011. BP committed to pay the trust $5 billion in each of the next four years. The question was how this obligation for the additional $17 billion was to be secured.

The proposal that BP made, and as I recall, had been agreed to by the Justice Department, was that BP would secure its obligation by giving the trust interests in its oil and gas production from various producing wells in the Gulf of Mexico. Thus, this kid from Brooklyn was going to have to become knowledgeable in the value of oil producing properties in the Gulf and the means of monetizing those assets if BP failed to meet its obligations to make required payments.

To meet our obligations, we needed the advice of expert geologists who would provide us with reasonable estimates of the amount of gas and oil that would be produced by the properties that would serve as the security for BP's obligation. Then we needed the advice of investment bankers to tell us how we should structure the financing agreement to be sure we could can convert our interest in the production of these properties into cash should BP default in its payment obligations. Of course we also needed the assistance of lawyers to draft the security agreements and to anticipate the protections that the trust would need if BP were to go bankrupt.

Fortunately, we were able to get excellent help in all of these areas. One thing I learned, however, is if there is such a thing as reincarnation, I want to come back as an investment banker. In order to get advice as to how to secure BPs obligation in a way that would ensure that we could convert our security to cash, we needed an investment banker's advice. When we reached out to a number of major investment bankers for help, only one of them was willing to make a proposal. The others all declined because they did not want to be in the position of having a conflict of interest that would prevent them from participating in other major BP financing. While I forget the precise amount we paid to the investment banker and probably could not disclose it for reasons of confidentiality, I was staggered by the amount they charged. As a lawyer I was used to billing by the hour but investment banking fees bore no relationship to the time involved. I am reminded of the story of the surgeon who was asked to explain to the patient how he came up with the charge of ten thousand dollars for an operation. The surgeon explained that $1,000 was for preoperative care, $1,000 was for time in the operating room, 1,000 was for postoperative care and $7,000 "was for knowing where to cut." Investment bankers knew where to cut.

Our efforts to negotiate the terms of the trust agreement and security took several weeks and involved a number of trips to Houston where BP was headquartered. Ultimately we agreed on the terms of the agreement and signed the appropriate contracts.

Once the contracts were signed, our job was limited to overseeing the investment of the funds that BP had put up and to be sure that any reimbursement to BP was properly documented. Since BP and the government had agreed that any money in the trust would be held in treasury securities, there was not a lot of discretion in the investment decisions made by Citibank, which was named as the corporate trustee to hold and manage the money.

Ultimately, BP provided the full $20 billion earlier than it was obligated to pursuant to the contract and the trust terminated.

Other Matters

I also handled a wide variety of arbitrations and mediations which were interesting but do not merit any detailed description. As noted earlier, one of the interesting parts of what I have done in my career is that almost every case requires you to learn something about the business involved. This was particularly true in the arbitrations.

One arbitration involved cost overruns in the construction of an electric power generating plant that was to be the model for the future. The plant involved a new process in which coal would be subject to a chemical process that would separate the natural gas in the coal from the other materials which enabled the company to burn natural gas to generate electricity rather than coal. This would enable the producer to meet stricter environmental standards without incurring the greater costs of natural gas.

The theory was great but, as the plant was being built, the economics changed dramatically when fracking lowered the cost of natural gas to a point where the process used to convert the coal to natural gas cost more than the purchase price of natural gas on the open market.

Another interesting arbitration involved a fire at a major chemical and chemical products manufacturing plant that occurred shortly before the major economic downturn of 2008 resulting from the collapse of the mortgage-backed securities market. The manufacturer was entitled to receive from its insurers the profit it had lost as a result of the shutdown of its manufacturing processes resulting from the fire. Although the manufacturer was able to show substantially lower amounts of sales of its product in the time between the fire and the repair of the facility, the difficulty was trying to determine what sales were lost because of the fire and what sales were simply the result of the general economic downturn. Unfortunately for the company, the insurers were able to introduce a number of public statements by the company's chief executive in which he talked about how much of a negative impact the economic downturn had on the company's income. As a result, the panel denied the company any recovery for lost profits because it had failed to produce any reliable evidence of what the loss was.

I also did a number of reports involving expert opinions. One of the benefits of these assignments is that it gave me the opportunity to work with my son John. In arbitrations and mediations I would rely on the materials given to me by the parties and would not do any independent research. With expert reports however, I had to be independent and therefore I had to do my own legal research. Having been years away from the time when I did not have law clerk or associate help with research, I did not want to rely on my own research skills. Since I could not rely on the lawyers in the case, I turned to John and informed the parties that he would be doing the research and he would be billed separately. As a result, I had not only the fun of working with John but also the opportunity to see firsthand what a good lawyer he is.

I served as a lawyer in one arbitration—a decision I greatly regret. The matter began when I was asked by a major law firm for whom I had done other arbitrations and mediations to provide their client with an independent opinion concerning their likelihood of success in a contract dispute. The client wanted that opinion to help it evaluate any settlement offer it might receive in an upcoming mediation.

I gave the client a memorandum setting forth my conclusion that they were likely to succeed in the litigation. The mediation was unsuccessful and the law firm advised me that their client would like me to participate with them as counsel in the arbitration and I agreed. The problem was that I was someone who was accustomed to being fully in charge of the litigation I conducted and that was not to be the case here. The result was that my advice was not always accepted and my role ultimately became more limited that had been agreed. This left me with a concern that my appearance as one of the attorneys, but with only a limited role, might convey the impression that I was retained simply with the hope that my appearance might influence the decision of the three former federal judges on the panel, all of whom I knew. At one point, I told the client and its lawyers that I would not any longer appear at the hearing. Ultimately, however, I was persuaded that my failure to appear might lead the panel to draw a negative inference against the client. I did appear and the client lost the case. I vowed never again to take a case where I was not fully in charge.

The assignments I liked best were those where I was asked to serve as a consultant with respect to a matter in court or arbitration. This might often begin when a law firm was about to become involved in a substantial motion in a pending case and I would be asked to serve as a moot court judge for a mock argument. In some of the cases I would then be asked to stay on as a consultant and to give my advice with respect to the various legal issues and proceedings that followed. This gave me the opportunity to work cooperatively with very able lawyers on interesting issues without having the responsibility for the day-to-day work involved.

I served as a consultant on a major case involving the liability of a middle eastern bank that had provided some financial services for what turned out to be terrorist organizations to the victims of those terrorists. Another case involved multimillion dollar claims against financial institutions that issued the complex mortgage-backed securities that went into default and caused the recession. I also provided advice in connection with a bankruptcy proceeding involving a major financial institution.

Fading Away

General MacArthur gave a famous farewell speech to Congress in which he paraphrased a well-known soldier song saying "old soldiers never die, they simply fade away." The same thing could be said about my practice. At 85, it has been almost 20 years since I retired from the bench. The lawyers who knew me from that time and would think of me when selecting an arbitrator and mediator are dying or retiring. As a result my practice is fading away, with fewer and fewer new matters coming my way as the years pass. I have no regrets, I am happy to have more free time and fortunately not dependent on the extra income.

About four years ago, Otto Obermaier retired and not long thereafter I realized that I had no need for a physical office. I did not have clients and my arbitrations and mediations could be conducted in the offices of the lawyers involved. Since people had told me they had heard that I retired and moved to Florida, I was anxious to maintain a New York presence. I spoke to Elkan Abramowitz and he agreed that, if I gave up my office, the firm would forward any mail to my assistant. I was able to keep my phone number by setting up an answering service with the phone company and could then operate from home without anyone knowing that I no longer had a physical office.

With little expense, I can continue taking on the limited number of new matters that come my way without having expensive overhead. As long as I am reasonably comfortable that my mental acuity has not been impaired, I will do whatever work is available. Although I enjoy playing golf, the intellectual stimulation I find in my work is something I do not wish to abandon.

Whatever happens in the future, I have had a great run. An interesting and exciting career, an extraordinary wife and wonderful children and grandchildren. Who could want more?

FIFTEEN

What I have Learned in Eighty-Five Years

The day Senator Moynihan announced that he was recommending me to be the United States Attorney for the Southern District of New York, I received a request for an interview from Arnold Lubash, who reported on the federal courts for the *New York Times*. He came to my office and spent over a half-hour questioning me about my background. After asking me for the names and ages of each of my siblings, he said, "do you know what this is for?" When I looked puzzled, he said, "your obituary."

When I die, the *Times* will probably run an obituary mentioning the important jobs that I held. The most important things in my life will be mentioned but only briefly; "He was married to Margaret Mary Conroy who predeceased him and is survived by his four children and nine grandchildren."

What is important is not how I will be remembered for my public service but how I will be remembered by those whom I loved. Public recognition can be briefly intoxicating but it can never bring the satisfaction and joy of a good relationship with your family and friends.

In that regard I was indeed fortunate. I had a marvelous wife who loved me as I loved her. Together we raised four children whom we dearly loved and who loved us and each other. They also gave us nine wonderful grandchildren.

All of my children have developed into wonderful human beings, who are kind and generous and thoughtful of their friends. They care about people and recognize their obligation to do something to help those less fortunate than themselves.

I told my son I think he is most successful lawyer I know. He has developed a legal practice that he enjoys while at the same time creating with his wife, Christy, a family of extraordinary children. Like my children, they love each other and their parents . They are intellectually gifted but that is not what makes them special. After all, with the gene pool they received from two parents who graduated from Yale, it was expected that they would do well academically. What is impressive about them is how well they have used the talents that have been given them and what kind and loving people they have become. When I brag about my older grandchildren I don't mention where they went to college, I talk about how each of them has taken time out of their busy lives to come to spend time with me after the death of my wife. What they will become in the future, I do not know but I have little doubt that they will be loving and giving adults.

My other five grandchildren are still developing but I am confident that they will all turn out well because they are being raised by loving and caring parents who love them and each other and who recognize that what goes on within the family is more important than anything else.

My daughter Kate, who has chosen not to get married and raise children of her own, has developed a wonderful relationship with her nieces and nephews who delight in her as she does in them. She fills their lives with her love, devotion, and nature walks. It is wonderful to see how excited the grandkids become when Aunt Kate walks through the door. Kate has developed a loving circle of friends who enrich her life as she enriches theirs. I know from visiting her office that those with whom she works cherish and respect her.

A Life Begun on Third Base

There is a tendency to think of people who hold prominent positions as people who are successful in life. It is not the position you hold that will make you successful, it is how you are viewed by those whose lives you touched. One of the most successful people I knew was a lifelong friend named Ed O'Connor. Ed played basketball for Manhattan College where for many years he held the single season scoring record. He got a degree in physical education and spent the rest of his life teaching and coaching in the public schools in New Jersey and working in a summer camp. When Ed died, Peggy and I drove to New Jersey for his wake. We stood for almost an hour in the rain with a long line of people whose lives had been touched by Coach O'Connor and who were there to show their respect and appreciation. In my view, Ed was more successful than any number of athletes whose busts you will find in the Hall of Fame. He made a difference in the lives of the people with whom he came in contact and earned their respect.

After I am gone, my children will find in my files a collection of letters I received over the years from people congratulating me on some important event in my life. There are many gracious letters from prominent individuals, but the ones of which I am most proud are those I received when I retired as a judge from people in the clerk's office of the court, from court reporters and from lawyers who had appeared before me thanking me for the way I treated them. I also cherish the letters I received from my colleagues on the court who thanked me for what I did outside the courtroom to make our court a better institution.

I hope I never let the fact that I held some important government position make me think that I was an important man. There are no important people, there are only important jobs filled by ordinary people. No one is more important than the lowest level person with whom they work.

My wife Peggy was someone who never treated people differently because of some position they held. While she was never disrespectful, she was not awed or cowed by anyone. I think one of the reasons our friendship with Thurgood and Cissy Marshall developed as it did was because Thurgood liked the fact that Peggy would not hesitate to challenge him if he said something with which she disagreed.

As I was walking my friend Father Richard Dillon to the elevator after he had administered the last rites to Peggy, he said, "When I first met Peggy, I was a little taken aback. When I would pontificate about something, she would not say "oh yes Father" as with most woman to whom I talked. She would actually challenge me." He loved and respected her for that.

One incident of her candor almost caused me apoplexy. Shortly after I became US Attorney in 1980, Peggy and I were at some fancy cocktail party talking to the then Chief Judge of the Second Circuit Bill Feinberg and his wife Shirley. I was new to the establishment and anxious to make a good impression on the Chief Judge. During our conversation Shirley asked Peggy what her maiden name was. When Peggy replied "Conroy," Shirley said "oh, then you are Irish. Our son is marrying an Irish girl." Without batting an eye Peggy said, "I bet her parents are as unhappy about it as you are." There was a pause and then Shirley started to laugh. Peggy had made another friend.

As a young lawyer I was somewhat awed by the judges before whom I appeared, and I felt it was appropriate to respect the institution that they represented. On becoming a judge, I found that these people were no different from myself or many others in our profession. What is most impressive about them is not their intellectual brilliance or professional competence, but rather the fact that they all seem motivated by the same desire to do the right thing for the parties who appear before them.

It is hard not become impressed with yourself when people spend the day referring to you as "Your Honor." That is when it helps to come home at night to a loving wife who asks you to take out the garbage or help with the dinner dishes. If we are lucky, we should all get to go home to a loving family that keeps us tethered to reality.

Some comedian once said "happiness can't buy money." However, as my former Chief Judge, Charlie Brieant, often said, "Remember, there are no pockets in a shroud."

He was right. There are a lot of millionaires buried in elegant mausoleums who were miserable and unhappy people. We should all live our lives thinking about how we will look back on what we have done with our lives in our later years and how we want to be remembered when we are gone.